E. M. Forster's *A Passage to India*

E. M. Forster's *A Passage to India* (1924) be generated decades of debate on issues as wide ranging as imperialism, modernism, ethnicity, sexuality and symbolism.

Taking the form of a sourcebook, this guide to Forster's challenging novel offers:

- extensive introductory comment on the contexts and many interpretations of the text, from publication to the present
- annotated extracts from key contextual documents, reviews, critical works and the text itself
- cross-references between documents and sections of the guide, in order to suggest links between texts, contexts and criticism
- suggestions for further reading.

Part of the *Routledge Guides to Literature* series, this volume is essential reading for all those beginning detailed study of *A Passage to India* and seeking not only a guide to the novel, but a way through the wealth of contextual and critical material that surrounds Forster's text.

Peter Childs is Professor of English at the University of Gloucestershire. His publications include *Modernism* (2000) and *The Twentieth Century in Poetry* (1998).

Routledge Guides to Literature*

Routledge Guides to Literature offer clear introductions to the most widely studied authors and literary texts.

Each book engages with texts, contexts and criticism, highlighting the range of critical views and contextual factors that need to be taken into consideration in advanced studies of literary works. The series encourages informed but independent readings of texts by ranging as widely as possible across the contextual and critical issues relevant to the works examined and highlighting areas of debate as well as those of critical consensus. Alongside general guides to texts and authors, the series includes "sourcebooks", which allow access to reprinted contextual and critical materials as well as annotated extracts of primary text.

Available in this series:

Geoffrey Chaucer by Gillian Rudd
Ben Jonson by James Loxley
William Shakespeare's The Merchant of Venice: A Sourcebook edited by S. P. Cerasano
William Shakespeare's King Lear: A Sourcebook edited by Grace Ioppolo
William Shakespeare's Othello: A Sourcebook edited by Andrew Hadfield
John Milton by Richard Bradford
Alexander Pope by Paul Baines
Mary Wollstonecraft's A Vindication of the Rights of Woman: A Sourcebook edited by Adriana Craciun
Jane Austen's Emma: A Sourcebook edited by Paula Byrne
Mary Shelley's Frankenstein: A Sourcebook edited by Timothy Morton
The Poems of John Keats: A Sourcebook edited by John Strachan
Charles Dickens's David Copperfield: A Sourcebook edited by Richard J. Dunn
Charles Dickens's Bleak House: A Sourcebook edited by Janice M. Allan
Herman Melville's Moby-Dick: A Sourcebook edited by Michael J. Davey
Harriet Beecher Stowe's Uncle Tom's Cabin: A Sourcebook edited by Debra J. Rosenthal
Walt Whitman's A Song of Myself: A Sourcebook and Critical Edition edited by Ezra Greenspan
Robert Browning by Stefan Hawlin
Henrik Ibsen's Hedda Gabler: A Sourcebook edited by Christopher Innes
Thomas Hardy by Geoffrey Harvey

* Some books in this series were originally published in the Routledge Literary Sourcebooks series, edited by Duncan Wu, or the Complete Critical Guide to English Literature series, edited by Richard Bradford and Jan Jedrzejewski.

Charlotte Perkins Gilman's The Yellow Wall-Paper: A Sourcebook and Critical Edition edited by Catherine J. Golden

Kate Chopin's The Awakening: A Sourcebook edited by Janet Beer and Elizabeth Nolan

D.H. Lawrence by Fiona Becket

The Poems of W. B. Yeats: A Sourcebook edited by Michael O'Neill

E. M. Forster's A Passage to India: A Sourcebook edited by Peter Childs

Samuel Beckett by David Pattie

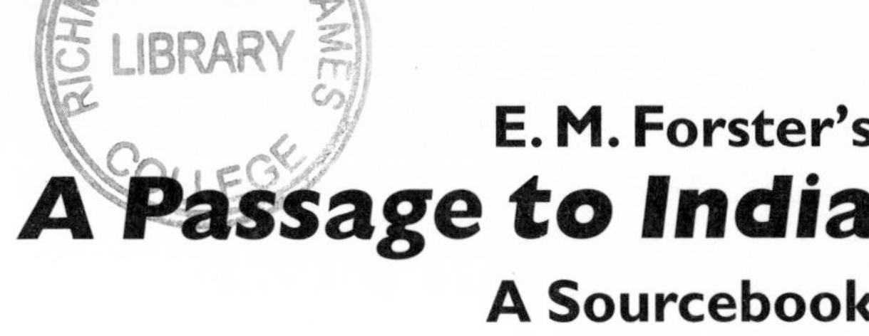

E. M. Forster's *A Passage to India*
A Sourcebook

Edited by Peter Childs

LONDON AND NEW YORK

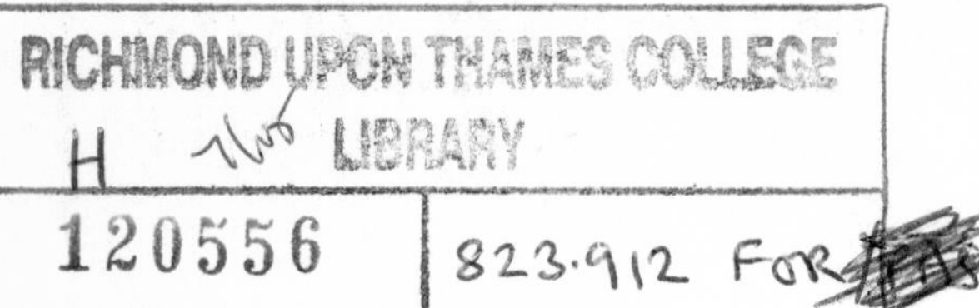

First published 2002 by Routledge
11 New Fetter Lane, London EC4P 4EE

Simultaneously published in the USA and Canada
by Routledge
29 West 35th Street, New York, NY 10001

Routledge is an imprint of the Taylor & Francis Group

This volume first published as *A Routledge Literary Sourcebook on E. M. Forster's A Passage to India*

Typeset in Sabon and Gill Sans by RefineCatch Limited, Bungay, Suffolk
Printed and bound in Great Britain by
TJ International Ltd, Padstow, Cornwall

British Library Cataloguing in Publication Data
A catalogue record for this book is available from the British Library

Library of Congress Cataloging in Publication Data
A Routledge literary sourcebook on E. M. Forster's *A Passage to India* / edited by Peter Childs
p. cm.—(Routledge literary sourcebooks)
Includes bibliographical references and index
1. Forster, E. M. (Edward Morgan), 1879–1970. A Passage to India. 2. India – In Literature.
I. Childs, Peter, 1962– . II. Series
PR6011.O58 P3817 2002
823'.912 – dc21 2001048681

ISBN 0–415–23822–6 (hbk)
ISBN 0–415–23823–4 (pbk)

To David and Andrea, David and Gina, and Keith

'if they turn me away I must go to the Dak'
(*A Passage to India*, ch. xxvi)

Contents

4: Further reading

Annotation and Footnotes

Annotation is a key feature of this series. Both the original notes from reprinted texts and new annotations by the editor appear at the bottom of the relevant page. The reprinted notes are preface by the author's name in square brackets, e.g. [Robinson's note].

Acknowledgements

The editor and publisher would like to thank the following copyright holders:

THE BRITISH LIBRARY, for image 447/3: A visit to the caves near Bangalore (figure)

COLUMBIA EMI WARNER DIST. LTD, for film still from David Lean's *A Passage to India*. Photo courtesy of Ronald Grant Archive

MACMILLAN LTD, for David Dowling, *Bloomsbury Aesthetics and Forster and Woolf*, published by Macmillan, 1985; G. K. Das, 'Through the Ruins of Empire' and 'Call Me a Non-Believer' in *E. M. Forster's India*, published by Macmillan, 1997

SOCIETY OF AUTHORS, for E. M. Forster, *A Passage to India* and *Aspects of the Novel*, as the literary representatives of the Provost and Scholars of King's College Cambridge

UNIVERSITY OF CHICAGO PRESS, for Charu Malik, 'To Express the Subject of Friendship: Masculine Desire and Colonialism in *A Passage to India*' in Robert K. Martin and George Piggford (eds), *Queer Forster*, published by University of Chicago Press, 1997

UNIVERSITY OF MINNESOTA PRESS, for Jenny Sharpe, 'The Indeterminacies of Rape' in *Allegories of Empire: The Figure of Women in the Colonial Text*, published by University of Minnesota Press, 1993

Every effort has been made to obtain permission to reproduce copyright material. If any proper acknowledgement has not been made, we would invite copyright holders to inform us of the oversight.

Introduction

Passage indeed O soul to primal thought,
Not lands and seas alone, thy own clear freshness,
The young maturity of brood and bloom,
To realms of budding bibles . . .
Passage to more than India!
–Walt Whitman, 'Passage to India' (ll.165–9, 224)

Though he lived for nearly fifty years after its publication, E. M. Forster did not write another novel after *A Passage to India* (1924). Almost as surprising is the fact that it appeared fourteen years after his previous novel, *Howards End* (1910). In the intervening years between his two most celebrated works, Forster was far from idle: during the First World War he worked for the Red Cross in Alexandria, about which city he published a book, *Alexandria: A History and a Guide*, in 1922; he travelled twice to India; he published a collection of short stories, *The Celestial Omnibus*, and a collection of essays and sketches on Alexandria entitled *Pharos and Pharillon*; and he even wrote another novel, *Maurice*, but its homosexual subject matter meant that it was not published until after Forster's death.

For the country in which Forster's new novel was to be set, India, this was also an eventful period. Between his first visit to the subcontinent in 1912 and his second in 1921, *A Passage to India* gestated in Forster's mind over a decade that spanned the First World War, the Rowlatt Acts (extending wartime repressive measures – including imprisonment without trial – to post-war India), Gandhi's return to India from South Africa and the start of his civil disobedience campaign, the first Government of India Act, an upsurge in Indian nationalist feeling, British promises of independence, and the most ignominious event in the raj's history: the infamous gunning down of Indian civilians, known as the Amritsar Massacre, in 1919. *A Passage to India* is firmly rooted in this history even though Forster argued that his book was about the human race's attempt to find a 'more-lasting home': that it was at its core about religion and metaphysics.

Over the course of this Sourcebook, the importance of both political and personal values for Forster will become apparent. The Sourcebook is divided into four sections, which cover different approaches to studying the novel. The first is concerned with contexts: biographical, literary and historical. The second focuses on interpretation: the history of the novel's criticism, early reviews and recent readings. The third section explores the book at the level of the text: after a brief summary of the narrative, there are detailed notes and discussion covering eleven key passages from the novel, from the opening paragraphs to the closing pages. Finally, the fourth section provides a note on the best available edition and a guide to recommended further reading. No single book can hope to cover every angle to reading and interpreting a novel, but this Sourcebook aims to provide the information that is most important to an understanding of its principal issues as well as the critical commentaries and debates surrounding them.

1

Contexts

Contextual Overview

This is indeed India; the land of dreams and romance, of fabulous wealth and fabulous poverty, of splendour and rags, of palaces and hovels, of famine and pestilence, of genii and giants and Aladdin lamps, of tigers and elephants, the cobra and the jungle, the country of a hundred nations and a hundred tongues, of a thousand religions and two million gods, cradle of the human race, birthplace of human speech, mother of history, grandmother of legend, great-grandmother of Tradition, whose yesterdays bear date with the mouldering antiquities of the rest of the nations – the one sole country under the sun which is endowed with an imperishable interest for alien prince and alien peasant, for lettered and ignorant, wise and fool, rich and poor, bond and free, the one land that *all* men desire to see, and having seen once, by even a glimpse, would not give that glimpse for the shows of all the rest of the globe combined.

Mark Twain, *Following the Equator*, vol. 2 (1897). *Stormfield Edition of the Writings of Mark Twain*, vol. 21, Harper and Brothers, New York and London, 1929, p. 16

Edward Morgan Forster was born in London on 1 January 1870, the year before his father's death, and educated at private schools in Eastbourne and Tonbridge. In 1887 he inherited £8,000 from his great-aunt, Marianne Thornton, about whom he later wrote a 'domestic biography'. From 1897, he attended King's College, Cambridge, where he read classics and history, partly under the supervision of Goldsworthy Lowes Dickinson, of whom he also wrote a biography. At Cambridge he came under the influence of the philosopher G. E. Moore and the aesthetic belief that the purpose of life is to contemplate beauty in art and to cultivate friendships in life. Forster was elected to the 'Apostles' clique of Cambridge intellectuals and through them met members of the Bloomsbury Group. After Cambridge, in 1901 he went on a one year's tour of Italy and Austria with his mother. Around this time he also began writing. The next year he taught at the Working Men's College and subsequently at the extra-mural department of the Cambridge Local Lectures Board, lecturing on Italian art and history. His first story, 'Albergo Empedocle', appeared in *Temple Bar* in December 1903 and in the following year he started contributing stories to the Cambridge-based journal *Independent Review*.

Forster's first published novel was *Where Angels Fear to Tread* (1905). It is a story about Anglo-Italian contrasts that sets the passionate world of Italy Forster had seen on his travels against the cool, reserved values of suburban England. A social comedy for most of its length, it ends as a tragedy with death and frustrated love as the English, briefly taken out of themselves, return to their narrow lives in the southern counties. In the year of its publication, Forster spent several months in Nassenheide, Germany, as tutor to the Countess von Arnim, an experience that, like his friendship with Virginia and Vanessa Stephen, would inform his portrait of the Schlegel sisters in *Howards End*. In 1907 he worked as a private tutor for an Indian Muslim, Syed Ross Masood, with whom he developed a close friendship and love, and to whom *A Passage to India* is dedicated. Also in 1907, Forster saw published the novel of his Cambridge days, *The Longest Journey*, which remained his favourite novel despite its comparatively low critical standing. It tells the story of an orphaned undergraduate and then struggling writer, Rickie, who abandons his close friend Ansell for a loveless marriage but is partially enlightened by the free spirit of his wayward, pagan, Wiltshire half-brother Stephen. At this time, Forster also associated more often with the Bloomsbury Group, becoming a close friend of the Woolfs, Lytton Strachey and Roger Fry. The following year his second Anglo-Italian novel, *A Room with a View*, was published: a story of misunderstandings and English snobbery which this time ends happily as the heroine, Lucy Honeychurch, realises in time her love for the impulsive George Emerson over the effete intellectual Cecil Vyse. However, it was *Howards End* in 1910 that was Forster's first considerable success, the book that secured his reputation. This is a condition-of-England novel about sections of the middle classes, which focuses on the question of who will inherit Howards End, Forster's metonym for England based on his childhood home of Rook's Nest. The story centres on the relationship between the intellectual German Schlegel sisters and the practical, male-dominated, business-oriented Wilcox family. In the novel, ambitiously if not wholly convincingly, Forster attempts to find a way for Wilcox money to become the support for Schlegel culture, and also for the future of rural England to be wrested from urban, commercial interests and placed once more in the hands of the yeomanry.

Now an established novelist, the hitherto prolific Forster was to publish only one novel in the rest of his life, though 1911 saw the release of a collection of his short stories, *The Celestial Omnibus*. In 1912–13 he made his first visit to India, with R. C. Trevelyan, Dickinson and G. H. Luce, and soon after Forster began writing an early draft of *A Passage to India*. He also worked on the homosexual novel that was not published until after his death, *Maurice: A Romance* (1971). This novel, circulated privately at the time, is a story of cross-class love that for the only time in Forster's fiction explicitly eschews the traditional orthodoxy of heterosexual romantic encounters for the homosexual love that Forster himself desired.

In 1915, after the war started, Forster began working for the International Red Cross in Alexandria and became a strong supporter of the poet C. P. Cavafy. He returned to England in 1919, after the war, but set off travelling again in 1921. On this trip to India he worked as the private secretary to the Maharajah of Dewas Senior, and his letters home from the two Indian trips were later published as *The Hill of Devi* (1953). In 1922 he published *Alexandria: A History and a Guide*, but copies were burned before distribution and the book was not republished until 1938. *Pharos and Pharillon*, Forster's essays on Alexandria together with some translations of Cavafy's poems, was published in 1923.

Over this time, Forster had been reworking his Indian novel, which was finally published in 1924, fourteen years after his previous novel. *A Passage to India* is the story of Adela Quested and Mrs Moore's journey to India to visit Adela's fiancé, and Mrs Moore's son, Ronny Heaslop. There they meet a college teacher, Cyril Fielding, who is Forster's surrogate in the novel, the Brahman Hindu Dr Godbole and the Muslim Dr Aziz, whose alleged assault on Adela is the fulcrum of the narrative. It was widely acclaimed but Forster gave up novel writing because he felt he could not write openly and honestly about (homo)sexual relations. In 1927 he gave the Clark lectures at Cambridge University, which were published as *Aspects of the Novel* the same year. He was also offered a fellowship at King's College, Cambridge, on the strength of them. In 1928, his second collection of short stories, *The Eternal Moment*, was published. This collection of six stories turns away from realism towards the styles of fantasy and romance.

In 1934, the year he published his first biography, *Goldsworthy Lowes Dickinson*, Forster became the first president of the National Council for Civil Liberties, an unsurprising decision for an active member of PEN (an association of writers founded in 1921 to promote the interests of literature) who had argued against the suppression of Radclyffe Hall's lesbian novel *The Well of Loneliness* in 1928 – he also spoke in defence of the overthrow of the ban on D. H. Lawrence's *Lady Chatterley's Lover* in the 1960s. Two years later, in 1936, Forster published his first assembly of essays and occasional pieces, *Abinger Harvest*. His mother died in 1945 and in the same year he was elected Honorary Fellow of King's, which entitled him to live at the college, as he did for the rest of his life. In 1947 he embarked on lecture tours in the United States, and two years later he refused a knighthood from the King. The same year he wrote the libretto for Benjamin Britten's opera *Billy Budd*, based on Herman Melville's novella.

The year 1951 saw the publication of Forster's second collection of essays and articles, *Two Cheers for Democracy*, 1953 the publication of *The Hill of Devi* and 1954 the assembly of his two short-story volumes as *Collected Short Stories*. His final book in his lifetime was *Marianne Thornton* (1956), a biography of the great-aunt whose gift in 1887 had allowed Forster to afford to go to Cambridge and subsequently to become a writer.

In 1969 Forster was awarded the Order of Merit. He died the following year in the home of friends on 7 June. The year 1971 saw the publication of *Maurice* and

1972 the release of his remaining, largely unpublished, short stories in *The Life to Come*.

Forster's early novels forged his reputation as one of the most thoughtful and capable novelists of the time, but it is probably only *A Passage to India* that stands as a masterpiece of twentieth-century fiction. Forster was principally an Edwardian novelist concerned with the restrictions placed on personal freedom by English sensibilities, but his later work, especially *A Passage to India* (1924), can be called modernist in its use of symbolism and its style of repetition-with-variation (which Forster called 'rhythm' in his 1927 book on fiction, *Aspects of the Novel*). In terms of the key aspects of his social, political and religious life, Forster was one of the less prominent figures in the Bloomsbury Group, a lifelong member of the Labour Party and an agnostic. He was also an avowed liberal humanist who believed strongly in personal relationships: he famously wrote in 'What I Believe' (1939) that he would sooner betray his country than his friend. His early novels and stories use Italy, and to a lesser extent Greece, as a vibrant, life-affirming antithesis to the stultifying repression of England.

To a degree, in his last novel Forster also uses India to represent a set of significantly different values and conventions from those of England. But India crucially differed from Italy and Greece in that it was a part of the British Empire and its relationship to England and the English was in many ways more complex. Here the English were rulers as well as foreigners, and their behaviour was always meant to represent something more important than themselves.

On 31 December 1600, Queen Elizabeth famously granted the year-old East India Company its first royal charter to trade – a monopoly that was not broken until 1813. The East India Company had been founded in 1599 to exploit the spice trade, which had previously been monopolised by the Dutch and the Portuguese. However, the first Englishman known definitely to have visited India did so in 1579. He was a Jesuit called Thomas Stevens, who served as a missionary in India for forty years. Knowledge of India in England at this time, when Shakespeare was writing his plays for example, was all second hand and entirely unofficial: merchants' and travellers' tales were all that informed reports and representations of India until after 1615, when James I sent out Sir Thomas Roe, funded by the East India Company, to initiate official Anglo-Indian diplomatic relations.

From 1640 onwards, England began to acquire land in India from trade, appropriation and inheritance. After 1757, when Robert Clive famously fought to retake Calcutta, which had been annexed by the Nawab of Bengal the previous year, there was considerable exploitation and plunder by the British, alongside an explosion of trade between the two countries. In 1773, the British government intervened to oversee the East India Company's affairs and British land control increased, with permanent settlements in Bengal and in the south around Madras. English language and culture were promoted in the 1830s, particularly in consequence of Thomas Macaulay's 'Minute on Indian Education'.

Exactly one hundred years after Clive of India's victory at the Battle of Plassey in 1757, sepoys in the Indian army turned against their officers. What followed was known by the British as the 'Indian Mutiny' of 1857 but by many Indians as the Indian Uprising or War of Independence. It centred on Delhi, Lucknow and Kanpur, involved soldiers and civilians, and developed into twelve months of violence and counter-violence. In 1858, Lord Canning quelled all opposition and became the first Viceroy of India as the British government took over rule of India, but a deep rift had been driven between Anglo-Indian and Indian society and the pretence of benign rule was impossible to maintain as the British became increasingly and intentionally isolated.

In 1876, Queen Victoria was proclaimed Empress of India. Indian opposition to British rule grew (with Hindu fundamentalism in the 1890s and the founding of the Muslim League in 1906) over the next few decades, to be spearheaded by Gandhi in 1915 when he returned to India after training to be a lawyer in England and practising in South Africa. Gandhi instigated a campaign of passive resistance, which he had already used successfully in South Africa, and at the end of the war he organised fasts and mass meetings in protest against the Rowlatt proposals, which recommended continuing wartime measures such as curfews into peacetime and in March 1919 became law. The terrible outcome of this battle of wills was the Amritsar massacre of April 1919, when hundreds of Indian civilians were mowed down by troops under the command of General Reginald Dyer at the Jallianwallah Bagh, a public meeting place in Amritsar.

Despite Gandhi's calls for non-violence and passive resistance, there were riots in the Punjab in 1919 and in Bombay in 1921. In 1922, Gandhi was imprisoned by the British but soon released (a pattern to be repeated over the coming years); his ability to unmask British rule as both unjust and unwanted made the raj's position increasingly untenable. This is the context for the battlelines drawn by the Anglo-Indians at the Club in *A Passage to India* and also for the impossibility of a friendship between Aziz and Fielding at the novel's close.

Over twenty years later, in 1947, following the war and the election of a Labour government in Britain, Indian independence was finally won.

Dramatis Personae: Some Key People in Forster's Life

J. R. Ackerley: A close friend of Forster's and author of, among other books, the travel memoir *Hindoo Holiday* (1932). Forster was instrumental in securing Ackerley's job as private secretary to the Maharajah of Chhokrapur [Chhatarpur], on which the book is based.

Vanessa Bell: Painter (also Virginia Woolf's sister). See Bloomsbury Group.

Bloomsbury Group: A select coterie of friends who began meeting in Bloomsbury from 1905. Based on shared interests in the arts and a belief in truth and friendship, this influential group is generally seen to have been in revolt against the conventions of Edwardian society. Forster was a member of the group, though not a central one.

Goldsworthy Lowes Dickinson: A historian at Cambridge who was a great friend of Forster's. His works, for example, *The Greek View of Life* (1896), were a great influence on the younger man. Forster wrote a biography of him in 1934.

Roger Fry: Painter and art critic. See Bloomsbury Group.

Duncan Grant: Scottish painter. See Bloomsbury Group.

John Maynard Keynes: Hugely influential economic theorist. See Bloomsbury Group

Maharajah of Dewas: The Maharajah for whom Forster became Private Secretary on his second visit to India, in 1921.

Syed Ross Masood: The Indian to whom Forster was tutor in 1906 before Masood went up to Oxford. They remained friends and *A Passage to India* is dedicated to Masood.

William Plomer: British writer, born in and associated with South Africa

Lytton Strachey: Biographer. Especially noted for his *Eminent Victorians* (1918), which revolutionised biography by refusing to minimise literary style or omit adverse personal judgements. See Bloomsbury Group.

Marianne Thornton: Forster's great-aunt and, via her will, chief benefactor.

Leonard Woolf: Novelist, critic and essayist. See Bloomsbury Group

Virginia Woolf: Novelist. See Bloomsbury Group.

Chronology

Bullet points are used to denote events in Forster's life, and asterisks to denote historical and literary events.

1876
* Queen Victoria made Empress of India

1879
• Forster born 1 January in London
* Anglo-Zulu War
* Alfred Lord Tennyson, 'Defence of Lucknow'
* Third Anglo-Afghan war

1880
• Forster's father dies
* Gladstone becomes Prime Minister
* First Anglo-Boer War

1882
* British occupy Egypt

1883
* Olive Schreiner, *Story of an African Farm*
* J. R. Seeley, *Expansion of England*

1884
* Berlin West
* Africa Conference

1885
* Gordon dies at Khartoum
* Indian National Congress formed
* H. Rider Haggard, *King Solomon's Mines*

1886
* Salisbury becomes Prime Minister
* Tennyson 'The Opening of the Indian and Colonial Exhibition by the Queen'

1887
* Golden Jubilee of Queen Victoria
* Haggard, *She*

1888
* Rudyard Kipling, *Plain Tales from the Hills*

1890
* Charles Dilke, *Problems of Greater Britain*
* Henry Stanley, *In Darkest Africa*

1892
* Gladstone becomes Prime Minister
* Kipling, *Barrack Room Ballads*

1895
* Salisbury becomes Prime Minister
* Jameson Raid
* Joseph Conrad, *Almayer's Folly*

1897
• Forster attends King's College, Cambridge (1897–1901)

1898
* Curzon becomes Indian Viceroy

1899
* Second Boer War (1899–1902)
* Conrad, *Heart of Darkenss*
* Kipling, 'White Man's Burden'

1900
* Sigmund Freud, *The Interpretation of Dreams*

1901
• Forster travels in Greece and Italy (1901–2)
* Edward VII accedes
* Conrad, *Lord Jim*
* Kipling, *Kim*

1902

- * Balfour becomes Prime Minister
- * A. E. W. Mason, *The Four Feathers*

1903

- • Forster has his first story published in *Temple Bar*
- * Empire Day is inaugurated
- * Samuel Butler, *The Way of All Flesh*
- * G. E. Moore, *Principia Ethica*

1904

- * Conrad, *Nostromo*

1905

- • *Where Angels Fear to Tread*
- * Bengal is partitioned
- * Einstein publishes his Special Theory of Relativity
- * H. G. Wells, *Kipps*
- * G. B. Shaw, *Man and Superman*

1906

- * Campbell-Bannerman becomes Prime Minister
- * John Buchan, *Lodge in the Wilderness*

1907

- • Forster becomes private tutor to Syed Ross Masood
- • *The Longest Journey*
- * Shaw, *John Bull's Other Island*

1908

- • *A Room with a View*
- * Asquith becomes Prime Minister
- * Robert Baden-Powell founds the Scout Association and publishes *Scouting for Boys*

1909

- * Morley–Minto reforms in India
- * Indian Council Acts
- * Wells, *Tono-Bungay*

1910

- • *Howards End*
- * George V accedes
- * Kipling, 'If'

1911

- • *The Celestial Omnibus*

* Delhi Durbar
* Suffragette riots
* Fletcher and Kipling, *School History of England*
* John Galsworthy, *Strife*

1912
• Forster visits India (1912–13) and begins writing *A Passage to India*
* Bengal Partition is revoked
* Alice Perrin, *The Anglo-Indians*
* Arthur Conan Doyle, *The Lost World*

1913
* Rabindranath Tagore wins Nobel Prize for Literature

1914
* Outbreak of the First World War

1915
• Forster works for the Red Cross in Alexandria (1915–18)
* Gandhi returns to India
* D. H. Lawrence, *The Rainbow*
* Virginia Woolf, *The Voyage Out*
* Ford Madox Ford, *The Good Soldier*

1916
* Lloyd George becomes Prime Minister
* James Joyce, *A Portrait of the Artist as a Young Man*

1917
* Russian Revolution
* T. S. Eliot, *Prufrock and Other Observations*

1918
* End of the First World War

1919
* Amritsar Massacre
* Government of India Act
* Somerset Maugham, *The Moon and Sixpence*
* John Maynard Keynes, *Economic Consequences of the Peace*

1920
• Forster is Literary Editor at *The Daily Herald*
* League of Nations founded
* Lawrence, *Women in Love*

1921

- • Forster visits India as Private Secretary to the Maharajah of Dewas Senior
- * Irish Free State established
- * Aldous Huxley, *Crome Yellow*

1922

- • *Alexandria: A History and Guide*
- * Bonar Law becomes Prime Minister
- * Eliot, *The Waste Land*
- * Katherine Mansfield, *The Garden Party*
- * Joyce, *Ulysses*
- * Woolf, *Jacob's Room*

1923

- • *Pharos and Pharillon* (sketches, literary and historical)
- * Freud, *The Ego and the Id*
- * Marie Stopes, *Contraception*

1924

- • *A Passage to India*
- * Empire Exhibition
- * First Labour government
- * I. A. Richards, *Principles of Literary Criticism*

1926

- * General Strike
- * Sean O'Casey, *The Plough and the Stars*

1927

- • Fellow of King's College Cambridge
- • *Aspects of the Novel*
- * Woolf, *To the Lighthouse*

1928

- • *The Eternal Moment*
- * Yeats, *The Tower*

1929

- * Stock market crash
- * Woolf, *A Room of One's Own*

1932

- * J. R. Ackerley, *Hindoo Holiday*

1934

- • First President of National Council for Civil Liberties

- *Goldsworthy Lowes Dickinson* (biography of friend)
- * *Left Review* begins
- * Peace Pledge Union
- * Baldwin becomes Prime Minister
- * George Orwell, *Burmese Days*

1936
- *Abinger Harvest* (essays)
- * Edward VIII accedes
- * George VI accedes
- * Spanish Civil War begins
- * Keynes, *A General Theory of Employment, Interest, and Money*
- * A. J. Ayer, *Language, Truth and Logic*
- * W. H. Auden, *Look, Stranger!*

1939
- *What I Believe*
- Starts wartime broadcasting for the BBC
- * Outbreak of the Second World War
- * Joyce, *Finnegans Wake*

1945
- Forster is elected Honorary Fellow of King's College, Cambridge
- Mother dies
- Last visit to India
- * First majority Labour government
- * End of the Second World War
- * Orwell, *Animal Farm*
- * Evelyn Waugh, *Brideshead Revisited*

1947
- * Indian independence
- * Malcom Lowry, *Under the Volcano*

1950
- * Doris Lessing, *The Grass is Singing*

1951
- *Two Cheers for Democracy* (essays)
- Libretto for Benjamin Britten's Billy Budd
- * Churchill becomes Prime Minister for the second time
- * Graham Greene, *The End of the Affair*

1952
- * Elizabeth II accedes

1953
- *The Hill of Devi*
- Samuel Beckett, *Waiting for Godot*

1954
- *Collected Short Stories*

* Iris Murdoch, *Under the Net*
* Kingsley Amis, *Lucky Jim*
* William Golding, *Lord of the Flies*

1956
- *Marianne Thornton* (biography of great-aunt)

* Suez Crisis
* John Osborne, *Look Back in Anger*

1960
- Witness for defence in *Lady Chatterley's Lover* trial

1961
- V. S. Naipaul, *A House for Mr Biswas*

1966
- Paul Scott, *The Jewel in the Crown*

1969
- Order of Merit

1970
- Forster dies 7 June

* Labour lose General Election

1971
- *Maurice* is published posthumously

1972
- *The Life to Come* (short stories)

Contemporary Documents

The English and their Empire

As a liberal humanist, Forster's attitudes were conditioned by his beliefs in such values as friendship, fairness, goodwill and liberty. His comments on the character of the English are thus far less celebratory than those of many of his contemporaries. His concern is far less with institutions than with social intercourse. The failure to form 'bridges' between the British and Indians in *A Passage to India* is largely a failure of national character, as the extracts below might indicate.

Forster, 'Notes on the English Character' (1920), *Abinger Harvest*, Harmondsworth: Penguin, 1967, p. 16 and 22

I spoke as a member of a prudent middle-class nation, always anxious to meet my liabilities. But my friend spoke as an Oriental, and the Oriental has behind him a tradition, not of middle-class prudence, but of kingly munificence and splendour. He feels his resources are endless, just as John Bull feels his are finite. As regards material resources, the Oriental is clearly unwise. . . . But, as regards the resources of the spirit he may be right.

. . . we are perfide Albion, the island of hypocrites, the people who have built up an Empire with a Bible in one hand, a pistol in the other, and financial concessions in both pockets.

Forster, 'Liberty in England' (1935), *Abinger Harvest*, Harmondsworth: Penguin, 1967, p. 76

I know very well how limited, and how open to criticism, English freedom is. It is race-bound and it's class-bound. It means freedom for the Englishman, but not for the subject-races of his Empire.

Forster, 'Reflections on India', *Nation and Athenaeum* (30) 21 January 1922, pp. 614–15

The decent Anglo-Indian of today realizes that the great blunder of the past is neither political nor economic nor educational, but social . . . [T]hough friendship between individuals will continue and courtesies between high officials increase, there is little hope now of spontaneous intercourse between two races. . . . Never in history did ill-breeding contribute so much towards the dissolution of an Empire.

Forster, 'Our Diversions: The Birth of an Empire' (1924), *Abinger Harvest*, Harmondsworth: Penguin, 1967, pp. 55–8

Feeling a bit lost, and lifting my feet like a cat, I entered the grounds of the British Empire Exhibition at Wembley a few days before their official opening. It was the wrong entrance, or at all events not the right one, which I could not find, and I feared to be turned back by the authorities, but they seemed a bit lost too, though they no longer lifted their feet. Useless for pussy to pick and choose in such a place; slap over one's ankles at the first step flowed the mud. A lady in the Victoria League had told me there was to be no mud; 'There was some, but we have dealt with it,' said she, and perhaps there is none at the proper entrance; the hundreds of shrouded turnstiles that I presently viewed from the inside were certainly clean enough. But the authorities seemed covered with mud; it disputed with grey paint the possession of their faces; they made no bones about mud at all, and were without exception courteous and cheerful. They were even leisurely; the idea that they were completing an entertainment which should be opened in less than a week had evidently been dismissed from their minds, and they went on living their lives. In this they showed their high imperial vision. Pray, did Clive settle the date when he would win Plassey, or Stanley and Livingstone decide exactly when and where they would shake hands? Certainly not. They were making history, not keeping to it, and Wembley does the same. Clocks may strike, suns rise and set, the moon herself accomplish an entire revolution, but the loftier enterprises of man have always ignored such promptings. What is time? And, after all (I thought), why should the Exhibition not be opened in a day or two. It is even open now.

I was bound for the Indian section, and received a good deal of sympathy and advice from the navvies I consulted. They agreed India was no ordinary journey, and far-away looks came into their eyes. 'It's a bit mucky that way. . . . Best try through that large building, but don't bear too much to the left or you'll get mixed up in the stuff.' I was already glad to be inside a building, for the mud seethed with railway trains, and if I attempted open country, gardeners complained it was their new grass lawn. But the building was so large that it failed in the normal immunities of an interior; more railway trains ran down its stupendous galleries, and there was the extra terror of motions overhead that shaved one's scalp. Some of the machines were exhibits and stood still, but, just as at Madame Tussaud's, one could never be sure the quietest creature would not shoot out a claw suddenly. Getting more and more mixed up in the stuff, I dodged among plesiosauri and waded through brown paper and straw – until, as in a dream, I wriggled through a small hole into the open air and saw across more central mud a mass of white minarets in the later Mogul style.

But how noble and severe was the nearer landscape! Almost overwhelmingly so, had it been complete. Gravely flowed a canal, Mr Kipling was going to name the streets, every street-lamp represented the terrestrial globe together with its axis, and two vast white buildings occupied the middle slopes of a hill, one of which now negotiated the approach of a super colossal horse. The horse was strapped upon a lorry; it lay upon its side, its stomach gleaming pallidly, and its hoofs sticking out like tureens. Bomph, squelch went the lorry, but the horse kept all of a piece. Did it propose to enter the building, like the stuffed animals, or to perch on its roof like a bird? I could not tell, nor waited to see, for neither the horse nor the building was then looking its best. No doubt both will gain in dignity when they come to terms; but they were ill at ease for the moment, so I passed on, aware that the building must be Australia, and the horse one of the Horses of the Sun. So the other building must be Canada, which lays more stress upon the tranquil afterglow. And the stern circular mass towering above them both, and executed in the loftiest Round-Tabular style of architecture – this must be the Stadium, aspiration's summit. Some advertisements of beer and biscuits topped the Stadium, and filled me with furtive relief, and I learn with regret that the public opinion of the Empire will have none of them and insists on their removal. I am sorry. Beer at tenpence the glass is surely the stuff to give them now and then, and, anyhow, the price I paid for the stuff at lunch. However, one must not become the least vulgar at Wembley, for there is a Petty Court inside it, where you can be had up in front of a couple of beaks if you enjoy yourself in the wrong way; that is said to be ready, anyhow. Pull the advertisements down. The Bishop of London has been prevailed upon to consecrate a small, aisleless church. The postage stamps have been admired by the King. In fact, with the exception of a cemetery, a seriously minded man will find through these turnstiles practically everything that he can require.

Walking along a duckboard, we reach India; some packing-cases in the entrance, labelled East Africa, prove it. Building better than they knew, the Native States appear in a most realistic and convincing state of confusion. It is impossible to settle their boundaries, to adumbrate their constitutions, to grasp their policy. I wriggled from cubicle to cubicle. In one of them, surrounded by parcels, a young lady smoked a cigarette. Asked where I was, she said Patiala. Asked what was in her parcels, she said she thought tigers, but was not sure. Indeed, no one did know what was in their parcels, and the East was unfastened amid cries of surprise and joy. 'Hilda, I had a topping time this morning . . .'; a stream of girls ran, leapt, and dived, swinging their attaché cases. Where had Hilda's friend come from, and what had she been up to? Other ladies followed, with dusty hair and bright eyes. Shrieks of 'We shall never be ready; I'm simply frantic, but they're worse; Oh, have you seen the little lacquer things?' Indians smiled charmingly, and gave incorrect information. It was all delightful; indeed, nothing was wanting except a few more exhibits.

I did come across one – a model of the Mosque of Wazir Khan at Lahore – and this was so lovely and stood so incidentally and accidentally upon a table, that it had all the magic of a real building, met by chance among squalid or pretentious streets. When I see it next, it will probably be glassed, docketed, and have lost its preternatural charm. The students of the Mayo College of Arts had made it, I was told, and perhaps have made models of the other Lahore buildings as well, but no one could be sure what the packing-cases would reveal. This mosque, and a peep-show of the Assuan dam, are the prettiest objects I hit at Wembley; there is plenty that is ludicrous, and all too much that is elevating, but little so far that is delicate, touching. Of course, beauty always does have a rough time in these shows – even rougher than in the actual world. The moment you put a picture into a Palace of Art it wilts like a cut flower, whereas a machine jibs for joy as soon as it gets into a Palace of Machinery. How triumphant the machines are! How imposing are the Horses of the Sun, and the stuffed necks and faces of the various wild animals, and cherries in bottles, and corn in shucks! They are the true denizens of Wembley, they flourish in its rich soil. The Mosque of Wazir Khan and its little friends have a very different summer before them, and I wish them happily through it, and a safe return to their homes.

Well, it is a show that will suit all tastes. Millions will spend money there, hundreds will make money, and a few highbrows will make fun. I belong to the latter class. Rule me out; go, think your own thoughts, don't forget your spats, and don't expect an Empire to be born too punctually.

On *A Passage to India*

Collected here are a number of comments Forster made on the novel itself, in interviews, letters and other writings. They are frequently cited by critics but of course do not constitute the 'truth' about the novel. They should be used as a way of opening up readings of the text, not closing them down.

Forster, *The Hill of Devi* (1953), Harmondsworth: Penguin, 1965, p. 153

I began [*A Passage to India*] before my 1921 visit, and took out the opening chapters with me, with the intention of continuing them. But as soon as they were confronted with the country they purported to describe, they seemed to wilt and go dead and I could do nothing with them. I used to look at them of an evening in my room at Dewas, and felt only distaste and despair. The gap between India remembered and India experienced was too wide. When I got back to England the gap narrowed, and I was able to resume.

Forster, letter to Syed Ross Masood, 27 September 1922, quoted in P. N. Furbank, *E. M. Forster: A Life*, vol. 2 [1978], London: Cardinal: Sphere, 1998, p. 106

When I began the book I thought of it as a little bridge of sympathy between East and West, but this conception has had to go, my sense of truth forbids anything so comfortable. I think that most Indians, like most English people, are shits, and I am not interested whether they sympathize with one another or not. Not interested as an artist; of course the journalistic side of me still gets roused over these questions.

Forster, letter to J. R. Ackerley (friend and author of *Hindoo Holiday*), 29 January 1924, in Mary Lago and P. N. Furbank (eds), *Selected Letters of E. M. Forster*, vol. 2, 1921–70, London: Collins, 1985

Your letters were a godsend to my etiolated novel. I copied in passages and it became ripe for publication promptly. I appreciated them myself very much too.

Forster, letter to G. L. Dickinson, 26 June 1924, quoted in P. N. Furbank, *E. M. Forster: A Life*, vol. 2 [1978], London: Cardinal: Sphere, 1998, p. 125

In the cave it is *either* a man, *or* the supernatural, *or* an illusion. And even if I know! My writing mind therefore is a blur here – i.e. I will it to remain a blur, and to be uncertain, as I am of many facts in daily life. This isn't a philosophy of aesthetics. It's a particular trick I felt justified in trying because my theme was India. It sprang straight from my subject matter. I wouldn't have attempted it in other countries, which though they contain mysteries or muddles, manage to draw rings round them.

Forster, letter to William Plomer, 28 September 1934, in Mary Lago and P. N. Furbank (eds), *Selected Letters of E. M. Forster*, vol. 2, 1921–70, London: Collins, 1985

I tried to show that India is an unexplainable muddle by introducing an unexplained muddle – Miss Quested's experience in the cave. When asked what happened there, *I don't know*.

Forster, 'Three Countries', in Elizabeth Heine (ed.), *Hill of Devi and Other Indian Writings*, New York: Abinger, 1983, p. 298

the book is not really about politics, though it is the political aspect of it that caught the general public and made it sell. It's about something wider than politics, about the search of the human race for a more-lasting home, about the universe as embodied in the Indian earth and the Indian sky. . . . It is, or rather desires to be – philosophic and poetic.

Forster, interview with P. N. Furbank and F. J. H. Haskell at King's College, Cambridge, 20 June 1952, in Malcolm Cowley (ed.), *Writers at Work: the 'Paris Review' interviews*, 1958

The Marabar Caves represented an area in which concentration can take place. A cavity. They were something to focus everything up: they were to engender an event like an egg. . . . [The section on the Hindu festival] was architecturally necessary. I needed a lump, or a Hindu temple if you like – a mountain standing up. It is well placed; and it gathers up some strings. But there ought to be more after it. The lump sticks out a little too much.

'Call Me a Non-Believer: Interview with E. M. Forster', in G. K. Das, *E. M. Forster's India*, London: Macmillan, 1977, pp. 117–19

Once again I had dropped in as before, but on this occasion it was midday; Mr Forster looked immaculate in his morning suit and did not have to suffer another session of our dialogue in his pyjamas.

I began by asking about the late W. S. Blunt. I said I had been reading Blunt's Diaries [reviewed by Forster in 1920] and was greatly struck by his strong pro-Indian feelings in the early days of the Indian movement for self-government. Mr Forster remembered his personal meeting with Wilfrid Blunt and described him as a 'very witty and entertaining man'. On my telling him how Blunt had once advised the late Mr Gokhale to carry a couple of bombs in his pocket when he went to the India Office Mr Forster laughed and remarked 'O yes, he was the sort of man who would say that . . . though he wouldn't have done it himself!'

Talking about the Indian political events of 1907–8 – the days when Gokhale was in London pleading for reforms – I expressed my doubts that Mr Forster should at such a time have remained untouched by the events. I said: 'Mr Forster, you say in your memorial essay on Syed Ross Masood that until you met him, i.e. until 1907 India was to you a vague jumble of rajahs, sahibs, babus and elephants, and that you were not interested in such a jumble. I find it difficult to take you seriously there. I find it difficult to believe that you were not interested in the political events that were then going on in India.'

Upon this Mr Forster remarked: 'I don't think really I turned my attention to India in any important way in those days', and he confessed in reply to my subsequent questions that he never met Gokhale, Tilak or Edwin Montagu, and had no connexion with the Liberal Club of Cambridge: 'Never been very much interested in politics . . . incidentally, of course, I have.'

We then talked of the reception of *A Passage to India* when it was first published, and answering my curiosity to hear something more about Lord Reading's reactions Mr Forster said: 'Lord Reading did not approve of me as far as he knew anything about me, I never met him myself.'

Continuing the topic of the British official reaction to the book I said in a lighter vein: 'Mr Forster, I have heard it said somewhere that some British civil servants on their voyage to India took to reading your book with great interest, but once they had read it, it seems they all threw their copies into the sea!'

'Did they indeed! How good for the sea!' Mr Forster interjected with laughter and added after a pause that 'it may only be gossip.'

'My book', Mr Forster said, 'when it came out, attracted very little notice. I think in the *Nation* it was well reviewed. I read some conservative papers who just dismissed it as trivial. It was not condemned, not noticed, not given that attention. *The Morning Post* was non-favourable – didn't think it important enough to be denounced.'

What *The Times* thought – if it said anything at all about the book – Mr Forster could not remember. (I discovered later that the review in *The Times Literary Supplement* was favourable though brief.) Mr Forster agreed that he never wrote anything for *The Times* apart from a couple of letters and the personal tribute to the Maharajah of Dewas in which he wanted to correct some errors in the Maharajah's official obituary published in that paper. '*The Times* is not very important now as you know', Mr Forster commented, and on my asking which papers he read he said, '*The Times*, generally, and *The Guardian*, a little.' While I was taking it down briskly, perhaps I gave Mr Forster the impression that approaching him through politics I was entirely at the wrong end and, possibly to revert me to his central position, he remarked: 'But, as you know, my own trend is not political. I am looking for other things.'

We turned to talk briefly about Godbole and Fielding. When I suggested that Godbole might have the peculiar shrewdness and power of a Chitpavan Brahmin Mr Forster appreciated the point, but to the question whether he had actually met Godbole's original at Dewas or elsewhere, Mr Forster answered: 'I never met anyone like him. Godbole was mainly constructed by me. He was to a large extent a created character.'

Concerning Fielding I remarked that his sympathies with the Indians came particularly close to Sir Malcolm Darling's social sympathies, and I quoted Sir Malcolm's own comments about this idea ('That is going into rather deep waters', Sir Malcolm had told me in the course of a recent interview with him). Mr Forster pondered for a moment and said: 'I don't think I thought of Darling when I was writing about Fielding.'

In the end our conversation turned on the question of Mr Forster's unbelief. On my asking in what particular way Hugh Meredith had influenced his unbelief Mr Forster remarked: 'Talking with him certainly influenced me. He became a professor at Belfast, as you know; he did a great deal of teaching and influencing people.'

The last question I picked on was a plain and straight one: 'Mr Forster, you will be ninety in the New Year ("Yes, good heavens!" he interjected), do you still regard yourself as an unbeliever?'

'Yes,' replied Mr Forster, 'I think I should call myself one.'

'Unbeliever?' I repeated.

'Yes, perhaps', answered Mr Forster and halting for a moment corrected himself: 'Non-believer perhaps – a better description.'

'I thought you were inclined to believe in Krishna, Mr Forster?'

'Not any more than any one else', Mr Forster remarked and (somewhat hopefully for me) added: 'I like things about Krishna worship.'

(This account of my interview with Forster in July 1968 was first published as 'Call Me An Unbeliever: Interview With E. M. Forster', *The Statesman*, Calcutta, 23 September 1968.)

India

Forster wrote extensively on India and it is useful to be able to place *A Passage to India* alongside some of his other writings. Included below therefore are three pieces that illuminate the text well. The first is a tribute to Syed Ross Masood, who introduced Forster to India and to whom Forster dedicated *A Passage to India*. The second is one of the most illuminating pieces Forster ever wrote about the subcontinent: 'India Again' is a return to the subject of the country twenty years after his famous novel. Written soon after his third visit to India in 1945, it contains many insights into Forster's views on the country in the year before it gained independence. The last piece included here is an extract from Forster's travel book *The Hill of Devi*, an account of his experience as the private secretary to the Maharajah of Dewas Senior in 1921. The extract concerns the Gokul Ashtami festival that Forster transmuted into fiction at the beginning of Part III of *A Passage to India*.

Forster, 'Syed Ross Masood' (1937), *Two Cheers for Democracy*, Harmondsworth: Penguin, 1965, pp. 296–8

Contributed to the Memorial Number of an Urdu Journal

Masood had many English friends, but I may claim to be the oldest and most intimate of them. I have known him since 1907, and we kept in touch the whole time. I have been with him in England and in Switzerland and have twice visited him in India[1] and have also been his guest in France and in Germany. I cannot speak of our affection here – it is not the time or the place – but I am thankful to pay this tribute to it and to his memory. There never was anyone like him and there never will be anyone like him. He cannot be judged as ordinary men are judged. My own debt to him is incalculable. He woke me up out of my suburban and academic life, showed me new horizons and a new civilization and helped me towards the understanding of a continent. Until I met him, India was a vague jumble of rajahs, sahibs, babus, and elephants, and I was not interested in such a jumble: who could be? He made everything real and exciting as soon as he began to talk, and seventeen years later when I wrote *A Passage to India* I dedicated it to him out of gratitude as well as out of love, for it would never have been written without him.

1 [Forster's note.] First at his home in Aligath, and then in Hyderabad, Deccan, where he was Director of Education.

Masood was essentially an artist. Those who knew him as an official may be surprised at this statement, but though his career was of a practical character his temperament was aesthetic. He lived by his emotions and instincts, and his standards were those of good taste. 'Don't be so damned inartistic,' he would say if he wanted to criticize my conduct. For logic, and for ethical consistency, he had very little use. He had an artist's recklessness over money; he was fantastically generous, incredibly hospitable, and always happiest when he was giving something away. He was a patron of the arts and a connoisseur; he loved good books, coins and engravings: when he went to Japan, he made a collection of coloured prints there, and gave them to me afterwards. His aesthetic judgements were not always sound but they were always vehement and came from the very depths of his being. As a young man he had an unbounded admiration for the poetry of Alfred de Musset, and in later life when a play of Tolstoy's was put on in London and took his fancy he went to see it eight times. A professional critic may smile at his enthusiasms, but men of wider outlook will understand them, and recognize their sincerity and their stimulating effect on others. One might disagree with him but he never left one cold. With his temperament, he naturally felt most at home in the country that has honoured art most, and that country is neither India nor England but France. He loved Paris, and he spoke French well.

What did he think of the English? He handled them splendidly. If they patronized him, he let them have it back, very politely, and I have often been amused at the way in which Englishmen and Englishwomen who had begun by giving themselves airs were obliged to drop them, and to yield to his masterful personality and his charm. There is a story that he was once involved in a 'railway-carriage' incident. He was stretched full-length in an empty compartment when a British officer bounced in and said 'Come on! get out of this.' Masood looked up quietly and said, 'D'you want your head knocked off?', whereupon the officer exclaimed, 'I say, I'm awfully sorry, I didn't know you were that sort of person,' and they became excellent friends. Whether this story be true or not, it is certainly true that on another occasion when returning on a P & O he contracted to shave an Australian miner all the way from Bombay to Marseilles for the sum of one guinea, and that he kept the contract. That was how he handled the Anglo-Saxons. He overwhelmed them by his energy and his unconventionality of address.

That was how he handled them, but what did he think of them? Leaving aside his English friends, whom he placed in a class apart, what did he feel about the Ruling Race as a whole? Perhaps his private thoughts are best expressed in a remark which has always amused me: 'As for your damned countrymen, I pity the poor fellows from the bottom of my heart, and give them all the help I can.' He was irritated by the English, he was sometimes bitter about them, but he realized that they were awkwardly placed in India, and he extended, half humorously, his sympathy towards them in their plight. He did not really dislike them, and I attribute his tolerance to his early upbringing; when he was a little boy at Aligarh, he lived with Sir Theodore and Lady Morison, and his life-long friendship with both of them coloured his outlook and made him less exacting.

Masood's real work, of course, lay with his own community in his own country, and those who shared it will write about him best. But I knew him very well, from a particular angle, and I have tried to keep to that angle in this inadequate contribution to his memory. When his official career is described, it must not be forgotten that he was essentially an artist, and I have tried to emphasize this. And when his services to Islam, to India, and to the Urdu language are commemorated, it must not be forgotten that he was loved and indeed adored by men and women who differed from him in creed, race, and speech, but were able nevertheless to recognize his genius and the greatness of his heart.

Forster, extract from broadcast talk 'India Again' (1946), in *Two Cheers for Democracy*, Harmondsworth: Penguin, 1965, pp. 323–7

It was a dull, cold Friday morning in October 1945 when I left England. Two days later, on the Sunday afternoon, I was in India. Below me lay the desert of Rajputana, baked by the sun and blotched with the shadows of clouds. The plane came down for half an hour near the dragon-shaped fort of Jodhpur, then took off again, and it was Delhi. I felt dazed. And we had travelled so fast that we were ahead of schedule, and had no one to meet us. Suddenly very slow, instead of very quick, we jogged in a tonga through the Delhi bazaars, our luggage in front, our legs hanging down behind, the dust rising, the sun setting, the smoke drifting out of the little shops. It became dark and the sky was covered with stars. Were we lost? No. An unknown host, an Indian, received us, and next day I stood on the high platform of the Great Mosque, one of the noblest buildings in India and the world. Profound thankfulness filled me. The sky was now intensely blue, and kites circled round and round the pearl-grey domes and the red frontispiece of sandstone, sounds drifted up from Delhi city, the pavement struck warm through the soles of my socks; I was back in the country I loved, after an absence of twenty-five years.

I was bound for a conference of Indian writers. The All-India centre of the P.E.N. club had invited us. The people I was to meet were nearly all Indians, of the professional classes – doctors, lawyers, public servants, professors at the university, business men. Many of them were old friends or the sons of old friends. They were what is termed 'intellectuals' and they lived in towns. I did not see much of the countryside nor of the industrial conditions. I met a few Englishmen but not many, and have often looked round a crowded room and observed that I was the only westerner in it. Such are my credentials, or, if you prefer, such are my limitations.

The big change I noticed was the increased interest in politics. You cannot understand the modern Indians unless you realize that politics occupy them passionately and constantly, that artistic problems, and even social problems – yes and even economic problems – are subsidiary. Their attitude is 'first we must find the correct political solution, and then we can deal with other matters'. I think the attitude is unsound, and used to say so; still, there it is, and they hold it much more vehemently than they did a quarter of a century ago. When I spoke about the necessity of form in literature and the importance of the individual vision, their attention wandered, although they listened politely. Literature, in their view, should expound or inspire a political creed.

Externally the place has not changed. It looks much as it did from the train. Outside the carriage windows (the rather dirty windows) it unrolls as before – monotonous, enigmatic, and at moments sinister. And in some long motor drives which I took through the Deccan there were the same combinations of hill, rock, bushes, ruins, dusty people and occasional yellow flowers which I encountered when I walked on the soil in my youth. There is still poverty, and, since I am older today and more thoughtful, it is the poverty, the malnutrition, which persists like a ground-swell beneath the pleasant froth of my immediate experience. I do not know what political solution is correct. But I do know that people ought not to be so poor and to look so ill, and that rats ought not to run about them as I saw them doing in a labour camp at Bombay. Industrialism has increased, though it does not dominate the landscape yet as it does in the West. You can see the chimneys of the cotton mills at Ahmadabad, but you can see its mosques too. You can see little factories near Calcutta, but they are tucked away amongst bananas and palms, and the one I have in mind has an enormous tree overhanging it, in whose branches a witch is said to sit, and from whose branches huge fruit occasionally fall and hit the corrugated iron roofs with a bang, so that the factory hands jump. No – externally India has not changed. And this changelessness in her is called by some observers 'the real India'. I don't myself like the phrase 'the real India'. I suspect it. It always makes me prick up my ears. But you can use it if you want to, either for the changes in her or for the unchanged. 'Real' is at the service of all schools of thought.

It is when you leave the country, or the streets of the town, and go into the private houses that you begin to notice a second great alteration, second only to politics – namely, the lifting of purdah, the increasing emancipation of women. It struck me particularly in cities which are largely Moslem, such as Lahore and Hyderabad, where women once kept rigidly behind the veil. I have been in my life three times to Hyderabad, some of my happiest Indian days were spent there, so I have been able to trace this change. My first visit was in 1912 and then I saw scarcely any Indian women. My second visit was in 1921, when I was admitted into some family circles and saw a good deal of what may be called 'semi-purdah' – ladies coming out into company, but not coming avowedly, and retiring at any moment behind the veil if they felt disposed to do so. Today, purdah has broken down at Hyderabad, except amongst the most conservative, and at the receptions to which I went the women sometimes outnumbered the men. Since they kept to their lovely Indian saris, the effect was exquisite; it was a delight to look round at so much gracefulness and graciousness, at so many and such well-chosen colours. I don't know how far into society this lifting of the veil has extended. But I imagine that sooner or later the change will extend to the villages and transform the Indian social fabric from top to bottom. Our world does not go back, though whether it progresses God alone knows, and in India, as in the west, women will shortly have the same opportunities as men for good and for evil.

The receptions I have been mentioning usually took the form of buffet dinners – they are an innovation since my time. Long tables are loaded with Indian food, and sometimes one table is labelled 'vegetarian' and the other 'non-vegetarian'. You help yourself, or are helped. I take away pleasant memories of these buffet dinners, memories of Indians moving elegantly through well-filled rooms, with well-filled plates in their hands, and miraculously conveying food to their mouths in the folds of a chapatti. There is rationing, but its workings are mysterious and I did not grasp them or suffer from them. For the well-to-do, life is much easier in India than in England. The shops are full of tinned delicacies for those who can afford them – butter, cheese, even plum puddings. For the poor, life is much harder there than here.

The Indians I met mostly talked English. Some of them spoke very well, and one or two of them write in our language with great distinction. But English, though more widely spoken than on my last visit, is worse spoken, more mistakes are made in it, and the pronunciation is deteriorating. 'Perpéndicule' for 'perpendicular'. 'Pip' into my office for 'pop'. Here are two tiny slips which I noted in a couple of minutes, and both of them made by well-educated men. The explanation, I think, is that Indians at the schools and universities are now learning their English from other Indians, instead of from English teachers as in the past. Furthermore, they have little occasion to meet our people socially and so brush it up; intercourse is official and at a minimum, and even where there are mixed clubs the two communities in them keep apart. So it is not surprising that their English is poor. They have learnt it from Indians and practise it on Indians.

Why talk English at all? This question was hotly debated at the P.E.N. conference of All-India writers. Writers from central or upper India were in favour of Urdu or Hindi as a common language for the whole peninsula. Writers from Bengal favoured Bengali, and it has great claims from the literary point of view. Writers from the south, on the other hand, preferred English. The debate, if I may say so, continues, and into it, as into everything, come politics. I mention it to indicate the trend of events, the change in emphasis. Meanwhile, in this uneasy interregnum, English does get talked and gets interlarded in the oddest way with the Indian vernacular. I was travelling one day to Baroda in a crowded second-class carriage. Indians, my luggage, their luggage, myself and a number of loose oranges were piled up together in confusion, and the Indians were arguing. Their language was Gujarati, but they used so many English words that I followed what they were saying. They were arguing about religion and free-thought. I intervened and was welcomed into the conversation, which was now carried on entirely in English out of courtesy to me. I did not follow it the better for that, but they peeled me an orange and we parted friends. Indeed, it is difficult to conclude an Indian railway journey on any other note. Their response to ordinary civility is immediate. I don't think they are particularly friendly in the street – if you ask them the way they are suspicious. But squashed in a railway carriage they seem to expand. And my reason for wanting English to be the common language for India is a purely selfish reason: I like these chance encounters, I value far more the relationships of years, and if Indians had not spoken English my own life would have been infinitely poorer.

My visit ended all too soon. On a Friday afternoon in December – it was again a Friday – I was walking about in the sunshine of Karachi. And on the Sunday evening I was in London. Our train was icy cold, it arrived at Waterloo two hours late, midnight, thick fog, refreshment-rooms closed, waiting-rooms closed, local trains gone, no taxi could leave the station. The grumpy railway policeman to whom we appeared was glad we were uncomfortable, and said so, while a poster on the wall exhorted us to practise even greater austerity, since it was peace time. It was not much of a return, it was not like the arrival in Delhi, and as the policeman's sulky bulky back disappeared into the gloom I found it understandable that not everybody should care for England.

Forster, *The Hill of Devi* (1953), Harmondsworth: Penguin, 1965, pp. 103–6

Old Palace
24 August

This ought to be an interesting letter. It is the fourth day of the Festival and I am getting along all right though I collapsed at first. The noise is so appalling. Hymns are sung to the altar downstairs without ceasing. The singers, in groups of eight, accompany themselves on cymbals and a harmonium. At the end of two hours a new group pushes in from the back. The altar has also a ritual which is independent of the singing. A great many gods are on visit and they all get up at 4.30 a.m. – they are not supposed to be asleep during the Festival, which is reasonable considering the din, but to be enjoying themselves. They have a bath and are anointed and take a meal, which is over about 9.0 a.m. At 12.0 is another service, during which three bands play simultaneously in the little courtyard, two native bands and one European, affecting a merry polka, while these united strains are pierced by an enormous curved horn, rather fine, which is blown whenever incense is offered. And still I am only at the beginning of the noise. Children play games all over the place, officials shout. Last night I had a dreadful dream about Verouka [our cat]. I thought I had shown him a mechanical doll that frightened him so that he went mad and raced round and round in a room overhead. I woke up to find it was the thudding of the old steam engine which we have tinkered up to drive our electric light. – As I said, the noise was too much at first, but Bapu Sahib's kindness and foresight for others never fail. I can always retire to the Guest House which is peaceful and now very beautiful since the Tank is full, and there is a complete staff of servants there and European food. I needn't stay here a moment longer than I like.

Well, what's it all about? It's called Gokul Ashtami – i.e. the *8 days* feast in honour of Krishna who was born at *Gokul* near Muttra, and I cannot yet discover how much of it is traditional and how much due to H.H. What troubles me is that every detail, almost without exception, is fatuous and in bad taste. The altar is a mess of little objects, stifled with rose leaves, the walls are hung with deplorable oleographs, the chandeliers, draperies – everything bad. Only one thing is beautiful – the expression on the faces of the people as they bow to the shrine, and he himself is, as always, successful in his odd role. I have never seen religious ecstasy before and don't take to it more than I expected I should, but he manages not to be absurd. Whereas the other groups of singers stand quiet, *he* is dancing all the time, like David before the ark, jigging up and down with a happy expression on his face, and twanging a stringed instrument that hangs by a scarf round his neck. At the end of his two hours he gets wound up and begins composing poetry which is copied down by a clerk, and yesterday he flung himself flat on his face on the carpet. Ten minutes afterwards I saw him as usual, in ordinary life. He complained of indigestion but seemed normal and discussed arrangements connected with the motor-cars. I cannot see the point of this, or rather in what it differs from ordinary mundane intoxication. I suppose that if you believe your drunkenness proceeds from God it becomes more enjoyable. Yet I am very much muddled in my own mind about it all, for H.H. has what one understands by the religious sense and it comes out all through his life. He is always thinking of others and refusing to take advantage of his position in his dealings with them; and believing that his God acts similarly towards him.

The Old Palace is built round a courtyard about 50 feet square, the Temple-Hall being along one side on the ground floor. The Hall is open to the court and divided into three or four aisles by thick pillars. The singers stand at one end of the chief aisle, the shrine is at the other end, red carpet between. The public squats against the pillars and is controlled, of course incompetently, by schoolboy volunteers. The heat is immense and, since H.H. disdains adventitious comforts, he has the electric fans turned off when his time comes to sing. – I don't think I can describe it better than this, and it is difficult to make vivid what seems so fatuous. There is no dignity, no taste, no form, and though I am dressed as a Hindu I shall never become one. I don't think one ought to be irritated with Idolatry because one can see from the faces of the people that it touches something very deep in their hearts. But it is natural that Missionaries, who think these ceremonies wrong as well as inartistic, should lose their tempers.

Next week I shall have the crisis of the Festival to describe the announcement of Krishna's birth (for he is not born yet!) and the procession from the Old Palace to the Tank, where a clay model of the village of Gokul will be thrown into the waters, and so it will end. Before I forget, though, we none of us wear shoes or socks inside the O.P. My feet suffered at first, but they can walk over heaps of coal now, as they have to whenever the Electric Light goes wrong. The costume is a turban (sãfar), a long coat, and a dhoti, which last resembles a voluminous yet not entirely efficient pair of bathing drawers. I have learnt to tie my own dhoti – the turban is much more difficult and I cannot acquire the knack. If you get the dhoti too short it is not thought elegant and if you get it too long you catch your bare foot in the folds and fall down.

My bedroom at the Old Palace is secluded (except for noise) since it is upstairs, through the Durbar Hall. This is fine – I described it in a letter eight years ago – and it is now free from mess, which has been carried below to adorn the Temple, so one can see its proportions. Nothing remains in it except the Gaddi, a sacred feather-bed with which the fortunes of the Dynasty are mysteriously connected. I am told – and I can well believe it – that some of the stuffing has been in that bed for generations. A row of little roses are placed on the bolster every day, and there are two lamps at night. H.H. comes up once in every twenty-four hours to worship the bed: except for this excursion he is forbidden to leave the ground floor of the palace. I shall never be at an end of the queernesses. But give every place its due. There are no smells and (as far as I can testify) no bugs. It is the noise, the noise, the noise, the noise which sucks one into a whirlpool, from which there is no re-emerging. The whole of what one understands by music seems lost for ever, or rather seems never to have existed.

I am finishing at the Guest House! The Tank looks so pretty and if it does not rain I shall take the boat out.

On Rhythm in Fiction

Forster used the term 'rhythm' to refer to the repeated suggestive use of phrases, words, incidents or characters to create a rhythmic effect in the development of a story's themes and meanings. The technique is apparent in *A Passage to India*, particularly in the echo that haunts Adela and Mrs Moore after their visit to the caves and itself seems to echo throughout the rest of the narrative.

Forster, *Aspects of the Novel* (1927), New York: Abinger, 1974, pp. 113–16

'Pattern and Rhythm'

Rhythm is sometimes quite easy. Beethoven's Fifth Symphony, for instance, starts with the rhythm 'diddidy dum', which we can all hear and tap to. But the symphony as a whole has also a rhythm – due mainly to the relation between its movements – which some people can hear but no one can tap to. This second sort of rhythm is difficult, and whether it is substantially the same as the first sort only a musician could tell us. What a literary man wants to say, though, is that the first kind of rhythm, the diddidy dum, can be found in certain novels and may give them beauty. And the other rhythm, the difficult one – the rhythm of the Fifth Symphony as a whole – I cannot quote you any parallels for that in fiction, yet it may be present.

Rhythm in the easy sense is illustrated by the work of Marcel Proust.[1] Proust's conclusion has not been published yet, and his admirers say that when it comes everything will fall into its place, times past will be recaptured and fixed, we shall have a perfect whole. I do not believe this. The work seems to me a progressive rather than an aesthetic confession, for with the elaboration of Albertine the author is getting tired. Bits of news may await us, but it will be surprising if we have to revise our opinion of the whole book. The book is chaotic, ill-constructed, it has and will have no external shape; and yet it hangs together because it is stitched internally, because it contains rhythms.

There are several examples (the photographing of the grandmother is one of

1 [Forster's note.] The first three books of *A la Recherche du Temps Perdu* have been excellently translated by C. K. Scott Moncrieff under the title of *Remembrance of Things Past* (Chatto & Windus).

them), but the most important, from the binding point of view, is the 'little phrase' in the music of Vinteuil. The little phrase does more than anything else – more even than the jealousy which successively destroys Swann, the hero and Charlus – to make us feel that we are in a homogeneous world. We first hear Vinteuil's name in hideous circumstances. The musician is dead – an obscure little country organist, unknown to fame – and his daughter is defiling his memory. The horrible scene is to radiate in several directions, but it passes.

Then we are at a Paris salon. A violin sonata is performed, and a little phrase from its andante catches the ear of Swann and steals into his life. It is always a living being, but takes various forms. For a time it attends his love for Odette. The love affair goes wrong, the phrase is forgotten, we forget it. Then it breaks out again when he is ravaged by jealousy, and now it attends his misery and past happiness at once, without losing its own divine character. Who wrote the sonata? On hearing it is by Vinteuil, Swann says: 'I once knew a wretched little organist of that name – it couldn't be by him.' But it is, and Vinteuil's daughter and her friend transcribed and published it.

That seems all. The little phrase crosses the book again and again, but as an echo, a memory; we like to encounter it, but it has no binding power. Then, hundreds and hundreds of pages on, when Vinteuil has become a national possession, and there is talk of raising a statue to him in the town where he has been so wretched and so obscure, another work of his is performed – a posthumous septet. The hero listens – he is in an unknown, rather terrible universe while a sinister dawn reddens the sea. Suddenly for him, and for the reader too, the little phrase of the sonata recurs – half heard, changed, but giving complete orientation, so that he is back in the country of his childhood with the knowledge that it belongs to the unknown.

We are not obliged to agree with Proust's actual musical descriptions (they are too pictorial for my own taste), but what we must admire is his use of rhythm in literature, and his use of something which is akin by nature to the effect it has to produce – namely a musical phrase. Heard by various people – first by Swann, then by the hero – the phrase of Vinteuil is not tethered: it is not a banner such as we find George Meredith using – a double-blossomed cherry tree to accompany Clara Middleton, a yacht in smooth waters for Cecilia Halkett. A banner can only reappear, rhythm can develop, and the little phrase has a life of its own, unconnected with the lives of its auditors, as with the life of the man who composed it. It is almost an actor, but not quite, and that 'not quite' means that its power has gone towards stitching Proust's book together from the inside, and towards the establishment of beauty and the ravishing of the reader's memory. There are times when the little phrase – from its gloomy inception, through the sonata, into the septet – means everything to the readers. There are times when it means nothing and is forgotten, and this seems to me the function of rhythm in fiction: not to be there all the time like a pattern, but by its lovely waxing and waning to fill us with surprise and freshness and hope.

Done badly, rhythm is most boring, it hardens into a symbol, and instead of carrying us on it trips us up. With exasperation we find that Galsworthy's spaniel John, or whatever it is, lies under the feet again; and even Meredith's cherry trees and yachts, graceful as they are, only open the windows into poetry. I doubt that it can be achieved by the writers who plan their books beforehand, it has to depend on a local impulse when the right interval is reached. But the effect can be exquisite, it can be obtained without mutilating the characters, and it lessens our need of an external form.

That must suffice on the subject of easy rhythm in fiction: which may be defined as repetition plus variation, and which can be illustrated by examples. Now for the more difficult question. Is there any effect in novels comparable to the effect of the Fifth Symphony as a whole, where, when the orchestra stops, we hear something that has never actually been played? The opening movement, the andante, and the trio-scherzo-trio-finale-trio-finale that composes the third block, all enter the mind at once, and extend one another into a common entity. This common entity, this new thing, is the symphony as a whole, and it has been achieved mainly (though not entirely) by the relation between the three big blocks of sound which the orchestra has been playing. I am calling this relation 'rhythmic'. If the correct musical term is something else, that does not matter; what we have now to ask ourselves is whether there is any analogy to it in fiction.

I cannot find any analogy. Yet there may be one; in music fiction is likely to find its nearest parallel.

The position of the drama is different. The drama may look towards the pictorial arts, it may allow Aristotle to discipline it, for it is not so deeply committed to the claims of human beings. Human beings have their great chance in the novel. They say to the novelist: 'Recreate us if you like, but we must come in,' and the novelist's problem, as we have seen all along, is to give them a good run and to achieve something else at the same time. Whither shall he turn? Not indeed for help but for analogy. Music, though it does not employ human beings, though it is governed by intricate laws, nevertheless does offer in its final expression a type of beauty which fiction might achieve in its own way. Expansion. That is the idea the novelist must cling to. Not completion. Not rounding off but opening out. When the symphony is over we feel that the notes and tunes composing it have been liberated, they have found in the rhythm of the whole their individual freedom. Cannot the novel be like that? Is not there something of it in *War and Peace*? – the book with which we began and in which we must end. Such an untidy book. Yet, as we read it, do not great chords begin to sound behind us, and when we have finished does not every item – even the catalogue of strategies – lead a larger existence than was possible at the time?

2

Interpretations

Critical History

Formalism and Liberal Humanism

Contemporary reviewers saw much that was political in Forster's novel[1] and considered it a meditation on the 'India question' – whether or not Britain should grant independence – but critics up to the 1970s more often focused on the novel's symbolism, structure, personal relationships and liberal values. As a liberal, Forster's politics were, as far as they could be, personal ones: he wrote an essay entitled 'What I Believe' in 1939, on the threshold of the Second World War, in which he said that 'tolerance, good temper and sympathy . . . are what really matter'. However, he worked on the novel in the light of a key political event of 1919: the Amritsar Incident, in which hundreds of Indians were brutally shot down for holding an illegal meeting. The massacre was ordered by a British officer in retribution for an attack on an English missionary woman, and events after the attack on Adela at the Marabar generate similar hostility and recriminations. Forster considered the Amritsar Incident to embody the antithesis of the principles in which he believed. Of equal importance to 'goodwill' for Forster was 'friendship', which blossoms in the 'Mosque' section at the start of the book – it is in this first part that Mrs Moore, Fielding, and to a lesser extent Adela, all make friends with Aziz. Quite probably this reflects Forster's personal reasons for going to India: to see Syed Ross Masood, the Muslim he was tutor to in 1907 and fell in love with. *A Passage* is dedicated to him. Because Forster follows this section with ones entitled 'Caves' and 'Temple' the religious development is from Islam to an ancient hollowness prior to all theistic religions and then on to Hinduism. In traditional criticism, the caves have been usually read as the nullity at the heart of the universe and the sense of alienation and incomprehension felt by Westerners in India. Yet, Forster was an agnostic not an atheist and he ends *A Passage to India* with the ambivalence he found in Hinduism: a constant calling to God to come or arrive, which is never answered. On the other hand, in terms of its

1 E. M. Forster, *A Passage to India* [1924], Harmondsworth: Penguin, 2000. All references are to this edition.

religious encoding 'Caves' seems to be substituted for 'Church' in the novel, and therefore its hollowness may appear to represent the position of the raj's spiritual emptiness sandwiched between the two major indigenous religions.

The first influential scholarly article on Forster was probably an essay of 1927 by the best known of the New Critics, I. A. Richards. 'A Passage to Forster: Reflections on a Novelist' was published in an American journal called *The Forum* (and is included in Malcolm Bradbury's 1966 assembly entitled *Forster: A Collection of Critical Essays*). Richards's cardinal point for later criticism was to direct attention to Forster's joint concerns with the spiritual and the social, with metaphysics and the mystical on the one hand, and with manners and morals on the other: twin preoccupations which early critics found hard to reconcile in terms of Forster's apparent symbolism.

It was Peter Burra's 1934 article 'The Novels of E. M. Forster', which Forster admired and which was then used as the introduction to the Everyman edition of *A Passage to India*, that tried to go beyond this critical impasse. Burra stressed Forster's use of pattern, motifs and rhythm (discussed by Forster in his 1927 lectures collected as *Aspects of the Novel*). For Burra, the novels had to be understood in terms of aesthetic ordering and Forster's characters had to be considered to express a juxtaposition of perspectives or attitudes whose reconciliation his narratives worked towards: the purpose of the novel as an art form was to order life's formless chaos. In 1938 there appeared the first monograph on Forster, *The Writings of E. M. Forster* by Rose Macaulay, another novelist. Macaulay perceived Forster as a liberal with no religious faith but with a spiritual sensibility, as a writer committed to the Bloomsbury creed of personal relationships but also intimating the possibility of transcending them. A review of Macaulay's book in *Scrutiny* by F. R. Leavis in 1938 was revised for his influential 1952 book *The Common Pursuit*. In it Leavis called *A Passage* 'a classic of the liberal spirit', but he found no position for Forster in his 'Great Tradition' because the other ironic social-comedies were weaker and overall Forster's vagueness and his Bloomsbury beliefs meant that Leavis felt Forster inadequately represented the life he advocated.

Another major, perhaps the most important, critical work to appear before 1945 was Lionel Trilling's book *E. M. Forster* (1943). Trilling's study also considers Forster in terms of the 'Liberal Tradition' – 'that loose body of middle-class opinion which includes such ideas as progress, collectivism and humanitarianism' – with which Trilling believes Forster's work to be both in deep sympathy and at odds. Forster emerges as an important writer against extremism, ideology, nationalism, prejudice and intolerance: an ambivalent, sceptical humanist more convincing and consistent in his oppositions than his convictions. The first key post-war reading of Forster was E. K. Brown's 1950 *Rhythm in the Novel* (though Brown had been writing on Forster since the mid 1930s). Brown successfully suggested that Forster had more in common with the modernists, such as Virginia Woolf and D. H. Lawrence, than had hitherto been thought by critics who considered his Edwardian criticisms of Victorian attitudes still firmly rooted in a realist aesthetic. Brown, like Frank Kermode after him (in an essay of 1958 for *The Listener* called 'Mr E. M. Forster as a Symbolist'), saw Forster as a writer who expressed his ideas more through repetitions, images and analogies than character or story. Forster now appeared as a modernist with as great a concern for form as content, with an interest in musical composition, and with art's ability to structure life's chaos into an ordered whole: most noticeable in his last novel's triadic form. The presentation of this method in *A Passage* was described in *Fields of Light* (1951) by Reuben A. Brower, in an essay title taken from the novel, as 'the twilight of the double vision'. Mrs Moore experiences this as the simultaneous awareness that neither the divine nor the human world is meaningful, that 'Everything exists, nothing has value', and, while Forster is able to suggest this spiritual, political and personal failure through rhythm and symbol in the early sections of the novel, Brower believes he does not succeed in showing a unified vision under the arching sky in the closing 'Temple' section. Several major studies of the 1960s subsequently focused on Forster as primarily a sceptical humanist and a formal symbolist. Frederick C. Crews's 1962 book *E. M. Forster: The Perils of Humanism* considers the novels to be dialectical, striving for balance, while deeply aware of, first, humanism's inability to root its transient values in anything beyond itself and, second, the liberal's dilemma, arising from a creed that professes the opposition to political extremism and intolerance combined with a refusal to use force. Wilfred Stone's 1966 partly psycho-analytical study *The Cave and the Mountain*[2] sees *A Passage to India* reaching successfully towards a unified vision of oneness above the mysteries, muddles, and personal failures in the novel. Lastly, George Thomson's 1967 book *The Fiction of E. M. Forster* used the manuscripts to *A Passage* to put forward a reading indebted to Carl Jung's theory of archetypes and to argue for the book as a mythic search for personal and spiritual transcendence. Forster's transformation in critical discussion from an Edwardian realist to a symbolist was by now complete.

Post-colonial and Political Readings

Over the last twenty-five years, analyses of Forster's novel have broadened out into a wide range of cultural and political readings, taking as their basis representations and constructions of the Other: in terms of orientalism, Indian nationalism, gender and homosexuality.[3] Above all, the novel has been read predomin-

2 Wilfred Stone, *The Cave and the Mountain*, Stanford: University of California Press, 1966.

3 For examples, on orientalism see Paul B. Armstrong, 'Reading India: E. M. Forster and the Politics of Interpretation', *Twentieth-Century Literature* 38: 4, Winter 1992; Zakia Pathak et al., 'The Prisonhouse of Orientalism', *Textual Practice* 5: 2, Summer 1991, pp. 195–218; Teresa Hubel, *Whose India?*, Chicago: University of Chicago Press, 1996, pp. 95–108; and Benita Parry, 'The Politics of Representation in *A Passage to India*', in John Beer (ed.), *A Passage to India: Essays and Interpretations*, London: Macmillan, 1985. On Indian nationalism see Frances B. Singh, '*A Passage to India*, the National Movement, and Independence', *Twentieth-Century Literature* 31: 2, 3, Summer/Fall 1985, pp. 265–77; Harish Trivedi, '*Passage* or *Farewell*? Politics of the Raj in E. M. Forster and Edward Thompson', in *Colonial Transactions: English Literature and India*, Manchester: Manchester University Press, 1995; G. K. Das, '*A Passage to India*: A Socio-Historical Study', in John Beer (ed.), *A Passage to India: Essays and Interpretations*, London: Macmillan, 1985, pp. 1–15. On (homo)sexuality see Robert K. Martin and George Piggford (eds), *Queer*

antly as emblematic of or suffused with the relationships between East and West, Britain and India, coloniser and colonised.

However, the shift away from formalist interpretations of the novel has brought out two key aspects of *A Passage to India* aside from colonialism: the representation of women and the importance of sexuality. In her essay '*A Passage to India* as "Marriage Fiction": Forster's Sexual Politics',[4] Elaine Showalter foregrounds the novel's concern with marriage from Mrs Moore's two husbands, alongside her view that too much fuss is made over marriage (p. 147), to parallels between Adela's sacrifice of herself to Ronny and Aziz's early belief in purdah and women as possessions. Because Forster appears hostile to marriage, and to the possibility of successful sexual relations more generally, many critics feel that Fielding's union with Stella at the end of the book is a compromise on Forster's part, and is no more satisfactory or convincing than Margaret Schlegel's marriage to Henry Wilcox in *Howards End*. Showalter argues that the burden of the incident at the caves is Adela's desire for not sex but emotional intimacy on the eve of her proposed marriage to Ronny: a loveless union that would amount to 'legalised rape'.

Frances L. Restuccia, in '"A Cave of My Own": E. M. Forster and Sexual Politics',[5] analyses the novel from both Anglo-American and French feminist perspectives. The first approach, she notes, would easily identify the misogyny exhibited by both the narrator and the principal male characters, combined with a general condemnation of Anglo-Indian women and a silence placed over Indian women, but would fail to come to terms with the indeterminacy of the caves. The second, French feminist, approach, by contrast, identifies the caves themselves as the entry to the female in the novel: they represent a vaginal opening after the mention of the Indian earth mother's breasts the party see from their elephant (pp. 152–3). Inside the caves, the pre-symbolic language that amounts only to ou-boum can be read as the semiotic voice of the female which challenges the rational systematising of the patriarchal raj and its official discourse. Together these approaches suggest that the caves can be identified with female subversion and Adela's reaction as a rebellion from the womb as she for the first time fully realises the threat of misogyny all around her.

An essay by Jenny Sharpe that combines a feminist and a post-colonial reading of the novel's gender politics is included on pp. 75–83, as are several essays that deal with the issues of masculinity and male desire in *A Passage to India*. Forster's world in the novel is largely a homosocial one, and even Mrs Moore and Adela

Forster, Chicago: University of Chicago Press, 1997; Parminder Bakshi, 'The Politics of Desire: E. M. Forster's Encounters with India', in Tony Davies and Nigel Wood (eds), *A Passage to India*, Buckingham: Open University Press, 1994; Christopher Lane, 'Volatile Desire: Ambivalence and Distress in Forster's Colonial Narratives', in Bart Moore-Gilbert (ed.), *Writing India 1757–1990*, Manchester: Manchester University Press, 1996; Joseph Bristow, *Effeminate England: Homoerotic Writing after 1885*, New York: Columbia University Press, 1995; and Bristow (ed.), *Sexual Sameness: Textual Differences in Lesbian and Gay Writing*, London and New York: Routledge, 1992.

4 Elaine Showalter, '*A Passage to India* as "Marriage Fiction": Forster's Sexual Politics', *Women and Literature*, 5, 1977, pp. 3–16.

5 Frances L. Restuccia, '"A Cave of My Own": E. M. Forster and Sexual Politics', *Raritan*, 9, 1989, pp. 110–28.

are unsexed by being pronounced by Aziz as too old and too unattractive (p. 85) respectively to impress themselves upon him as women. Arguably, they can therefore be seen as examples of Forster's surrogate men, as connectors who bring the males together and constitute only the subplot in comparison with Forster's interest in Aziz and Fielding.

Following the favourable reviews and essays that praised the political balance and the character portrayals in the novel, the first substantial strike in the backlash against Forster was made in 1954 by Nirad Chaudhuri, who, in his article 'Passage To and From India',[6] criticised the book for its Muslim protagonist (unrepresentative of a predominantly Hindu country or of the 'India question' the novel in some ways sought to address), and for its reduction of political history to a liberal's preoccupation with personal relationships. Since then, much discussion of the novel has shifted gradually away from its presentation of the 'twilight of the double vision' to its representation of Indo-British relationships (some of these analyses are included below and I will not discuss them in detail here).

It was not until the 1970s that this strain of criticism became established: a decade notable for Forster's death and the general knowledge of his homosexuality, P. N. Furbank's biography and the proliferation of new literary theories, of which the one that will most preoccupy us here is the inauguration of postcolonial studies in the Western academy with the publication of Edward Said's *Orientalism*.[7] One of the earliest critics to write from the angle of Indo-British relationships was Benita Parry, in both her 1972 book *Delusions and Discoveries: Studies on India in the British Imagination, 1880–1930*[8] and her essay for G. K. Das and John Beer's 1979 *E. M. Forster: A Human Exploration* (revised in 1985 as 'The Politics of Representation in *A Passage to India*').[9] Parry's readings of the novel assert the context of the colonial 'historical situation' as important both to the study of Forster's story and to the meaning of literary texts: European fiction inherits and informs the Empires' practices of domination over the colonies, through force and representation. For example, a clear instance of stereotyping is McBryde's belief in 'Oriental pathology'. McBryde's 'scientific' theory that Indians are lustful and threatening in fact underlies aspects of the entire narrative. Its stereotype of the lascivious East pervades the 'Marabar Caves incident' (when Dr Aziz is accused of assaulting Adela Quested), which serves to bring the English together at the club, to assert their Englishness and to condemn the 'Oriental'. McBryde's selective characterisation of Aziz typifies this fetishisation of the Other, mixing disavowal and desire: McBryde distastefully represents Aziz as a (stereo)typical Indian who reads pornography, visits prostitutes and, because of the climate, is a born criminal. The stereotype is only explicitly challenged when Fielding tells McBryde that he also goes to the brothels in Calcutta, a comment

6 Nirad Chaudhuri, 'Passage To and From India' [1954], in Rutherford (ed.), *Twentieth Century Interpretations of* A Passage to India, Englewood Cliffs: Prentice-Hall, 1970.

7 Edward Said, *Orientalism* [1978], Harmondsworth: Penguin, 1991.

8 Benita Parry, *Delusions and Discoveries: Studies on India in the British Imagination, 1880–1930*, London: Allen Lane, 1972.

9 Benita Parry, 'The Politics of Representation in *A Passage to India*', in John Beer (ed.), A Passage to India*: Essays in Interpretation*, London: Macmillan, 1985.

that merely throws doubt on Fielding for McBryde. The ambivalence of McBryde's fixation is drawn out at the trial when he asserts that the 'darker' races are attracted to the 'fairer' – a narcissistic conviction that also signals the anxiety felt by the coloniser – and a member of the audience responds by asking if it works this way around even when the English person (Adela) is so less attractive than the Indian (Aziz).

Another important early essay in terms of post-colonial studies is Abdul R. JanMohamed's 'The Economy of Manichean Allegory: The Function of Racial Difference in Colonialist Literature'.[10] JanMohamed posits 'imaginary' and 'symbolic' kinds of colonialist writing, instancing Forster's novel as an example of 'symbolic' literature, which shows an awareness of 'potential identity' (while 'imaginary' literature is characterised by aggression and a projection of the coloniser's self-alienation onto the colonised). He discusses *A Passage to India* as one of the two early twentieth-century English novels that 'offer the most interesting attempts to overcome the barriers of racial difference' (cf. Christopher Lane's 'Managing the "White Man's Burden": The Racial Imaginary in Forster's Fiction'[11]). Through a consideration of Forster's complex symbolism, JanMohamed marries the different emphases of New Critical interpretations with the kind of approach taken in more recent political commentaries. He shows that since the 1980s there has been a broad range of readings that have focused on different aspects of the novel: colonialism, Forster's homosexuality, feminist readings of Adela's portrayal, the elements of mimicry and ambivalence, the central absence in the text (the lack of description of what happened in the caves), representations of India, *A Passage's* highly wrought structure and Edward Said's concept of 'Orientalism'.

Said, indebted to Ferdinand de Saussure's theory of definition through difference in language, and to Michel Foucault's argument that cultural and political divisions are discursively constructed by interested parties, states that:

> [The Orient] is not merely *there*, just as the Occident is not just *there* either. We must take seriously Vico's comment that men make their own history, that what they can know is what they have made, and extend it to geography: as both geographical and cultural entities – to say nothing of historical entities – such locales, regions, geographical sectors as 'Orient' and 'Occident' are man-made.
>
> (Said, *Orientalism*, p. 244)

This acknowledges the way in which images of the East and the West have been constructed antithetically, through their supposed differences. Indeed, as D. C. Goonetilleke[12] notes: 'It has been a common tendency for people of developing

10 Abdul R. JanMohamed, 'The Economy of Manichean Allegory: The Function of Racial Difference in Colonialist Literature', in Henry Louis Gates Jr (ed.), *'Race', Writing and Difference*, Chicago: University of Chicago Press, 1986.

11 Christopher Lane, 'Managing the "White Man's Burden": The Racial Imaginary in Forster's Fiction', *Discourse*, 15: 3, 1993.

12 D. C. R. A. Goonetilleke, *Images of the Raj*, London: Macmillan, 1988.

countries to look at the West and for Europeans to look at developing countries, in romantic fashion' (p. 7). However, Goonetilleke's arguments generally serve to illustrate his view that when looking at colonial fiction there always remains the likelihood of finding a distorted reflection that needs close examination, whereas Said's analysis suggests the post-structuralist perspective that nothing exists outside of its constructions in language and so representations cannot be divided into the authentic and the inauthentic, only into inscriptions that serve different power interests.

Another influential critic, Sara Suleri,[13] perhaps thinking of, amongst others, Colonel Creighton's Indian survey in *Kim*, in which every camp and village is recorded, characterises colonial fiction's treatment of geographical distinctions in this way (partly thinking of Forster's travelogue opening to *A Passage to India*):

> Typically, the narrator is a cartographer, the only locus of rationality in an area of engulfing unreliability, so that ultimately the narrative mind is the only safe terrain the texts provide. India itself, like a Cheshire cat, functions as a dislocated metaphor for an entity that is notoriously remiss in arriving at the appointed place at the correct time. As a consequence, it becomes a space that imposes its unreality on western discourse to the point where the narrative has no option but to redouble on itself, to internalize the symbolic landscape of India in order to make it human. Thus geography is subsumed into the more immediate and familiar territory of the liberal imagination, in the act of recolonizing its vagrant subject with the intricacies of a defined sensibility.
>
> Such is the imagination, of course, that legitimizes a text like *A Passage to India* as a humanely liberal parable of imperialism, and allows a reader like Trilling to interpret the novel's depiction of Eastern action as a metaphor for the behaviour of the West. In other words, the only difference of India inheres in the fact that it is symbolic of something the western mind must learn about itself.
>
> (Suleri, 'The Geography of *A Passage to India*', p. 245)

Suleri argues that, in the use of metaphoric geography, the West's Others most often appear as (dark) holes, spaces, lacunae, places uninhabited by civilised people, God, or Western morality: 'Forster . . . constructs a symbolic geography that provides western narrative with its most compelling and durable image of India, which is, of course, the figure of India as a hollow, or a cave' (ibid., p. 246). This corresponds with other faults (such as muddle and contradiction) that Forster attributes to India, whether in the space of cave, temple or mosque. However, Suleri's stress on hollows fails to emphasise the Christian element of *A Passage to India*; the 'Caves' section is also symbolic of Western spiritual vacancy, sandwiched between the holy buildings of a Muslim 'Mosque' and a Hindu 'Temple', where the Christian 'Church' ought to reside (or perhaps the 'Court' of the Indian

13 Sara Suleri, 'The Geography of *A Passage to India*', in D. Walder (ed.), *Literature in the Modern World*, Milton Keynes: Open University Press, 1991.

Princely States). Suleri's argument also seems at odds with much of Forster's presentation of infinity and boundlessness – of the overarching sky, the circles of people that no earthly invitation can embrace, the silence beyond the remotest echo. The small spaces in the novel are more often the places resorted to by the English body and mind unable to cope without limitations. It is the openness that tires the 'souls' of Forster's characters, Indian and British, and encourages them to retreat 'to the permanent lines which habit or chance have dictated' (ibid., p. 247).

Suleri's discussion of the novel is representative of many recent studies that, since Gillian Beer's 1980 essay[14] on *A Passage*'s use of 'negation', have emphasised their recognition of the silences, omissions and gaps in Forster's text to develop political and post-colonial readings (cf. Moffat (1990)[15]). The characterisation of India as a place without bounds does however complement Forster's inscription of it as an inexplicable country without rationality: 'Hassan [. . .] found it possible not to hear him; heard and didn't hear, just as Aziz had called and hadn't called. "That's India all over . . . how like us . . . there we are" ' (*A Passage to India*, pp. 114–15). Though Forster is keen to emphasise the other-worldliness of India to the European mind, this seems in some ways a continuation of Cromer's view, popular in Europe, that logic is ignored by 'the Oriental'.

In Forster's metaphoric system it is also the topography of India that keeps East and West necessarily apart (in other words it defines their limits), and proscribes contact or connection. Suleri writes that:

> Finally, what prevents the European and the Indian from completing their embrace is the obliterating presence of the landscape. The European wants the completion of his desire in the present moment, yet the narrative gives the last word to the land's great power to deny and disappear.
>
> (ibid., pp. 249–50)

The importance of natural and political geography in much colonial writing lies in its enabling of a crude definition of East and West and the people found in each. For the Europeans, the foreign, alien soil of India becomes a metaphor for those who live on it, and the West's response to it is a correlative of its response to 'non-Europeans'. Said notes:

> we are left with a sense of the pathetic distance still separating 'us' from an Orient destined to bear its foreignness as a mark of its permanent estrangement from the West. This is the disappointing conclusion corroborated (contemporaneously) by the ending of E. M. Forster's

14 Gillian Beer, 'Negation in *A Passage to India*', *Essays in Criticism*, 30, 1980, pp. 151–66. Also included in John Beer (ed.), A Passage to India: *Essays in Interpretation*, London: Macmillan, 1985.

15 Wendy Moffat, '*A Passage to India* and the Limits of Certainty', *Journal of Narrative Technique*, 20, 1990, pp. 331–41.

A Passage to India, where Aziz and Fielding attempt, and fail at, reconciliation.

(Said, *Orientalism*, p. 244)

Yet, Forster discussed the Empire in *A Passage to India* in terms of Western exclusion: 'We must exclude someone from our gathering, or we shall be left with nothing' (p. 58): the 'nothing' that is precisely the message of the caves. Forster places this in comparison with the inclusion he finds typical of India and Indians: 'I invite you all' is a representative phrase for Forster to give to Aziz (p. 86). This inclusiveness is equated with a lack of discrimination evident in all life on the subcontinent.

> Perhaps [the wasp] mistook the peg for a branch – no Indian animal has any sense of an interior. Bats, rats, birds, insects will as soon nest inside a house as out; it is to them a normal growth of the eternal jungle, which alternately produces houses trees, houses trees. There he hung, asleep, while jackals in the plain bayed their desires and mingled with the percussion of drums.
>
> (*A Passage to India*, p. 55)

Pitted against this is the division that Forster implies is derived from the Indian soil. Such a sentiment is present in the famous last sentence of the novel, but also earlier: 'he had challenged the spirit of the Indian earth, which tries to keep men in compartments' (p. 141). Forster's decision to situate division in the soil as much as in human relations is at odds with an anti-colonial perspective which would lay the blame at the door of the strong inclination towards hierarchy inherent in England's class-steeped society. These divisions have usually been encoded in the language of Orientalism. That is, alongside the systems of hierarchy applied to the Empire, a vocabulary arose in the nineteenth century for the discussion of 'non-Europeans' as the subjects of study by a Western world whose sense of superiority necessitated strict discrimination. Said explains it thus in *Orientalism*: 'What [mid-nineteenth-century scholars] did was to place Orientalism on a scientific and rational basis. This entailed not only their own exemplary work but also the creation of a vocabulary and ideas that could be used impersonally by anyone who wished to become an Orientalist' (p. 10).

Forster, as an early twentieth-century European writer, worked within this discourse, but he also had a desire to overcome the attitude that 'East is East and West is West'. Cyril Connolly[16] says the following: 'the novels of Forster state the general conflict which is localised in the political conflict of today. His themes are the breaking down of barriers: between white and black, between class and class, between man and woman, between art and life. "Only connect . . .", the motto of *Howards End*, might be the lesson of all his work' (*Enemies of Promise*, p. 18). Despite this, a number of criticisms have been levelled at Forster by critics such as

16 Cyril Connolly, *Enemies of Promise* [1938], Harmondsworth: Penguin, 1961.

Chaudhuri and Suleri. There are undoubtedly generalisations about Indians made by the narrator of *A Passage to India* that are for the most part unmatched by similar observations on (all) Britons: 'like all Indians, [Aziz] was skilful in the slighter impertinences' (p. 296). Remarks such as this build up the impression that Forster is writing to 'us' about 'them'.

Using the work of Frantz Fanon as well as Said, Brenda R. Silver[17] also analyses issues of control and resistance throughout the novel in terms of gender, race and sex (e.g. Indian women are figured as rapable, Indian men are metonymically represented as penises). Where Sara Suleri has argued that the centre of the book is the vacancy of the Marabar Caves (mirroring European beliefs about the emptiness of India, a land simply of heat and dust), Silver maintains that at its heart is the 'unspeakable' colonial trope of rape (cf. Sharpe's essay, pp. 75–83). Again, while Suleri says that 'To the imperial English mind, India can only be represented as a gesture of possible rape' ('The Geography of *A Passage to India*', p. 246), Silver argues that Aziz 'reduced to his sexuality, becomes simultaneously rapist and object of rape' ('Periphrasis, Power and Rape in *A Passage to India*', p. 94). A simple expression of this in another novel, published within a decade of Forster's, comes in Orwell's *Burmese Days*:[18] 'To [Mrs Lackersteen's] mind the words "sedition", "Nationalism", "rebellion", "Home Rule", conveyed one thing and one only, and that was a picture of herself being raped by a procession of jet-black coolies with rolling white eyeballs' (p. 156).

One of the most influential critics in this area is Homi Bhabha, whose work can lead towards a post-colonial perspective on a word at the heart of *A Passage to India*, and of Forster's writing generally: 'muddle.' Different commentators have placed various emphases on this Forsterian keyword. In the novel itself the term is likened to a 'mystery' (e.g. in chapters 7 and 29). In critical discussions, Tony Davies[19] has compared Forster's 'muddle' to deconstruction's 'aporias' (Davies and Wood, *A Passage to India*, p. 15), while Wilfred Stone[20] has written that it 'describes a condition of separateness, of doubleness, that hints at everything that divides people and rives them into separate religions, races and political parties' (Beer (ed.), A Passage to India: *Essays in Interpretation*, p. 24). Stone thinks that in the novel doublings characterise the things that divide (and trinities – such as Mosque, Caves, Temple, or Cold Weather, Hot Weather, Rains, or Animal, Vegetable, Mineral – the things that connect). Yet, if the effect of muddles is to separate, their action is usually to conflate, confuse and commingle. Consequently, they can be considered in terms of Bhabha's theory of hybridity.[21] Hybridity for Bhabha is not simply a fusion of two things, it represents a 'mud-

17 Brenda R. Silver, 'Periphrasis, Power and Rape in *A Passage to India*', *Novel* 22, Fall 1988, pp. 86–105.
18 *Complete Novels of George Orwell*, Harmondsworth: Penguin, 1983.
19 Tony Davies and Nigel Wood, (eds), *A Passage to India*, Buckingham: Open University Press, 1994.
20 Wilfred Stone, 'The Caves of *A Passage to India*', in John Beer (ed.), A Passage to India: *Essays in Interpretation*, London: Macmillan, 1985.
21 Homi Bhabha, *The Location of Culture*, London: Routledge, 1994. Unless otherwise stated, references are to the essays in this collection.

dle', a confusion that results from a meeting of cultures in the colonial contact zone. Hybridity is illustrated by Bhabha in several essays. The first one I want to mention is an example from a missionary in India in the early nineteenth century (see 'Signs Taken for Wonders: Questions of Ambivalence and Authority under a Tree outside Delhi, May 1817') about the keen acceptance of Bibles in Bengal. It transpired that the distributed copies of the Bible were not read but willingly received by Indians to be sold or bartered, and to be used as waste or wrapping paper. Meanwhile, back in England, 'the public are hearing of so many Bibles distributed, they expect to hear soon of a correspondent number of conversions' (p. 122). This muddle is one sign of the effects of hybridity, the tension the missionary feels at the borderline between cultures which have vastly different expectations of the uses to which a copy of the Bible might be put. Bhabha writes that 'If the effect of colonial power is seen to be *the production* of hybridisation rather than the noisy command of colonialist authority or the silent repression of native traditions, then an important change of perspective occurs [. . .] enabl[ing] a form of subversion, founded on the undecidability that turns the discursive conditions of dominance into the grounds of intervention' (p. 112). The simple spreading of what the Europeans present as the unitary, unchangeable Word of God is undermined by the natives' responses: '*how can the word of God come from the flesh-eating mouths of the English*?'; and later '*how can it be the European book, when we believe it is God's gift to us*?' (original emphasis). The Indians' questions require that authority and its texts engage with cultural difference and so become not mirrored or brought into a dialectic but hybridised, which Forster presents as 'muddle'. Another example of hybridity occurred in India when vegetarian Hindus understood Christian communion in terms of a kind of cannibalism, eating the flesh of Christ, or vampirism, drinking his blood.

In this way, Bhabha says, 'in the very practice of domination the language of the master becomes hybrid – neither the one thing nor the other' (p. 33). Every concept the coloniser brings to the colonised will itself be reborn, renewed, reinterpreted in the light of the Other's culture. As he says elsewhere, 'the important thing about the hybrid site is to see that the contenders in any antagonistic interaction are never unitary . . . and their interaction therefore has the possibility always of setting up other sites.'[22] Hybridity shifts power, questions discursive authority, and suggests that colonial discourse is never wholly in the control of the coloniser: in *A Passage to India* this is seen in the endless muddles and mysteries engendered by cultural difference.

In a discussion that has much relevance to the response of the Anglo-Indian community to Adela's experience at the Marabar Caves, Bhabha also expands on the notion of colonial paranoia, which he seems to pick up from a comment of Edward Said's: 'Orientalism is a form of paranoia, knowledge of another kind, say, from ordinary historical knowledge' (Said, *Orientalism*, p. 72). Bhabha discusses paranoia as an effect of hybridity, which 'represents that ambivalent

22 Homi Bhabha, 'The Postcolonial Critic: Homi Bhabha interviewed by David Bennett and Terry Collits', *Arena*, 96, 1991, p. 61 .

"turn" of the discriminated subject into the terrifying, exorbitant object of paranoid classification – a disturbing questioning of the images and presences of authority' (p. 113) Paranoia is here defined as an aggression projected onto the other: s/he hates or deceives me – manifest in the stereotypes of the lying native or the duplicitous Oriental. Thus, the effect of hybridity on the coloniser is paranoia, a feeling of persecution, an anxiety spread throughout authority.

If we look at the examples in the novel of 'muddle', they often appear as signs of cultural difference: the invitation from Mrs Bhattacharya; Aziz's collar stud; the reasons for the Bridge Party; who Fielding has married; and, of course, what happened in the Marabar Caves. The novel repeatedly uses the obfuscatory words 'muddle' and 'mystery' to characterise what is happening in the narrative, but it is a matter of interpretation how far this is a reflection of Forster's pessimism, of Imperial uncertainty, or of British-Indian relationships.

Lastly, the view that hybridity is figured as 'muddle' by Forster is supported by his 1921 experience in Dewas of the Hindu festival celebrating the birth of Krishna, an incarnation of the God Vishnu:

> Well, what's it all about? It's called Gokul Ashtami – i.e. the *8 days* feast in honour of Krishna who was born at *Gokul* near Muttra, and I cannot yet discover how much of it is traditional and how much due to H.H. What troubles me is that every detail, almost without exception, is fatuous and in bad taste. The altar is a mess of little objects, stifled with rose leaves, the walls are hung with deplorable oleographs, the chandeliers, draperies – everything bad. [. . .] Yet I am very much muddled in my own mind about it all [. . .] There is no dignity, no taste, no form, and though I am dressed as a Hindu I shall never become one. I don't think one ought to be irritated with Idolatry because one can see from the faces of the people that it touches something very deep in their hearts. But it is natural that Missionaries, who think these ceremonies wrong as well as inartistic, should lose their tempers.
>
> (*The Hill of Devi*, pp. 104–5)[23]

In the fictional reworking of this experience in *A Passage to India*, Forster writes: 'They sang not even to the God who confronted them, but to a saint; they did not one thing which the non-Hindu would feel dramatically correct; this approaching triumph of India was a muddle (as we call it), a frustration of reason and form' (p. 282).

A frustration of Enlightenment reason and European form is precisely what happens throughout Forster's novel, and the terms he uses to describe the British experience of cultural shock in India enunciate the disturbing effect of hybridity on the coloniser: India's 'approaching triumph' is the raj's 'muddle'.

23 E. M. Forster, *The Hill of Devi* [1953], Harmondsworth: Penguin, 1965.

Early Critical Reception

In the main, reviews of *A Passage to India* in 1924 were very favourable, praising the novel's fairness, characterisation and verisimilitude. Hostile reactions were almost only found among reviews by and letters in the Anglo-Indian press. The *Calcutta Statesman* thought the trial scene preposterous and 'full of technical error' while the *Calcutta Englishman* took the book to be a tissue of prejudices. The contemporary response from the Indian press was generally sympathetic and acknowledged that Forster's novel would provoke hatred among the British in India. One critic, Bhupal Singh, quoted on pp. 56–8, wrote in 1934 that it contained a 'a subtle portraiture of the Indian', while another, Nihal Singh, said in the year of publication, in the Calcutta *Modern Review*, that it showed 'how the British in India despise and ostracise Indians, while on their part the Indians mistrust and misjudge the British'. From the press in Britain, the response in general began with the view that a novel from Forster after a fourteen-year wait was reason enough to celebrate, and concluded with the opinion that it was Forster's best work. For an extended discussion of responses to the novel see P. N. Furbank's biography of Forster, pp. 126–30.

The following extracts are taken from Philip Gardner (ed.), *E. M. Forster: The Critical Heritage*, London: Routledge, 1973.

Rose Macaulay (1881–1958), 'Women in the East', *Daily News*, 4 June 1924, p. 8

Mr E. M. Forster is, to many people, the most attractive and the most exquisite of contemporary novelists (for a contemporary novelist he has, fortunately, now once more become). Further, he is probably the most truthful, both superficially and fundamentally. His delicate character presentation – too organic to be called drawing – his gentle and pervading humour, his sense and conveyal of the beauty, the ridiculousness, and the nightmare strangeness, of all life, his accurate recording of social, intellectual and spiritual shades and reactions, his fine-spun honesty of thought, his poetry and ironic wit – these qualities have made him from the first one of the rather few novelists who can be read with delight.

No one now writing understands so well as he the queer interaction of fantasy and ordinary life, the ghosts that halo common persons and things, the odd, mystic power of moments. Neither does anyone, I think, understand quite so well, or convey with such precision and charm, what ordinary people are really like, the way they actually do think and talk. His people are solid, three-dimensioned, and he sees them both from without and within.

A Passage to India is his fifth novel, and his first for fourteen years. Those who fear that his peculiar gifts may be wasted in a novel about India can be reassured; they have full scope. He can make even these brown men live; they are as alive as his Cambridge undergraduates, his London ladies, his young Italians, his seaside aunts; they are drawn with an equal and a more amazing insight and vision. And in the Anglo-Indians, male and female, he has material the most suitable ready to his hand.

The Ruling Race

Never was a more convincing, a more pathetic, or a more amusing picture drawn of the Ruling Race in India. A sympathetic picture, too, for Mr Forster is sympathetic to almost everyone. Here, for instance, is the Club, after a supposed insult offered by an Indian to an English-woman:

> They had started speaking of 'women and children' – that phrase that exempts the male from sanity when it has been repeated a few times. Each felt that all he loved best in the world was at stake, demanded revenge, and was filled with a not unpleasing glow. . . . 'But it's the women and children,' they repeated, and the Collector knew he ought to stop them intoxicating themselves, but had not the heart.

Somewhere between the two camps, the Anglo-Indians and the Indians, are the newcomers to India – an old lady and a girl, not yet hardened and harrowed into the Anglo-Indian outlook, but full of honest, interested curiosity. These two women are alive with all the imaginative actuality with which Mr Forster invests his old and his young females. He is almost alone in this, that he enters into the minds of old ladies, and attributes to them those sensitive reactions to life, those philosophic, muddled speculations as to the universe and personal relationships, which most novelists only find younger persons worthy to contain or to emit. The old lady in this book is the most clear-sighted, sensitive, civilised and intellectually truthful person in her circle. She speculates like a male or female undergraduate. 'She felt increasingly (vision or nightmare?) that, though people are important, the relations between them are not, and that in particular too much fuss has been made over marriage. Centuries of carnal embracement, yet man is no nearer to understanding man. And to-day she felt this with such force that it seemed itself a relationship, itself a person who was trying to take hold of her hand.' What other novelist would attribute such thoughts to a lady of sixty-five who has just been told of the engagement of her son?

It is such patient, imaginative realism as this that distinguishes Mr Forster from most writers. His young woman, too, is an achievement – a queer, unattractive, civilised, logical, intellectually honest girl, who wanted to understand India and the Indians, and came up against the wall of Anglo-India between herself and them. *A Passage to India* is really a story about this Anglo-Indian wall, and the futile occasional attempts, from either side, to surmount it. I suppose it is a sad story, as most truthful stories of collective human relationships must be; it is an ironic tragedy, but also a brilliant comedy of manners, and a delightful entertainment. Its passages of humour or beauty might, quoted, fill several columns. But they cannot profitably be isolated; Mr Forster is not, in the main, a detachable epigrammist; his wit and his poetry are both organically contextual. This novel has a wider and a deeper range than any of his others.

He has quite lost the touch of preciousness of exaggerated care for nature and the relationships of human beings, that may faintly irritate some readers of his earlier books. He used once to write at times too much as a graduate (even occasionally as an undergraduate) of King's College, Cambridge (perhaps the most civilised place in the world), who has had an amour with Italy and another with the god Pan. In *A Passage to India* (as, indeed, in *Howards End*), Pan is only implicit, the mysticism is more diffused, the imagination at once richer, less fantastic, and more restrained. It is a novel that, from most novelists, would be an amazing piece of work. Coming from Mr Forster, it is not amazing, but it is, I think, the best and most interesting book he has written.

But I should like very much to know what Anglo-Indians will think of it.

Leonard Woolf (1880–1969),[1] 'Arch beyond Arch', *Nation and Athenaeum*, 14 June 1924, p. 354

A little while ago I wrote in these columns that the book of this publishing season to which I looked forward most eagerly was Mr E. M. Forster's new novel, *A Passage to India*. And now it has appeared and I have read it and – Well, there are few things more exciting than to look forward to the publication of a new book, by a living writer, to read it, and to find one's hopes realized. That, at least, has happened to me with *A Passage to India*. But it only adds to the difficulty of writing about it. It is very easy to criticize a book which you know to be bad or which you think to be good; your real difficulties begin with a book by a contemporary which seems to you to be very good. There is, for instance, that terrible question: 'How good?' a question which, in the case of Mr Forster, it is hopeless to try to answer in 1,200 words.

There are, first, certain obvious things which must be said about *A Passage to India*. It is superbly written. Mr Forster seems now to have reached the point at which there is nothing too simple or too subtle for his pen; he is able to find words

1 Husband of Virginia Woolf and co-founder with her of the Hogarth Press; also an important political theorist and a member of the Fabian Society.

which exactly fit, which perfectly express, every thought which comes to him, and neither the thought nor the words are those which would come to anyone else in the world except Mr Forster. If that is not one of the essential characteristics of a great writer or of great writing, then I have no knowledge or understanding of either. Let me quote: –

> She had come to the state where the horror of the universe and its smallness are both visible at the same time – the twilight of the double vision in which so many elderly people are involved. If this world is not to our taste, well, at all events there is Heaven, Hell, Annihilation – one or other of those large things that huge scenic background of stars fires blue or black air. All heroic endeavour, and all that is known as art, assumes that there is such a background just as all practical endeavour, when the world is to our taste, assumes that the world is all. But in the twilight of the double vision, a spiritual muddle is set up for which no high-sounding words can be found; we can neither act nor refrain from action; we can neither ignore nor respect Infinity. Mrs Moore had always inclined to resignation. As soon as she landed in India it seemed to her good, and when she saw the water flowing through the mosque-tank, or the Ganges, or the moon, caught in the shawl of the night with all the other stars, it seemed a beautiful goal and an easy one. To be one with the universe! So dignified and so simple. But there was always some little duty to be performed first, some new card to be turned up from the diminishing pack and placed, and while she was pottering about the Marabar struck its gong.

In this book there are all the elements which made Mr Forster's previous novels of such promise. There is the extraordinarily subtle and individual humour, the lifelikeness of the characters, the command of dialogue, the power of opening windows upon what is both queer and beautiful. The difference between *A Passage to India* and the former novels is that now Mr Forster knows exactly how to use the elements of his genius. The promise of *Where Angels Fear to Tread* was renewed, but not fulfilled, in *Howards End*. None of these former books 'came off;' and there were in them disconcerting lapses into 'silliness,' if I dare say so – the silliness, not of a stupid but of a clever man. But there is no silliness, no lapse, no wobbling in *A Passage to India*; it marches firmly, triumphantly, even grimly and sadly – the adverbs can only be explained by reading the book – through the real life and politics of India, the intricacy of personal relations, the story itself, the muddle and the mystery of life.

I have left my last paragraph for what I shall find most difficult to say. I ought, I know, to have said something about the plot, the story, the novel. They are extraordinarily interesting, but they are the superficies of the book. Even what I have been writing about in the previous paragraphs is on, or only just below, the surface. Nearly all great books, certainly nearly all great novels, have deep beneath their surface a theme or themes which are what give to the whole book its form, real meaning, greatness. Most writers are content with a single informing idea of this sort as the basis of their book, but what makes Mr Forster's novel so remarkable is that he has a large number of such 'themes,' which, interwoven with great imaginative subtlety, weave a strange and beautiful texture for the book itself. The old lady, Mrs Moore, a superb character in the book, felt that 'outside the arch there seemed always an arch, beyond the remotest echo a silence.' I feel the same about the book, when I look back on it, if one adds, perhaps, that beyond the remotest silence there is again an echo. There is the story itself with the two ladies who wanted to see India, the Anglo-Indian society of Chandrapore, and Aziz the only living Indian whom I have ever met in a book, and his friendship – which failed to be a friendship – with the Englishman Fielding. Behind that is an arch of politics, the politics of Anglo-India and the nationalist India. And beyond that is another arch, half mystery, half muddle, which permeates India and personal relations and life itself – 'and all the time,' as Mrs Moore says, 'this to do and that to do and this to do in your way and that to do in her way, and everything sympathy and confusion and bearing one another's burdens. Why can't this be done and that be done in my way and they be done and I at peace? Why has anything to be done, I cannot see.' And beyond that the terrible arch of 'personal relations' – do 'we exist not in ourselves, but in terms of each other's minds'? – and 'the friendliness, as of dwarfs shaking hands.' And beyond that the still more terrible arch of disillusionment – 'the shadow of the shadow of a dream.' So the book builds itself up, arch beyond arch, into something of great strength, beauty, and also of sadness. The themes are woven and interwoven into a most intricate pattern, against which, or in which, the men and women are shown to us pathetically, rather ridiculously, entangled. That is how the book presents itself to me immediately after having read it, and perhaps my description may be hardly intelligible to anyone who has not read it. If so, all I can do is to advise him to rush out to the nearest bookseller, buy a copy of the book, and read it for himself.

H. W. Massingham (1860–1924),[1] 'The Price of India's Friendship', *New Leader*, 27 June 1924, p. 10

I read the other day a notice, in *The Nation*, of Mr E. M. Forster's novel, *A Passage to India*. It was a very laudatory notice, written by a gentleman who expressed, with evident sincerity, his sense of the æsthetic and spiritual qualities of Mr Forster's book, and gave an alluring picture of the delicacy and complexity of its structure, built up in 'arch beyond arch' of individual and personal and political relationships. At that point the criticism came to an end, with an asseveration of the extreme beauty of this production of Mr Forster's. But on the actual subject of his work, beyond a general remark that it dealt with India, with the

1 Journalist and Editor of the *Daily Chronicle*, died two months after this review appeared. His mention of the Dyers and O'Dwyers of India is a reference to General Dyer, who ordered the Amritsar Massacre in 1919, and Sir Michael O'Dwyer, Lieutenant-Governor of the Punjab at the time, who supported Dyer's action.

politics of Anglo-India, with Nationalist India, and with the visit of two English ladies to India, the article threw no light whatever. For all that one could tell, Mr Forster might have written in a sketchy-spiritual way anything about India that had come into his head to write. The one palpable fact which was made clear to the reader was that he had strongly impressed Mr Leonard Woolf with the beautiful way he had written it.

A Satire of Contrasts

Now, this habit of our latter-day critics of writing on literature as if its form-pattern, or its spiritual rhythm, and not its meaning and content, were the most important thing about it, is very characteristic of them, and it is quite true that Mr Forster's wonderful style offers itself to this kind of admiration. He has the modern writer's gift of analysis, of spiritual discernment of the concealed or half-concealed sides of human nature. The irony of the contrast between what we say and even think, and the dark current of instinctive life that flows on beneath all this seeming, presses on his mind, just as it presses on the sterile, not to say the malign, genius of Mr D. H. Lawrence. He has the art of presenting both the thoughts of men and the scenes in which they develop – witness the brilliant descriptions of the trial at Chandrapore and the festival of Krishna in Mau, the Indian State. And his detail is at once rich and curious. None of his contemporaries has a finer power of suggesting the colour and movement of life, and can be at once so disdainful and so sympathetic about it.

Nevertheless, it is just as informing to talk merely of the beautiful manner in which *A Passage to India* is written as it would be to remark of the *Decline and Fall* that 'Mr Gibbon had composed a wonderful architectural work on the early and late Roman Empire.' Gibbon, of course, had the most definite thing to say about Imperial and Christian Rome, and he took care to say it on nearly every one of his thousands of crowded pages. In the same way, Mr Forster has something extremely pointed to say about India, and he says it directly and passionately, or ironically and suggestively, just as the current of his thought sweeps him along.

That is by no means to say that he has written a pamphlet. *A Passage to India* is, indeed, a satire of contrasts, much in the same sense that the *Voyage to Lilliput* is a satire of contrasts. As Swift sets against the grossness of Gulliver the pettiness of the race of little men, so Mr Forster portrays the super-sensitiveness, the impulsiveness, the charm and the weakness, of Mohammedan and Hindu India, in order to emphasise the honesty, the arrogance, the intellectual shallowness, the physical courage and the moral tremors of the governing caste, in all its haughty and unimaginative segregation. In effect, the book is addressed to the Dyers and the O'Dwyers of India, and to those who keep up the political repute of these people in this country. It says: 'Keep your bad manners if you will, but realise that they are losing you India, if they have not already lost it.' Only all this is said or inferred in the manner of the artist, not of the didactic writer. The latter can bring theory, rhetoric, argument, into the case. The artist can only contribute his love or his æsthetic and moral aversions.

Now Mr Forster's temperament draws him towards native India, as it draws him away from the temper and spirit of Anglo-Indianism. Thus the exquisite picture of Dr. Aziz is touched with sympathy, as the picture of Major Callendar is deeply bitten with disdain. But both sketches are in proportion. Mr Forster knows well where the weakness of a non-English India, an India from which we had withdrawn in anger or despair, would be – an India in which the affinities and repulsions of Professor Godbole, the Brahman, met the affinities and repulsions of Dr. Aziz, the Mohammedan, without the screen of British indifference thrown between them. And he seems – perhaps he only seems – to suggest that if such Englishmen as Mr Fielding and such Englishwomen as Mrs Moore could have their say, the irreconcilable might be reconciled, the all-but-impossible accomplished. But Mr Forster's serio-comic picture of the India of to-day is not of a thing that can last. It is the image of a phantasm, almost a joke of the Time-spirit. If India is governed from the bridge-tables and tennis-courts of Chandrapore – well, the day is coming when she will be so no longer.

Warring Spiritualities

This, then, is the theme of *A Passage to India*. Its illustration is in the main through a single piece of portraiture. Dr. Aziz, the victim of an hysterical woman and an equally hysterical society, is also the hero of the story. He is imagined in such a glow of feeling and drawn with such delicacy of touch that it seems natural to guess an original. But it is clear that Mr Forster means us to take him for a good deal – not all – of India. In the rich profusion and confusion of her creeds and loyalties he stands out for something tangible, to be apprehended with sympathy and won, as far as India is to be won at all, with a price. Mrs Moore wins him in a moment, with a single touch of spiritual generosity. The Collector and the 'Bridge Party' lose him again, it seems for ever. Mr Fielding attempts a recapture, and the effort fails, because both men feel that the time of Anglo-Indian reconciliation is not yet. There is too much between – too little character and clear purpose on the one side, not enough understanding on the other. Perhaps when the problem of Krishna and his worship, the problem of Professor Godbole and his food, and the problem of 'Ronny' and his rawness, have all been solved together, the peace-makers can begin to talk.

Therefore it is not enough to ignore the subject of Mr Forster's story, and to content oneself with the delicate ornament that so delights Mr Woolf and the rest of the readers of *A Passage to India*. Yet it is true to say that its charm lies equally in its precision of detail, and in the way in which, when once the vivid impression of reality is attained, the study as a whole recedes into a mystical background, where the half-revealed forces have their play – the dim prophecies and blank misgivings of Mrs Moore, the ecstasies and (to the European mind) the absurdities of the Brahman, to whom mere happenings are nothing, and 'whose conversations frequently culminated in a cow.' Obviously, the Anglo-Indian scene is a tangle of such obscure and warring spiritualities as these. But it is also a little absurd. Absurd are the Collector and the frightened gathering in the Chandrapore club, scenting a second Mutiny because Miss Quested has had an attack of nerves.

[Quotation follows.]

Absurd, too, is Aziz himself, melting in a moment when the governing caste behaves a little decently to him, and blazing up into wrath as it falls back to its habitual mood of cold intolerance. Mr Forster's conclusion is, perhaps, a little difficult to state. Fear, and the concealment of thought that fear brings, govern, to his mind, the whole Anglo-Indian relationship. The Indian dreads the fury of a second Amritsar. The Englishman knows himself hated, a stranger in an unknown and a complicated land, and feels that the hatred is unjust. Reconciliation might come through love and understanding. But how can India understand our shy, distant race? And what is an Englishman to make of a people that bows down to the strangest kinds of idols, and yet somehow enjoys the easy and scandalous intimacy with Godhood which Mr Forster describes in his brilliant picture of the celebration of the Birth of Krishna?

[Quotation follows.]

Alas! it seems impossible for an Englishman (unless he is a Scotchman) to enjoy God. But it ought to be within his competence to begin to realise what a task the Indian spirit has laid upon him, and to resort to such interpreters of it as the author of *A Passage to India*.

Extracts from Bhupal Singh, 'Forster's Picture of India', *A Survey of Anglo-Indian Fiction*, Oxford: Oxford University Press, 1934, pp. 221–32

Mr Forster's *A Passage to India* is an oasis in the desert of Anglo-Indian fiction. It is a refreshing book, refreshing in its candour, sincerity, fairness, and art, and is worth more than the whole of the trash that passes by the name of Anglo-Indian fiction, a few writers excepted. It is a clever picture of Englishmen in India, a subtle portraiture of the Indian, especially the Moslem mind, and a fascinating study of the problems arising out of the contact of India with the West. It aims at no solution, and offers no explanation; it merely records with sincerity and insight the impressions of an English man of letters of his passage through post-War India, an Englishman who is a master of his craft, and who combines an original vision with a finished artistry. Like all original books it is intensely provoking. It does not flatter the Englishman and it does not aim at pleasing the Indian; it is likely to irritate both. It is not an imaginary picture, though it is imaginatively conceived. Most Anglo-Indian writers, as we have seen, write of India and of Indians with contempt; a very few (mostly historians) go to the other extreme. Mr Forster's object is merely to discover how people behave in relation to one another under the conditions obtaining in India at present. That he does not win applause either from India or Anglo-India is a tribute to his impartiality.

Mr Forster's theme bristles with difficulties. He takes for his subject the conflict of races. Race feeling is strong in the English; it is stronger in Anglo-Indians for reasons which can be easily understood. Indians, on the other hand, are very sensitive to insults, real or imagined. Though a conquered people, they have not forgotten their past, nor their ancient culture or civilization. It is what Mr Ralph Wright has called 'this almost fratricidal subject' that Mr Forster has chosen as the theme of his novel.

[Two sections follow, summing up the plot and giving examples of Forster's presentation of Anglo-India.]

Mr Forster's portraiture of Anglo-Indian life has called forth bitter protests from Anglo-India, and he has been accused of ignorance, if not of unfairness, in his delineation of the English colony at Chandrapore. It has to be admitted that most of the Anglo-Indians, from the Collector downwards, do not appear in a favourable light. Turton is a 'burra sahib', much too conscious of his position, before whom other Europeans cringe. His hectoring manner to Fielding is specially offensive and typical of the attitude of a 'Heaven-born' towards a by-no-means unimportant officer of the Indian Educational Department. But Turton's behaviour is the result of Fielding's pro-Indian proclivities. Fielding is not 'pukka'. That is his main fault. His profession inspires distrust, his ideas are fatal to caste. Though the sahibs tolerated him for the sake of his good heart and strong body, it is their wives who decided that he was not a sahib, and for that reason disliked him. He had to pay a heavy price for associating with Indians, and for his unconventionality and independence. Those critics who see in Turton's behaviour to Fielding something unreal, forget that it is not as types that Fielding and Turton have been delineated by Mr Forster. They are individuals. All Collectors are not Turtons, as all college Principals are not Fieldings. Major Callender [*sic*], similarly, is not representative of Civil Surgeons. His treatment of Aziz is not typical of the treatment by Englishmen of their Indian subordinates. But Callender's natural contempt and insolence are heightened by the knowledge that his subordinate is more efficient as a surgeon than himself. Mr Forster is always careful to individualize his characters, even when he is painting them as representatives of a class. The traces of exaggeration, unreality or unnaturalness that Anglo-Indians find in these characters are perhaps due to their habit of confounding the character with the type. The individual and class characteristics have been so cleverly combined in almost all the characters of Mr Forster's novel, that even his minor characters have an exquisite sense of completeness. Mr Forster is not so much a portrait painter as a psychologist. He observes human beings under certain conditions. Environment as affecting character is specially marked in his novels. He knows, as 'Affable Hawk' is careful to explain in the *New Statesman*, that often the atmosphere 'distorts human relations, making people behave wildly and foolishly who, under other circumstances, would be neither wild nor foolish'. Just as in the novels of Mr Wells, clashes of class consciousness and the confusions of the social order make it impossible for people to behave properly towards each other, similarly in *A Passage to India* racial consciousness and the contradictions of a system once established firmly on the distinction between a conquering race and a subject people, but now in the process of rapid decay, make the Turtons and Burtons and Callenders of Chandrapore behave so foolishly that they appear to be 'wildly improbable and unreal'. Turton and Callender, however, are minor characters.

[A section follows on the character of Ronny Heaslop.]

In spite of differences of opinion as regards the reality of Anglo-Indian portraits, and in spite of a few mistakes, Mr Forster's knowledge of Anglo-India shows insight and penetration.

[An approving summary follows of Forster's presentation of Moslem India.]

It is doubtful whether Mr Forster knew Hindus intimately. Professor Godbole's conservatism and his religious ecstasy, his good nature and his small lies, his tranquillity and his 'polite enigmatic' manner, are all caught by the deft pen of Mr Forster. But he is not interesting, any more than Dr. Panna Lal, Mr Das the Magistrate, the Battacharyas [*sic*] or Ram Chand. Mr Forster's description of the Gokul Ashtami in an Indian State is a beautiful picture of Hindu superstitions, faith and fervour, vulgarity and mysticism.

Mr Forster is not a propagandist. He is scrupulously fair. He has no didactic aim either. But it is possible that in one of the self-communings of Aziz, he is communicating his own vision of India of the future.

> This evening he longed to compose a new song which should be acclaimed by multitudes and even sung in the fields. In what language shall it be written? And what shall it announce? He vowed to see more of Indians who were not Mohammedans, and never to look backward. It is the only healthy course. Of what help, in this latitude and hour, are the glories of Cordova and Samarcand? They have gone, and while we lament them the English occupy Delhi and exclude us from East Africa. Islam itself, though true, throws cross-lights over the path to freedom. The song of the future must transcend creed.

Modern Criticism

Extract from Nirad Chaudhuri, 'Passage To and From India', *Encounter* (2) June 1954, pp. 19–24. Reprinted in Andrew Rutherford (ed.), *Twentieth-Century Interpretations of A Passage to India*, Englewood Cliffs: Prentice-Hall, 1970, pp. 68–74

Chaudhuri's essay was the first since Indian independence to consider Forster's novel in terms of its colonial aspect: 'as a political essay on Indo-British relations.' It continued to be a strikingly different analysis alongside the various Anglo-American readings that saw *A Passage* in terms of symbolism and structure, religion and rhythm, until the 1970s. Chaudhuri considers Forster's novel to have been contributory to, if not partly responsible for, a growing indifference to India and Empire amongst the British between the wars, culminating in a peremptory and almost dismissive granting of independence in 1947. He then goes on to suggest that the novel was both unrepresentative in its choice and inaccurate in its delineation of characters, faults that Chaudhuri believes culminated in a misrepresentation of the Indo-British relationship.

Reading *A Passage to India* some time ago, I was led to think not only of the final collective passage of the British from India but also of Mr Forster's contribution to that finale. Such an association of ideas between a novel and an event of political history may be objected to, but in this case I think the association is legitimate. For *A Passage to India* has possibly been an even greater influence in British imperial *politics* than in English literature.

From the first, the more active reaction to it followed the existing lines of political cleavage, its admirers being liberal, radical, or leftist sheep and its detractors conservative, imperialist, and diehard goats. The feud between English liberalism and the British empire in India was as old as the empire itself. Except for a short period of quiescence when Liberal-Imperialism was in vogue, it raged till 1947. Mr Forster's novel became a powerful weapon in the hands of the anti-imperialists, and was made to contribute its share to the disappearance of British rule in India.

On those, also, who did not follow clear party cues in respect of India, its influence was destructive. It alienated their sympathy from the Indian empire. As it was, the British people taken in the mass were never deeply involved in this empire, emotionally or intellectually. To them it was rather a marginal fact of British history than what it really was – a major phenomenon in the history of world civilisation. Mr Forster's book not only strengthened the indifference, it also created a positive aversion to the empire by its unattractive picture of India and Anglo-Indian life and its depiction of Indo-British relations as being of a kind that were bound to outrage the English sense of decency and fair play. Thus, the novel helped the growth of that mood which enabled the British people to leave India with an almost Pilate-like gesture of washing their hands of a disagreeable affair.

Even intrinsically, the novel had a political drift. There is of course no necessary connection between a writer's own intentions and the manner in which he is accepted or exploited by his public. It has even been said that it is only when they are debased or deformed that philosophical ideas play a part in history. But in regard to *A Passage to India*, it can be said that the author's purpose and the public response more or less coincided. The novel was quite openly a satire on the British official in India. Perhaps in a veiled form it was also a satire on the Indians who were, or aspired to be, the *clientes* of the foreign patriciate. As such it was, at one remove, a verdict on British rule in India. At the risk of depriving it of its nuances, but perhaps not misrepresenting its general purport, I might sum it up as follows. This rule is the cause of such painful maladjustment in simple human relations that even without going deeply into the rights and wrongs of the case it is desirable to put an end to it. The intention seems to have been to bring even English readers to agree with the last outburst of the hero of the novel, Aziz: 'We shall drive every blasted Englishman into the sea, and then you and I shall be friends.'

Accordingly, one is almost forced to appraise the novel as a political essay on Indo-British relations, and as soon as it is considered as such, a striking gap in Mr Forster's presentation of these relations fixes attention. It is seen that the novel wholly ignores the largest area of Indo-British relations and is taken up with a relatively small sector. The ignored area is the one I watched at first hand from the age of seven to the age of fifty. The other sector, in contrast, was known to me only by hearsay, because I feared its contact almost as much as a Pharisee feared the contact of publicans and sinners.

The Indo-British relations I was familiar with were contained, for the most part, within the conflict between Indian nationalists and the British administration. Here I saw great suffering and distress, but also exultation, a brave acceptance of ill-treatment and conquest of weak tears. The longer the men had been in jail, the more they had been persecuted, the more 'sporting' they seemed to be. In the other sector, the conflict was between associates, the British officials and their Indian subordinates or hangers-on, and had all the meanness of a family quarrel. It sizzled without providing any ennobling or even chastening release for passion, only distilling rancour. It contributed much to the pathology of Indo-British relations but virtually nothing to the final parting of ways. If we can at all speak of having driven the 'blasted Englishman into the sea,' as Aziz puts it, it was not men of his type who accomplished the feat. Those who fought British rule in India did not do so with the object of eventually gaining the Englishman's personal friendship. Just as personal humiliation did not bring them into the conflict, personal friendship did not also lure them as a goal.

But of course there was good reason for Mr Forster's choice. The reason is not however that the political conflict was impersonal and could not be treated in a novel. It could be, though the result would have been a tragedy of mutual repulsion and not a tragi-comedy of mutual attraction. Mr Forster chose the sector of which he had personal knowledge. As an Englishman paying a short visit to India, he naturally saw far less of Indians in general than of his own countrymen and of the Indians with whom the latter had official business or perfunctory social relations. Being an Englishman, of humane sensibilities, he was also shocked by the state of these relations, as among others Wilfrid Blunt was before him. On the other hand, he could not observe the larger and the more important area without going considerably out of his way and making a special effort.

There is also another and not less fundamental reason for Mr Forster's choice. That is the character of his political consciousness. I should really call it humanitarian consciousness. For his is an appeal in a political case to the court of humane feelings to what he himself calls 'common humanity' in a later essay. Now, the relationship between common humanity and politics is even more complex than that which exists between morality and politics. I firmly believe that ultimately, politics and morals are inseparable; even so, the most obvious moral judgement on a political situation is not necessarily a right judgement, and for humane feelings to go for a straight tilt at politics is even more quixotic than tilting at windmills.

The consequences of pitting humane feelings against a political phenomenon are well illustrated in *A Passage to India*. One consequence is that it leads to pure negation. In the sphere of Indo-British relations the novel has no solution to offer except a dissolution of the relationship, which is not a solution of the problem but only its elimination. The good feeling that such a dissolution can generate, and has in actual fact generated between Indians and the British after 1947, is the sort of kindly feeling one has for strangers or casual acquaintances. It is of no use whatever for a sane ordering of political relations which one is struggling to raise from an amoral or even immoral level to a moral one.

Another consequence is that the humanitarian prepossession leads Mr Forster to waste his politico-ethical emotion on persons who do not deserve it. Both the groups of characters in *A Passage to India* are insignificant and despicable. I have, however, my doubts about Mr Forster's delineation of his countrymen. I am no authority on the life of White officials in India, for I never cultivated them. Still, observing them in their public capacity, and at times laying incredible stupidities at their door, I did not consider them quite so absurd a class as Mr Forster shows them to be.

Of one implied charge I will definitely acquit them. Mr Forster makes the

British officials of Chandrapore nervous about the excitement of the Muharram to the extent of making the women and children take shelter in the club, and after the trial of Aziz he makes them reach home along by-ways for fear of being manhandled by a town rabble. Of this kind of cowardice no British official in India was to my mind ever guilty, even in their worst time since the Mutiny, in the years 1930 to 1932, when the Auxiliary Force armoury at Chittagong in Bengal was raided by a band of young revolutionaries, British officials were shot dead in Calcutta and the districts, and attempts were made on the life of the Governor of Bengal and the Police Commissioner of Calcutta. As a class, the British officials kept their head. The courage shown by the District Magistrate of Chittagong on the night of the raid, when an insurrection of unknown magnitude and danger faced him, was admirable. The shortcoming of the British official was not in courage, but in intelligence.

On the other hand, Mr Forster is too charitable with the Indians. Aziz would not have been allowed to cross my threshold, not to speak of being taken as an equal. Men of his type are a pest even in free India. Some have acquired a crude idea of gracious living or have merely been caught by the lure of snobbism, and are always trying to gain importance by sneaking into the company of those to whom this way of living is natural. Another group of men are more hardboiled. They are always out to put personal friendship to worldly profit, perhaps the most widespread canker in Indian social life even now. Indian ministers and high officials feel this even more strongly than Ronny in Mr Forster's novel. These attempts at exploitation are making them more outrageously rude than any British official, and all the more so because in India there is no tradition of kindliness among people in power. In British days this bickering gave rise to a corrosive race conflict, now it is fomenting an equally corrosive class conflict. But it is futile to grow censorious over this, no sane or satisfactory human relations can be built up with such material.

Mr Forster appears to have felt this himself. He is too intelligent to be able to overlook the weak points in the Indian character, and too honest to suppress them in his book. Indeed, he shows himself so acute in seizing them that it is impossible to imagine that he was representing Aziz and his associates as fine fellows who deserved to be treated as equals by the British, and was not conscious of their utter worthlessness. I detect a personal admission in the comment he puts in the mouth of Ronny about the Nawab Bahadur, the 'show Indian': 'Incredible, aren't they, even the best of them?' So I am not surprised to find a streak of satire even in his presentation of Indians. But such satire not being his aim, he is driven into a corner, from where he can plead for satisfactory Indo-British relations on the only basis which could be proof against disillusionment, the basis of the least respect and the largest charity. Inevitably he has also to make a moralist's impossible demand on human nature.

But even if Mr Forster's Indians had been good as individuals as they are malodorous, he would not have had a very much stronger case. For he had not chosen his Indian types happily. In regard to the Hindu characters, he relied mostly on the types found in the Princely States. Certainly they were more traditional than those in British India, but they were so traditional that they did not represent modern India at all. For instance, to those of us who are familiar with the teachings of the Hindu reformers of the 19th century, Godbole is not an exponent of Hinduism, he is a clown. Even for us, friendly personal relations with these men became possible only if we assumed we were in an anthropological reserve. Although the States have now been incorporated in India, the unevenness persists, and it presents a serious problem of *Gleichschaltung* for the future.

But Mr Forster's more serious mistake was in taking Muslims as the principal characters in a novel dealing with Indo-British relations. They should never have been the second party to the relationship in the novel, because ever since the nationalist movement got into its stride the Muslims were playing a curiously equivocal role, realistic and effective politically, but unsatisfying in every other respect. The Muslims hated the British with a hatred even more vitriolic than the Hindu's, because it was they who had been deprived of an empire by the British. Yet they found themselves wooed by the latter as a counterpoise to the Hindu nationalists, and they did not reject these overtures.

They were shrewd in their calculations. They knew that their own battle was being fought by the Hindus and that in an eventual victory their share of the spoils was guaranteed. In the meanwhile, it was profitable to exploit the British, make the best of both worlds. This game, played with boldness and hardheaded realism, succeeded beyond expectation and created an independent state for the Muslims of India.

But a colossal Machiavellian game of politics like this could be played without moral risks only by men of very great strength of character, as indeed all the Muslim leaders, from Sir Sayyid Ahmad Khan to M. A. Jinnah, were. On the rank and file of the Muslims, so far as this policy influenced them, it had a deplorable effect. It left one section unweaned from its barren and rancorous hatred and made another pine for British patronage. Aziz and his friends belong to the servile section and are all inverted toadies. With such material, a searching history of the Muslim destiny in India could have been written, but not a novel on Indo-British relations, for which it was essential to have a Hindu protagonist.

But I think I know why Mr Forster would not have a Hindu. He shares the liking the British in India had for the Muslim, and the corresponding dislike for the Hindu. This was a curious psychological paradox and in every way unnatural, if not perverse. On the one hand, the Islamic order was the natural enemy of the Christian-European, and the British empire in India was in one sense the product of the secular conflict between the Christian West and the Islamic Middle East, which is still running its course. More than one British Foreign Secretary found the pitch of British policy queered by the incurable phil-Islamic attitude of the British Indian Government, and once Sir Edward Grey expressed frank annoyance at it.

On the other hand, there was between European civilisation and the Hindu in its stricter form a common Indo-European element, which was discovered and described by British Orientalists in the first century or so of British rule, but which came to be forgotten and ignored by Englishmen in later times. Modern Hindu thinkers did not, however, lose sight of the affinity. Swami Vivekananda, speaking at the end of the last century, said that two branches of the same people placed in different surroundings in Greece and India had worked out the problems of life, each in its own particular way, but that through the agency of the British people the ancient Greek was meeting the ancient Hindu on Indian soil, and thus 'slowly and silently the leaven has come, the broadening out, the life-giving revivalist movement that we see all around us.' The British in India never gave this fruitful idea any encouragement. They were taken in by the deceptive simplicity of the Muslim and repelled by the apparent bizarrerie of Hinduism and its rococo excrescences. I wonder if it was the Hebraic element in the British ethos which was responsible for this.

This leads me straight to my objections to the politics of *A Passage to India* and my one positive comment on its central theme. My most serious criticisms are the following. It shows a great imperial system at its worst, not as diabolically evil but as drab and asinine; the rulers and the ruled alike are depicted at their smallest, the snobbery and pettiness of the one matching the imbecility and rancour of the other. Our suffering under British rule, on which a book as noble as Alfred de Vigny's *Servitude et grandeur militaires* could have been written, is deprived of all dignity. Our mental life as depicted in the book is painfully childish and querulous. Lastly, attention is diverted away from those Indians who stood aloof from the world the book describes and were aristocratic in their way, although possessing no outward attribute of aristocracy. When I consider all this I feel Mr Forster's literary ability, which has given the book its political importance, as a grievance.

At the root of all this lies the book's tacit but confident assumption that Indo-British relations presented a problem of personal behaviour and could be tackled on the personal plane. They did not and could not.

Extract from G. K. Das, 'Through the Ruins of Empire', *E. M. Forster's India*, London: Macmillan, 1977, pp. 81–90

Das provides a more sympathetic reading than Chaudhuri but he begins with a similar premise: that Forster intended the novel to represent an attempt, however flawed, to comprehend India. The essay serves as a response to Chaudhuri's, and reorients Forster's political purpose, seeing it as a fitting condemnation of the contemporary colonial situation. Das's conclusion is that the book is a 'comprehensive' and 'fully evocative' approach to India, not an interpretation of it. Just as interesting, Das casts Forster's portrayal of Indian characters in a more sympathetic light, and also introduces discussion of the court punkah-wallah, who was such an important character to Forster.

To understand India is the keynote of Forster's approach in the novel. The complexities of India's past traditions, the great variety presented by the range of her physical nature, the more intriguing variety of her people, and the intricacies of the contemporary political situation too – all these subjects are approached in order to be understood, and they are presented in the novel in an artistic form that is fully comprehensive and distinctive. In dealing with its immense theme and purpose, *A Passage to India* attains to a status of creative writing which is more lively than actual history and more meaningful than normal fiction. It presents historical facts with imagination, and tempers imagination with factual observation. Its creative approach is essential for comprehending the complexity and vastness of the subject: any approach to India other than for understanding, other than the deep and the creative, would be inadequate.

The story of the novel is itself significantly concerned with illustrating the limitations in a conventional approach to India. Adela Quested, 'the queer, cautious girl' from England, has come on a visit to India in the company of Mrs Moore, an elderly lady, to meet Mrs Moore's son, Ronny Heaslop, the city magistrate at Chandrapore, whom there is a possibility of her marrying: she is also anxious to 'see the real India'. Her approach to India has the excitement of a conventional visit, although she assumes herself to be unconventional. The India of her imagination is composed of the usual items of publicised romantic glamour: 'an elephant ride', and 'catching the moon in the Ganges'; and she insists that Mrs Moore too must not miss seeing that India – 'I will fetch you from Simla when it's cool enough. I will unbottle you in fact . . . We then see some of the Mogul stuff – how appalling if we let you miss the Taj! – and then I will see you off at Bombay'.[1] Mrs Moore, on her part, is in India because she has been commissioned by her son to bring Adela from England; she has a duty to perform in seeing her son married; and, incidentally, she is interested in seeing 'the right places' too.

At the English club at Chandrapore where no Indians are admitted, it is suggested by Fielding, the principal of the local Government College, that in order to see the real India one has to 'try seeing Indians'. Fielding is sympathetic to Indians and has friends among them, but at the club he is disliked, and his idea of trying to see Indians is mocked: 'As if one could avoid seeing them', sighs Mrs Lesley. Fielding's idea, however, appeals to Adela, for it has the appearance of unconventionality. 'I am tired of seeing picturesque figures pass before me as a frieze . . . It was wonderful when we landed, but that superficial glamour soon goes',[2] she says, and she wants to meet Indians.

A 'bridge party' is arranged under 'British auspices' at the Collector's bungalow, for Adela and Mrs Moore to meet Indians. It is not a success, for the Indian guests were awkward: they arrived early and 'were only gazing sadly over the lawn'. Adela and Mrs Moore are later introduced by Fielding to Aziz, a doctor at Chandrapore hospital, who invites them all to a picnic on the Marabar hills, where there are the 'famous' caves. The expedition to Marabar fills Adela with excitement: she likes to hear from Dr Aziz about the Moguls, about Akbar's universal religion, and she thinks, inspired temporarily by Akbar's 'fine' idea, that the barriers are to be broken down in India, and that there will be 'universal brotherhood'. The picnic, however, ends in disaster: Adela, while being shown the caves by Dr Aziz, has a hallucination that she is molested by him. In a fit she is brought back to the 'civil station'; Dr Aziz is arrested and has to appear on trial.

1 [Das's note.] *A Passage to India*, ch. XIV, p. 143.
2 [Das's note.] Ibid., ch. III, p. 30.

The English and the Indian communities of Chandrapore are roused to bitter hostility against each other. Indians, long embittered because they are hated and also deprived of jobs by the English, look at the case of Aziz as an insult to the whole of India – to Hindus as well as Muslims – and are all united against the English. The English meet at the club to discuss the situation. They think that the law must be enforced, justice must be done; it is also suggested that the situation should have been left in the control of troops. The Collector, however, decides that there should be the least possible provocation of the natives lest there be a riot. The women and children are sent off to the hills for safety.

The case against Aziz is tried by an Indian magistrate, a subordinate of Ronny. (The English community is angered by the idea that an Indian should be judge over an English girl.) There is a well-formulated charge against Aziz, prepared by the English Superintendent of Police; and to defend him Indians have brought a strongly anti-British Hindu barrister from Calcutta. The elaborate preparations on both sides, however, prove of little use, as the trial ends in a simple and unexpected way when Adela confesses during the trial that Dr Aziz did not follow her into the cave.

Aziz is released, and the Indians celebrate their 'victory' over the English. In bitterness against the English, Aziz leaves Chandrapore to work and live in the Hindu native state of Mau, outside the limits of British India. Adela returns to England, getting 'the worst of both worlds': she has antagonised the Indians, and has also 'renounced her own people' in India by asserting Aziz's innocence. Ronny cannot marry her, 'it would mean the end of his career'. 'Disaster had shown her limitations'; she understands that she has suffered because her whole approach to India has been senseless, and she assents when Fielding reminds her: 'You have no real affection for Aziz, or Indians generally . . . The first time I saw you, you were wanting to see India, not Indians, and it occurred to me: Ah, that won't take us far. Indians know whether they are liked or not – they cannot be fooled here. Justice never satisfies them, and that is why the British Empire rests on sand'.[3]

Mrs Moore's approach to India, like Adela's, is conventional, though in another way. She does not look at India with Adela's eye for anything superficially curious, she applies her own simple and benevolent Christian outlook instead: ' "India is part of the earth. And God has put us on the earth in order to be pleasant to one another. God . . . is . . . love." She hesitated . . . but something made her go on. "God has put us on earth to love our neighbours and to show it, and He is omnipresent, even in India, to see how we are succeeding." '[4] With her intuitive sympathy and pious tenderness Mrs Moore has endeared herself to both Aziz and Professor Godbole, though only in a vague way; and similarly (though only by the curious fact of her being absent from India at the time of the trial of Dr Aziz, which she did not wish to see) her memory among the Indians at Chandrapore has turned into a charming and inexplicable popular legend. There is no real

3 [Das's note.] Ibid., ch. XXIX, p. 270.
4 [Das's note.] Ibid., ch. V, p. 55.

dimension of life in her contact with India: her simple, pious outlook is too soon confounded, and, wearied and pushed into 'the twilight of the double vision in which so many elderly people are involved',[5] she wishes for relief by departing from India:

> So Mrs Moore had all she wished; she escaped the trial, the marriage, and the hot weather; she would return to England in comfort and distinction, and see her other children. At her son's suggestion, and by her own desire, she departed. But she accepted her good luck without enthusiasm . . . Mrs Moore had always inclined to resignation. As soon as she landed in India it seemed to her good, and when she saw the water flowing through the mosque tank, or the Ganges, or the moon, caught in the shawl of night with all the other stars, it seemed a beautiful goal and an easy one. To be one with the universe! So dignified and simple. But there was always some little duty to be performed first, some new card to be turned up from the diminishing pack and placed, and while she was pottering about, the Marabar struck its gong.[6]

Mrs Moore's departure from India is described in the novel with expressions of pity, pathos and irony. Her naive idea of India in the days of her arrival in the country is seen also in her thoughts at the time of her departure:

> The swift and comfortable mail-train slid with her through the night, and all the next day she was rushing through Central India, through landscapes that were baked and bleached, but had not the hopeless melancholy of the plain. She watched the indestructible life of man and his changing faces, and the houses he has built for himself and God, and they appeared to her not in terms of her own trouble, but as things to see. There was, for instance, a place called Asirgarh which she passed at sunset and identified on a map – an enormous fortress among wooded hills. No one had ever mentioned Asirgarh to her . . .[7]

While the train descends through the Vindhyas [*sic*] Mrs Moore sees only a half-view of Asirgarh. She arrives at the end of her journey in Bombay, and is filled with regret that her visit to India has been incomplete. Her old longing for India is revived when she is to sail back:

> 'I have not seen the right places', she thought, as she saw embayed in the platforms of the Victoria Terminus the end of the rails that had carried her over a continent, and could never carry her back. She would never visit Asirgarh or the other untouched places; neither Delhi nor Agra nor the Rajputana cities nor Kashmir, nor the obscurer marvels that had

5 [Das's note.] Ibid., ch. XXIII, p. 216.
6 [Das's note.] Ibid., pp. 216–17.
7 [Das's note.] Ibid., pp. 217–18.

> sometimes shone through men's speech: the bilingual rock of Girnar, the statue of Shri Belgola, the ruins of Mandu and Hampi, temples of Khajraha, gardens of Shalimar. As she drove through the huge city which the West has built and abandoned with a gesture of despair, she longed to stop, though it was only Bombay, and disentangle the hundred Indias that passed each other in its streets. The feet of the horses moved her on, and presently the boat sailed and thousands of coconut palms appeared all round the anchorage and climbed the hills to wave her farewell. 'So you thought an echo was India; you took the Marabar caves as final?' they laughed. 'What have we in common with them, or they with Asirgarh? Good-bye!'[8]

Mrs Moore's, and Adela's, general outlook on India at least acquires an edge of sensitivity as a result of their experiences during their visit, but the British living in India, with the exception of Fielding, all remain insensitive. The principal figures among them are all officials – the collector, the superintendent of police, the civil surgeon, and the city magistrate whose only interest in India is in governing her: 'to do justice and keep the peace'.[9] They are not interested in knowing Indians socially, nor are they interested in Indian art, literature, or culture: 'Their ignorance of the Arts was notable, and they lost no opportunity of proclaiming it to one another; it was the public school attitude, flourishing more vigorously than it can yet hope to do in England. If Indians were shop, the Arts were bad form'.[10] The officials' wives are portrayed as more indifferent to India than their husbands. They are dull, they express racial hatred openly, and they are also inhuman: Mrs Callendar, the civil surgeon's wife, thinks that 'the kindest thing one can do to a native is to let him die'.[11]

There is, on the whole, an element of dramatic exaggeration in Forster's portrayal of the Anglo-Indian official,[12] but the exaggeration is deliberate, and is intended to show the futility of an outlook to India that is based chiefly on officialdom. Forster was, in fact, not ignorant that it could be possible for an Anglo-Indian official to be true to his 'duty', and perform it within the context of a larger and more meaningful outlook on India. (His high appreciation for men like Alfred Lyall and Malcolm Darling has already been referred to in the third chapter.) He illustrates that outlook in the character of Fielding. Fielding is not portrayed as an ideal character, or as a perfect spokesman for the author's views: his past life 'had included going to the bad and repenting thereafter'; in middle age, when he entered India, he 'bribed a European ticket inspector' to take his luggage into his compartment in the train at Victoria terminus; and it may be

8 [Das's note.] Ibid., ch. XXIII, pp. 218–19.
9 [Das's note.] Ibid., ch. V, p. 53.
10 [Das's note.] Ibid., p. 43.
11 [Das's note.] Ibid., ch. III, p. 29.
12 [Das's note.] In a long newspaper correspondence on this question which appeared soon after *A Passage to India* was published, E. A. Home of the Indian Educational Service, who had spent 'the last fourteen years of [his] life in Chandrapore [Patna] itself', criticised Forster's portrayal of Anglo-Indians as unreal – showing an ignorance of actual Anglo-Indian life and manners.

remembered also that his nomination to the principalship of the 'little college' at Chandrapore was obtained 'through the influence of friends'. But however incomplete in his private life, Fielding has an essentially personal approach to society in general, which he also applies to the society of Anglo-India. He believes in the value of fellowship between individuals, and in human culture, and he cannot sympathise with the communal barrier between the British and Indians: 'Neither a missionary nor a student, he was happiest in the give-and-take of a private conversation. The world, he believed, is a globe of men who are trying to reach one another and can best do so by the help of goodwill plus culture and intelligence – a creed ill suited to Chandrapore, but he had come out too late to lose it'.[13] If he has no racial feeling against Indians, he does not sympathise with the Indians' communal feeling against the British either. He is disliked by his fellow Anglo-Indians and is considered a renegade when he openly sympathises with Aziz during his trial, but he stands by his own personal loyalty to the individual, and not by his community. His role in the novel illustrates that it was possible for an Englishman to live in British India in terms of a social and personal relationship with Indians, and provides a basis for the kind of outlook towards India which *A Passage to India* encourages.

Yet the total outlook of the novel (which may for present purposes be regarded as Forster's own outlook) is larger than Fielding's. Fielding is unable to grasp that his desire for friendship with Indians must recognise and absorb the condition of the Indians' political aspirations as well. He cannot imagine that the British Empire will be abolished or that India can become a nation; when Aziz emotionally portrays the future of India as a nation with 'no foreigners of any sort', Fielding mocks the idea: 'India a nation! What an apotheosis! Last comer to the drab nineteenth century sisterhood! Waddling in at this hour of the world to take her seat! She, whose only peer was the Holy Roman Empire, she shall rank with Guatemala and Belgium perhaps!'[14] It was sad that in contemporary India the possibility of friendship between an Englishman and an Indian was dependent on whether India was going to be politically free of Britain's domination, but it was the reality, and the situation had to be looked at realistically. Fielding had illusions about a relationship with India and Indians within the continuity of Britain's imperial presence in India, which Forster himself had not. Forster had understood that the Empire was no longer a reality, and that a link with India and Indians must be sought independently of Britain's imperial interests, within the terms of the real situation.

For this reason *A Passage to India* puts the contemporary political situation into persepctive. In its picture of the British administration at Chandrapore it shows the imperialist policies in their worst form, and also draws attention to the Indians' political demand for complete freedom from British domination. In a criticism[15] of the political theme in *A Passage to India* it has been pointed out that

13 [Das's note.] *A Passage to India*, ch. VII, pp. 65–6.
14 [Das's note.] Ibid., ch. XXXVII, p. 335.
15 [Das's note.] See Andrew Shonfield, 'The Politics of Forster's India', *Encounter*, XXX, no. I, January 1968, pp. 62–9.

the novel does not take into account the fact that the imperial administration was also sensitive to Indian feelings; although the administration had been actually involved, since the Reforms of 1919, in the work of preparing Indians for self-government by giving them an increasing share of power and authority, there is, the critic maintains, no trace of this side of the picture in Forster's account. It is true of course that the emphasis in the novel's political picture is on showing the lapses in the imperial policies; but it is false to say that the novel does not take notice of the new progressive elements in the imperial machinery – the effects of the recent constitutional provisions of dyarchy, 'Indianisation' of the Civil Service, and other democratic reforms. The effects of 'Indianisation' are seen in the novel's general picture of British and Indian officials working together, holding important posts in the administration at Chandrapore. It is also shown in the story of Aziz's trial, where Das, a 'subordinate' Indian magistrate, presides over the trial (it may be remembered that the case is a criminal case involving an English girl, and that a subordinate Indian magistrate did not have the authority before the reforms of the Indian Criminal Procedure in 1923, to try such a case); by making Das preside the novel throws light on an entirely new development in the imperial system.[16] There are, besides, other instances in the novel where direct reference is made to the new sympathetic imperial policies: for example, it is pointed out that the Collector of Chandrapore is reluctant to call troops to control the situation in the city, because he knows not only that important Indians like the Nawab Bahadur would be annoyed, but that the Government of India and the British Parliament are also watchful.[17] Thus the political theme in the novel is not blind to the new policies which were in operation in the 1920s; but, by focusing attention on the main political issue of the time, which was the irreconcilable Indian national challenge to the Empire, it shows that the effects of the reforms had been minimal. Politically awakened Indians, like Aziz, thought that reforms and attempts at conciliation were useless as long as the Indian people were not treated as equals by the British.

Apart from drawing attention to the fact that the Indians' political aspirations were a part of their enlightenment, and that these aspirations could not be ignored,[18] the political theme of *A Passage to India* does not have any other relevance within the context of the novel's total outlook on India. Forster's interests in looking beyond the confines of Anglo-India at the face of Indian society and civilisation are stimulated, first of all, by distinctive qualities of the Indian way of life and of individual Indians. He is struck deeply by the peace and

16 [Das's note.] Prior to 1923 the Indian Criminal Procedure discriminated between the Indian and European communities on the ground of racial distinctions, and outside the Presidency towns of Calcutta, Bombay and Madras the subordinate Indian magistrate had no jurisdiction over the Europeans living in his area.

17 [Das's note.] Cf. *A Passage to India*, ch. xx, p. 191.

18 [Das's note.] Asked what political influence *A Passage to India* had 'on the "Indian question" of the time', Forster is reported to have said: 'It had some political influence – it caused people to think of the link between India and Britain and to doubt if that link was altogether of a healthy nature . . .' (See K. Natwar-Singh (ed.), *E. M. Forster: A Tribute, with Selections from His Writings on India*, New York, 1964, p. xiii.)

restfulness, and the traditional warmth and generosity of Indian social life, which he sees as the marks of a civilisation unknown to the West:

> Civilization strays about like a ghost here, revisiting the ruins of empire, and is to be found not in great works of art or mighty deeds, but in the gestures well-bred Indians make when they sit or lie down. Fielding, who had dressed up in native costume, learnt from his excessive awkwardness in it that all his motions were makeshifts, whereas when the Nawab Bahadur stretched out his hand for food or Nureddin applauded a song, something beautiful had been accomplished which needed no development. This restfulness of gesture – it is the Peace that passeth Understanding, after all, it is the social equivalent of Yoga. When the whirring of action ceases, it becomes visible, and reveals a civilization which the West can disturb but will never acquire. The hand stretches out for ever, the lifted knee has the eternity though not the sadness of the grave. Aziz was full of civilization this evening, complete, dignified, rather hard . . .[19]

The three Indians who are offered for study in their distinct individuality as comprehending the vast range of attraction and complexity in the Indian character are Aziz, Godbole and the man who pulled the punkah in the Court at Chandrapore. Aziz is a well-bred, enlightened, anglicised, modern Indian, whose personality includes an attractive blend of intensely individual and traditional features, with elements of influence from English education. He is spontaneous, imaginative, fond of poetry, sentimental, deeply generous, hospitable, proud of his own Muslim community and of his motherland as a whole, prejudiced against the Hindus temperamentally, but deeply prejudiced against the Anglo-Indians as a class. He is happy in his private life with his children, sentimental about his dead wife and content in his profession – despite the irritant of the relationship with his superior, Major Callendar, the civil surgeon. His curiosity about 'Post-Impressionism' in the West, which was ignored by Fielding, his independence, which was looked down upon by Ronny Heaslop as making 'the spoilt Westernized' type, his personal generosity, which was abused in a racially divided society, his conception of the value of pathos in personal life and in art, his inborn religious prejudices and his emotional feeling for his nation – all these qualities in Aziz show him as a modern and enlightened Indian, not simply a product of British India, but truly and deeply 'Indian', his complex character the result of contacts with many civilisations.[20]

19 [Das's note.] *A Passage to India*, ch. XXVII, p. 261.

20 [Das's note.] Aziz's character disappoints the Indian critic, Nirad C. Chaudhuri, who thinks that Forster ought to have chosen for his protagonist in the novel an Indian of the stature of Rammohun Roy or Bankim Chandra Chatterji. . . . Chaudhuri's criticism might have been apt if Forster's intention behind the portrayal of Aziz was to present the image of a great Indian national figure, and to present him within the specific context of Indo-British relations. But Forster's intention was apparently more modest: he has tried (not limiting his study to the particular environment of British India) to look at Aziz as a modern, average, individual Indian, whose mental qualities may not be highly extraordinary, but are deeply interesting and attractive for him personally.

Against the enlightened and sophisticated Aziz is set the character of Professor Godbole, presented in the novel as an essentially conservative, conventionally religious, uncertain, yet mysteriously attractive figure. He is not studied purely as a type (against Aziz, say, who happens to be a Muslim) to represent the traditional Hindu character in general; yet his portraiture is composed from certain elements which Forster had gathered chiefly from his contacts with society in the Hindu states of Dewas and Chhatarpur. Godbole appears on the whole rather enigmatic – corresponding, evidently, to some elements in Forster's own experience in the Native States; in a significant way, however, he is seen as a more intriguingly Indian character than Aziz. (This point will be illustrated in the next chapter, where Godbole's character is scrutinised in the context of Forster's view of Hinduism in general.)

All the other Indians in the novel including Aziz's poor relative, Mohammed Latif, belong, like Aziz and Godbole, to a particular social level which however complex has evolved, in one way or another, in contact with intelligible trends of civilisation. But the Indian who is seen as distinct from everyone else – from Indians belonging to society as well as from the British – is the man 'of low birth',[21] the outcaste Indian, who is employed to pull the punkah in the city magistrate's Court. He is humble, 'splendidly formed', beautiful, and strong. He is shown sitting almost naked, on the floor of a raised platform, in the back of the Court. The proceedings of the trial are not understood by him, the social and political conflicts between the British and Indians do not touch his mind. Forster's portrayal of this unique figure in the Indian world is drawn with deep feeling, and it has a central relevance to the total outlook of the novel. He is drawn realistically, and also as a symbolic presence. By portraying him as he is – deprived and condemned by society – Forster draws attention to one most enigmatic feature of the Indian social tradition, and also comments on the actual scene of social inequality, poverty and deprivation in India: 'This man would have been notable anywhere; among the thin-hammed, flat-chested mediocrities of Chandrapore he stood out as divine, yet he was of the city, its garbage had nourished him, he would end on its rubbish heaps'.[22]

Symbolically, the punkahwallah's presence in the court room reflects on the meaninglessness of the communal and class conflicts in Anglo-India. Physically naked, he is presented in the novel as a man in his natural form, as the human individual, who is equal with all other indivduals[23] and higher than communities and religions. His presence points out, in the novel's local context, that the British

21 [Das's note.] See *A Passage to India*, ch. XXIV, p. 226. Forster's portrayal of 'the untouchable' inspired the writing of the courageous and powerful Indian novel, *Untouchable* (London, 1935), which deals with the life of the outcaste Indians. The author, Mulk Raj Anand, writes about his debt to Forster: 'I could not have started off writing my first book, *Untouchable*, if I had not noticed your own sympathy for the outcastes of India in your famous book after I had stayed in the Sabarmati Ashram of Mahatma Gandhi'.

22 [Das's note.] *A Passage to India*, ch. XXIV, p. 226.

23 [Das's note.] Cf. Forster's comment elsewhere: 'Naked I came into this world, naked I shall go out of it! And a very good thing too, for it reminds me that I am naked under my shirt, whatever its colour' (*Two Cheers for Democracy*, p. 85).

in the days of their imperial power might have looked at Indians as equals; and in the wider context it points out the way that any individual human being might look at any other.

The portrayal of Indian life in the novel is seen alongside an intelligent portrayal of Indian nature. Forster has said that the three sections into which *A Passage to India* is divided 'also represent the three seasons of the Cold Weather, the Hot Weather, and the Rains, which divide the Indian year'.[24] Evocations of the great variety of Indian nature, linked in a correspondence with Indian life in various ways, can be seen in some of the most poetic passages in the novel. In the opening chapter, for example, the description of the city of Chandrapore, viewed from the slope of the 'little civil station', is characteristic:

> It is a tropical pleasance washed by a noble river. The toddy palms and neem-trees and mangoes and peepul that were hidden behind the bazaars now become visible and in their turn hide the bazaars. They rise from the gardens where ancient tanks nourish them, they burst out of stifling purlieus and unconsidered temples. Seeking light and air, and endowed with more strength than man or his works, they soar above the lower deposit to greet one another with branches and beckoning leaves, and to build a city for the birds. Especially after the rains do they screen what passes below, but at all times, even when scorched or leafless, they glorify the city to the English people who inhabit the rise, so that newcomers cannot believe it to be as meagre as it is described, and have to be driven down to acquire disillusionment.[25]

In contrast to such a picture where nature is shown in close association with Indian life, there is the short prosaic description of the 'civil station' where the British officials live in a society, aloof and small, of their own:

> As for the civil station itself, it provokes no emotion. It charms not, neither does it repel. It is sensibly planned, with a red-brick Club on its brow, and farther back a grocer's and a cemetery and the bungalows are disposed along roads that intersect at right angles. It has nothing hideous in it, and only the view is beautiful; it shares nothing with the city except the overarching sky.[26]

The correspondence between the Indians' life and nature is shown always in the form of a pageant which is deeply imaginative, and at the same time real. When the hot weather comes to Chandrapore and stifles human activity, its horror is evoked with the same touches of imagination and realism with which the

24 [Das's note.] See 'Author's Notes', *A Passage to India*, p. XXIX. (The notes were specially written for the Everyman's Library edition, London, 1965.)
25 [Das's note.] *A Passage to India*, ch. I, p. 10.
26 [Das's note.] Ibid.

atmosphere at Mau at the coming of the monsoon rains is described. Here are two excerpts to illustrate the point:

> The heat leapt forward in the last hour, the street was deserted as if a catastrophe had cleaned off humanity during the inconclusive talk . . .
>
> All over the city and over much of India the same retreat on the part of humanity was beginning, into cellars, up hills, under trees. April, herald of horrors, was at hand. The sun was returning to his kingdom with power, but without beauty – that was the sinister feature. If only there had been beauty! His cruelty would have been tolerable then.[27]

> The sky grey and black, bellyfuls of rain all over it, the earth pocked with pools of water and slimy with mud. A magnificent monsoon – the best for three years, the tanks already full, bumper crops possible. Out towards the river (the route by which the Fieldings had escaped from Deora) the downpour had been enormous; the mails had to be pulled across by ropes. They could just see the break in the forest trees where the gorge came through, and the rocks above that marked the site of the diamond mine, glistening with wet. Close beneath was the suburban residence of the Junior Rani, isolated by floods, and Her Highness, lax about purdah, to be seen paddling with her handmaidens in the garden and waving her sari at the monkeys on the roof . . .[28]
>
> The rain settled in steadily to its job of wetting everybody and everything through, and soon spoiled the cloth of gold on the palanquin and the costly disk-shaped banners. Some of the torches went out, fireworks didn't catch, there began to be less singing, and the tray returned to Professor Godbole, who picked up a fragment of the mud adhering and smeared it on his forehead without much ceremony . . .[29]

Viewing contemporary social and political events in the wider perspective of the traditional and more permanent aspects of Indian life and nature *A Passage to India* thus portrays an India of perennially attractive interest; it portrays an India whose people, their stream of life, their civilisation, religions and culture, all have peculiar attractions. Its account is not an exhaustive account, but it has the distinction of being comprehensive and fully evocative. While meaning to present a book about India Forster was deeply aware of the magnitude of his task; he knew that the immensity of his subject could always be approached, each approach being rewarded with a greater understanding; only a complete and final interpretation of India would always elude the grasp:

> How can the mind take hold of such a country? Generations of invaders have tried, but they remain in exile. The important towns they

27 [Das's note.] Ibid., ch. x, pp. 119–20.
28 [Das's note.] Ibid., ch. xxxv, pp. 309–10.
29 [Das's note.] Ibid., ch. xxxvi, p. 329.

> build are only retreats, their quarrels the malaise of men who cannot find their way home. India knows of their trouble. She knows of the whole world's trouble ... She calls 'Come' through her hundred mouths, through objects ridiculous and august. But come to what? She has not defined. She is not a promise, only an appeal.[30]

Forster's interests in India were sustained, after the publication of *A Passage to India*, through his many connections with the country. He continued to contribute a number of articles to periodicals, all written in a direct and interpretative style, on various aspects of Indian society, of the traditions of Indian religions, of Indian art and architecture, and of contemporary Indian thought. He was engaged in broadcasting to India on subjects of literary interest for a period during and after the Second World War,[31] and invited by the All-India centre of the P.E.N. club he also visited in India, for the third time, in 1945. Through all these ways his contacts with India became deeper, and his writings, which took the form of detailed observations on individual items of interest concerning India, were to provide valuable supplementation to his interpretation in *A Passage to India*.

Jenny Sharpe, section entitled 'The Indeterminacies of Rape' from the chapter 'The Unspeakable Limits of Civility: *A Passage to India*', *Allegories of Empire: The Figure of Woman in the Colonial Text*, Minneapolis and London: University of Minnesota Press, 1993, pp. 118–27

Sharpe's discussion of the novel is informed by feminism and post-colonial studies. In this extract, she turns her attention to the central omission of the text, traditionally phrased as 'What happened in the Marabar Caves?' Sharpe is not concerned directly here with Forster's desire to suggest mystery and confusion, but with the circulation of desire around the question of 'rape', a word that Brenda Silver has noted is significantly missing from *A Passage*. To an extent, the traditional question about the novel's enigmatic middle/muddle elides the issues in and around the novel of sexual and racial politics, reducing these concerns themselves to an impersonal and vague theorising over 'what happened', and when the charge brought against an Indian man by an English

30 [Das's note.] Ibid., ch. XIV, pp. 142–3.
31 [Das's note.] John Arlott writes: 'During the Second World War the B.B.C., within its Eastern Service, built up a programme-grouping called "English to India" ... Forster was the one contributor the programme *had* to have if it was to command respect in India. He accepted that fact and became its only regular contributor throughout the war and for some three years afterwards. He did not do these broadcasts for the usual reasons; he was not concerned with what he might earn from them, and he had neither the need nor the wish to create a reputation as a broadcaster ... His strongest motive was his liking for the Indians ... He was eager as *A Passage to India* would suggest to establish understanding, trust, and affection between Indians and people like himself. At a slightly lower level, he was anxious to show Indians that people like himself did exist in Britain ...' ('E. M. Forster at the Microphone', *Listener*, 2 January 1969, p. 809.)

woman, in a novel by a homosexual English man, is 'indecent assault', or attempted rape. It is, crucially, a charge brought under the colonial rule of the raj in India, with its history of the 1857 rebellion or 'Mutiny', and with the 1919 Amritsar massacre still fresh in the minds of the novel's readers in 1924. An 'attempted rape' is in fact tried by Ronny (ch. V; p. 69).

> The unspeakable attempt presented itself to her as love: in a cave in a church – Boum, it amounts to the same.
>
> – E. M. Forster, *A Passage to India*

A Passage to India holds up for public scrutiny the racialization of colonial relations by generating its narrative desire through the indeterminate status of a rape. Adela Quested, who is English, accuses an educated Muslim, Dr. Aziz, of molesting her in one of the Marabar caves. Since the reader is not privy to what happened, we are faced with the contradictory evidence of Adela's accusation and Aziz's denial. Her accusation sets off a judicial machinery that condemns Aziz before he is even brought to trial. Victimized by an unjust colonial system, he becomes a *cause célèbre* for Indian nationalists. The plot then undergoes a strategic reversal. The accuracy of Adela's judgment is undermined during the trial when, upon interrogation, she claims that she was mistaken. The roles of assailant and victim are now dramatically reversed as the novel reveals the 'real crime' to be an abuse of power that can only lead to the demise of colonialism. Forster's staging of the court scene around the reversal of a rape charge disrupts the taken-for-grantedness of the racially motivated assumption that, to use the words of the prosecution, 'the darker races are physically attracted by the fairer, but not *vice versa*' (*PI*, 218–19). Yet it is never revealed whether the attempted rape was real or imagined, and the question of what happened in the Marabar caves continues to intrigue readers. Whereas earlier inquiries investigated the mystery for what it revealed about Forster's narrative technique or Indian metaphysics, recent criticism has shifted the terms of the debate toward issues of race and gender.

Forster's critical look at colonialism presents a problem that is particularly vexing for feminists. Upon questioning whether the real crime is Adela's accusation or Aziz's assault, *A Passage to India* sets up an opposition between the English woman and Indian man. If one decides, in keeping with its anti-imperialist theme, that the crime lies in a system capable of reducing an Indian man to his pathological lust for white women, then even the slightest hint of an actual rape cannot be entertained. Conversely, a defense of Adela's accusation involves condemning the Indian patriarchy and Aziz's objectification of women as sex objects. The ambiguity surrounding the alleged rape thus forces the critic to defend either the native man or the white woman against his/her opponent. It is this either/or decision (but never both) that has divided readings of *A Passage to India* along gender lines.

Critical opinion tends to favor Adela's hallucination as the most likely explanation for what happened in the caves.[1] Offering her sexual repression as evidence, such accounts discredit her charge against Aziz as not only mistaken but also misguided. Even those readings that critically engage the problems of colonial representation treat Adela's cry of rape as the sign of her repressed desire. Although *A Passage to India* does suggest the imaginary nature of the attack, it does not provide sufficient evidence for presupposing that Adela's musings on Aziz's handsome appearance should translate into a sexual fantasy of rape.

In his screen adaptation of the novel, David Lean legitimates this common reading by adding a scene that eliminates any doubt that, on at least one other occasion, the unattractive Adela suffered a bout of sexual hysteria. The scene shows her leaving the safety of the European compound to venture out on a bicycle alone. She chances upon an ancient Hindu temple, whose sexually explicit carvings arouse her curiosity and interest. The threatening aspect of her sexual arousal is figuratively represented in the aggressive monkeys that swarm over the statues and scare her away. Adela returns to Chandrapore breathless, pale, and sweating. Having just broken off her engagement to Ronny Heaslop, she now says she will marry him. His query – 'What happened?' – and her response 'Nothing' – are emblematic of the film's message regarding the cave scene. In a flashback of Adela staring fixedly at Aziz's silhouetted shape looming in the cave's entrance, Lean repeats the image of her pale and frightened face after her encounter with the monkeys. The conclusion to be drawn is so obvious that he provides no further elaboration.

A masculinist explanation of the mystery in the cave (such as Lean's) is based on the 'common knowledge' that frigid women suffer from sexual hysteria and that unattractive women desire to be raped. This interpretation works backward from the imaginary rape, metaleptically positing the effect of an effect as its cause. The argument consequently produces its own tautology: Adela hallucinated the rape because she was sexually repressed, the proof of which lies in her hallucination. Feminist criticism of *A Passage to India* has dismantled this tautology by revealing the 'making into meaning' of its assumptions. Rather than discounting the imaginary nature of the attack, feminists respond to the critical verdict against Adela by retracing her hallucination to a 'first cause' of patriarchal authority instead of sexual hysteria. Elaine Showalter, for instance, reads the hallucination in terms of Adela's apprehensions about committing herself to a loveless marriage that is nothing short of 'legalized rape.'[2] Brenda Silver also links the imaginary

1 [Sharpe's note.] The following select list gives some indication of the pervasiveness of the explanation that the accusation of rape is the product of a sexually repressed woman's imagination: Louise Dauner, 'What Happened in the Cave? Reflections on *A Passage to India*,' in *Perspectives on E. M. Forster's A Passage to India*, ed. V. A. Shahane (New York: Barnes, 1968), 51–64; Benita Parry, *Delusions and Discoveries: Studies on India in the British Imagination* (London: Allen Lane, 1972), 294–95; Barbara Rosencrance, *Forster's Narrative Vision* (Ithaca, N.Y.: Cornell University Press, 1982), 207; Abdul R. JanMohamed, 'The Economy of Manichean Allegory: The Function of Racial Difference in Colonialist Literature' in *'Race' Writing and Difference*, ed. Henry Louis Gates, Jr. (Chicago: University of Chicago Press, 1986), 94–95; David Rubin, *After the Raj: British Novels of India Since 1947* (Hanover: University Press of New England, 1986), 66; Sara Suleri, 'The Geography of *A Passage to India*,' in *E. M. Forster's* A Passage to India, ed. Harold Bloom (New York: Chelsea House, 1987), 109–10.

2 [Sharpe's note.] Elaine Showalter, '*A Passage to India* as "Marriage Fiction": Forster's Sexual Politics,' *Women & Literature* 5 no 2 (1977): 3–16.

rape to the gender roles suggested by marriage. Since Adela enters the cave disturbed about her forthcoming marriage to Ronny Heaslop, she is forced to acknowledge her social status as a sex object and thus to confront 'the material and psychological reality of what it means to be rapable.'[3]

Although they are correct to situate the alleged rape within the larger frame of women's oppression, Showalter and Silver fail to address the historical production of the category of rape within a *system of colonial relations*. Feminist criticism has thus replaced one tautology with another. The feminist tautology goes something like this: Adela experiences the conditions of rape because she is objectified as a woman, the proof of which lies in her experience of rape. What does it mean for an English woman's experience of her oppression to be staged as a scenario in which she is the potential object of a native attack? In other words, how does the feminist critic negotiate the either/or opposition between the colonizing female and the colonized male that the novel sets up? I would begin by insisting that Adela's confrontation of 'what it means to be rapable' is framed by race relations that cannot be understood as yet another form of patriarchal oppression.

What is immediately noticeable about gender hierarchies in *A Passage to India* is the discrepancy between Adela's social positioning and that of Anglo-Indian women. From the early pages of the novel there are suggestions that, due to racial segregation, colonial women are protectively cloistered behind an anachronistic code of chivalry and honor. 'Windows were barred lest the servants should see their memsahibs acting,' the narrator informs us, 'and the heat was consequently immense' (*PI*, 24). Fielding's refusal to be 'lively and helpful' toward women 'would have passed without comment in feminist England' (*PI*, 62) but not in Anglo-India. Unfamiliar with their customs, Adela is surprised that club members have chosen to perform *Cousin Kate*, a play that Showalter reminds us is 'a mildly antifeminist comedy.'[4] Thus establishing an opposition between the emancipated women of England and the stalled liberation of memsahibs, *A Passage to India* plots Adela's movement from one side of the East–West divide to the other.

It is not just that Adela enters the cave contemplating a marriage that will subsume her identity into that of her husband. More important, she recognizes the danger of assuming the Anglo-Indians' racist assumptions about India and its inhabitants. 'Well, by marrying Mr Heaslop, I shall become what is known as an Anglo-Indian,' she says to Aziz as they make their way toward the caves:

> He held up his hand in protest. 'Impossible. Take back such a terrible remark.'
>
> 'But I shall! it's inevitable. I can't avoid the label. What I do hope to avoid is the mentality. Women like ——' She stopped, not quite liking to

3 [Sharpe's note.] Brenda Silver, 'Periphrasis, Power, and Rape in *A Passage to India*,' *Novel* 22 (Fall 1988): 100. A shorter version of this essay appears in *Rape and Representation*, ed. Lynn A. Higgins and Brenda R. Silver (New York: Columbia University Press, 1991), 115–37.

4 [Sharpe's note.] Showalter, '*A Passage to India* as "Marriage Fiction"'. [*Cousin Kate* is a comedy by H. H. Davies (1876–1917). It was first performed in 1903.]

mention names; she would boldly have said 'Mrs Turton and Mrs Callendar' a fortnight ago. (*PI*, 145)

Adela's inability to identify Mrs Turton and Mrs Callendar as the insensitive colonialists that they are, demonstrates her newfound loyalty to Anglo-Indian women. Her transformation into a memsahib was already under way the moment she agreed to marry Ronny Heaslop. 'She was labelled now' (*PI*, 94), she thought to herself at the time. If the label is inevitable, the mentality is inescapable. A disregard for Indians to the degree of rendering them invisible is an offense that Anglo-Indian women repeatedly commit. Mrs Turton addresses Indian women in the third person, as if they do not exist, and Mrs Callendar stares right through Aziz when she takes his carriage. Forster has justifiably been taken to task for situating the evils of colonialism in the attitudes of Anglo-Indian women. What I am attempting to do here, however, is to read the strategic deployment of the memsahib in colonial discourse, one that demands her scapegoating in the anti-imperialist message of *A Passage to India.*

By the time Adela enters the cave, her self-consciousness about what it means to be an Anglo-Indian is forgotten. After presuming that, as a Muslim, Aziz has more than one wife, she is oblivious to having offended him and, being so wrapped up in her own thoughts, is not even aware of his presence. 'Quite unconscious that she had said the wrong thing, and not seeing him, she also went into a cave, thinking with half her mind "sight-seeing bores me," and wondering with the other half about marriage' (*PI*, 153). Only half of Adela's mind is on thoughts of marriage; the other half expresses a boredom with Aziz's elaborate efforts to show her 'the real India.' Her divided mind reveals a tension between the double positioning of the English woman – as inferior sex but superior race. It is a contradiction that must be addressed in any discussion of the alleged assault.

When Adela emerges from the cave accusing Aziz of rape, she consolidates the identity she would rather deny. Which is to say, she reconfirms the racist assumption that, given the slightest opportunity, the native will revert to his barbaric ways. In her haste to escape, she flees through cacti, lodging thousands of minuscule spines into her flesh. Her mutilated condition confirms the violence of the attack, but it also reduces her sensibility to her tortured body. 'Everything now was transferred to the surface of her body, which began to avenge itself, and feed unhealthily' (*PI*, 193). Her fellow expatriates react to the news of the sexual assault from within a code of chivalry; they treat Adela as a mere cipher for a battle between men. 'Miss Quested was only a victim, but young Heaslop was a martyr; he was the recipient of all the evil intended against them by the country they had tried to serve; he was bearing the sahib's cross' (*PI*, 185). The term *sahib's cross* is a parody of the idea of the white man's burden that represents colonialism as an act of martyrdom. It is also an indictment of the masculinist perception that the sexual humiliation of English women is an indirect attack on men. The objectification of Adela into a passive victim denies her an entry into the great narrative of the white man's burden even as it confirms the self-sacrifice of the men who serve that mission. *She* cannot save the natives from their depravity, but neither can she save herself. Adela, the memsahib, the Anglo-Indian woman, has strayed far from the borders of feminist England. She may have entered the caves with some semblance of her former identity, but she leaves it as a violated body bearing the visible signs of the native's ingratitude. Behind the novel's reference to Adela's tortured body are the Mutiny reports on the rape and mutilation of English women.

The racial memory that echoes across the Mutiny novels as a horrific nightmare is also silently constitutive of *A Passage to India*. The (mis)representation of the object of the 1857 uprisings is so closely imbricated with the racial stereotype of brown-skinned men desiring white women that the Mutiny serves as a convenient name for expressing colonial fears and fantasies over the intermingling of two races. The Anglo-Indian residents of Chandrapore think of Aziz's 'crime' as 'the unspeakable limit of cynicism, untouched since 1857' (*PI*, 187), while the district superintendent of police, Mr McBryde, advises Fielding to 'read any of the Mutiny records' (*PI*, 169) for evidence of the Indian criminal mind. By alluding to the Mutiny as *the* representative crime of a sexual assault, the Anglo-Indians not only invoke the memory of those earlier 'unspeakable crimes' but also reproduce its effect. I take from Forster's presentation of the alleged rape within the frame of 1857 the license to read his novel as a critical intervention in a discourse that codes anticolonial rebellion as the assault of English women. By intertwining the lives of individuals with the history of decolonization, his plotting of sexual violence contends with the ideological effect of a colonial discourse of rape.

The drama surrounding Aziz's arrest reenacts the precariousness of the colonialist mission under threat of native insurrection. It is a vulnerability that hides behind a representation of the Indian male's sexual desire for white women as the cause of colonial conflict. As the court case draws nearer, the novel recreates the explosive atmosphere of 1857 and 1919 in a scene showing club members who debate what they should do about the hostile mobs demanding that Aziz be released. Their discussion centers on defending their women and children, a particularly charged phrase for eliciting cries of revenge. One young, golden-haired woman, whose husband is away, is afraid to go home 'in case the "niggers attacked"' (*PI*, 181). Her fellow Anglo-Indians invest the image of 'her abundant figure and masses of corn-gold hair' with the full value of colonialism; for them, 'she symbolized all that is worth fighting and dying for' (*PI*, 181). Parodies of this sort can be read as sobering reminders of the retributions against a rebellious Indian population that were committed in the name of English womanhood. If, as de Man informs us, 'all true criticism occurs in the mode of crisis,'[5] Forster's parody is critical in the sense that it revives the racial memory of the Mutiny not in order to manage the crisis of the 1920s in colonialism but to force it.

Instead of invoking 'the protection of women and children' as an excuse for police and military action (which is what Thompson does), *A Passage to India* shows that the catch phrase conveniently exculpates English men from any wrongdoing. 'They had started speaking of "women and children,"' comments

5 [Sharpe's note.] Paul de Man, 'Crisis and Criticism,' *Blindness and Insight: Essays in the Rhetoric of Contemporary Criticism*, 2nd ed. (Minneapolis: University of Minnesota Press, 1983), 8.

the narrator, 'that phrase that exempts the male from sanity when it has been repeated a few times' (*PI*, 183). The novel is also critical of the tendency to blame English women for racial violence. Upon being confronted with protests in his district the Collector directs his anger and frustration at Adela: '"After all, it's our women who make every thing more difficult out here," was his inmost thought, as he caught sight of some obscenities on a long, blank wall, and beneath his chivalry to Miss Quested resentment lurked, waiting its day – perhaps there is a grain of resentment in all chivalry' (*PI*, 214). Here, Forster shows that a colonial cult of chivalry excuses military action; elsewhere, he draws attention to the role of a discourse of rape in the management of anticolonial demonstrations. The major's uncontrollable outburst that they should 'call in the troops and clear the bazaars' (*PI*, 187) is reminiscent of General Dyer's directive at Amritsar. And Mrs Turton's command that every native who dare look at an English woman should crawl from Chandrapore to the Marabar caves echoes the infamous 'crawling order.' An ironic restaging of British honor and punishment, however, does not overturn the Mutiny narratives but merely questions their premises. What does reveal the fictionality of colonial truth-claims is the indeterminacy introduced to the certainty of a sex crime confirming the native's depravity.

By generating its narrative desire through the indeterminate status of a sexual assault, *A Passage to India* drives a wedge of doubt between a colonial discourse of rape and its object. During the trial, Adela delivers a verdict that throws the courtroom into chaos. 'Dr. Aziz never followed me into the cave,' she declares. 'I withdraw everything' (*PI*, 229). When situated within the racial memory of the Mutiny, Adela's extension and withdrawal of the charge interrupt a plotting that establishes a causal relation between the native assault of English women and British suppression of rebellion. Forster does not replace the certainty of an attack with its negation; rather, he replaces it with a narrative suspension that opens up the space for a mystery. Upon addressing this 'space,' we should keep in mind the historical usage of 'mystery' in a colonial discourse of power. 'Mystery' not only names the place where the logic of colonialism breaks down but also resolves a contradiction by making a question serve as its own answer.

After the trial, Fielding explores with Adela four possible explanations for what happened: Either Aziz did molest her, she claimed he did out of her own malice, she hallucinated the attack, or someone else followed her into the cave (the guide and a Pathan are offered as two likely assailants). Although Fielding rules out the first two possibilities, Adela gives no indication to him (or the reader, for that matter) whether she reacted to a real or an imaginary assault. She finally admits that the only one who knows for sure is Mrs Moore, who she claims acquired her knowledge through a telepathic communication. As he keeps forcing Adela to return to the question of what happened in the caves, Fielding soon realizes that the very multiplicity of explanations offers no easy resolution to the mystery: 'Telepathy? What an explanation! Better withdraw it, and Adela did so. . . . Were there worlds beyond which they could never touch, or did all that is possible enter their consciousness? They could not tell. . . . Perhaps life is a mystery, not a muddle; they could not tell' (*PI*, 263). As readers, we are perhaps less satisfied than

Fielding with the 'life is a mystery' response. Critics have and still do search their imaginations for an explanation.

Forster himself imagined one outcome of the attempted rape that did not appear in the published version of his novel. The deleted scene contains such a detailed description of the assault in the cave that it would be practically impossible to read what transpired there as Adela's hallucination. Here we have no helpless woman seeking the protection of others, but one who calculates the right moment to make her move and fights off her attacker:

> At first she thought that <she was being robbed,> he was <holding> \taking/ her hand \as before/ to help her <out>, then she realised, and shrieked at the top of her voice. 'Boum' <went> \shrieked [?]/ the echo. She struck out and he got hold of her other hand and forced her against the wall, he got both her hands in one of his, and then felt at her <dress> \breasts/. 'Mrs. Moore' she yelled. 'Ronny – don't let him, save me.' The strap of her Field Glasses, tugged suddenly, was drawn across her throat. She understood – it was to be passed once around her neck, <it was to> she was to be throttled as far as necessary and then . . . [Forster's suspension points] Silent, though the echo still raged up and down, she waited and when the breath was on her wrenched a hand free, got hold of the glasses and pushed them at \into/ her assailant's mouth. She could not push hard, but it was enough to <free her> hurt him. He let go, and then with both hands \on her weapon/ she smashed <him to pieces> \at him again/. She was strong and had horrible joy in revenge. 'Not this time,' she cried, and he answered – or <perhaps it was> the cave \did/.[6]

Like the behavior of the English women who survived the 1857 uprisings, Adela's act of self-defense is at odds with a dominant discourse that constructs her as a passive victim. As a consequence, one cannot help but notice a resemblance between the absent text of her struggle and an official discourse that erases colonial women's agency. In fact, feminist critics have submitted Forster's deletion of this scene as the sign of a more pervasive silencing of women in his novel.[7] What remains unacknowledged, however, is that the deleted script replaces woman-as-victim with woman-as-agent, but only at the risk of confirming the alleged rape. A clearing up of the mystery in favor of Adela's guilt or innocence consequently adheres to the terms of a discourse that displaces racial signification away from colonial relations onto narratives of sexual violence. We see that a restoration of the silenced stories of English women in itself does not unravel a colonial plotting of rape.

If we are to study literature for its disruption of a discourse that prevents social change, we can no longer afford to restrict readings to the limits of the literary text. The racial and sexual signification of rape in *A Passage to India* does not

6 [Sharpe's note.] *The Manuscripts of A Passage to India,* 242–43.

7 [Sharpe's note.] Silver, 'Periphrasis, Power, and Rape,' 86; Frances Restuccia, '"A Cave of My Own" The Sexual Politics of Indeterminacy,' *Raritan* 9, no. 2 (Fall 1989): 117.

issue from Adela's experience in the cave; the answer is not to be found there. Like Fielding and Adela, who confront the mystery in a multiplicity of explanations, we should recognize that there are no easy answers. To clear up the mystery of what happened by searching our imagination for the missing details means reading Forster's novel according to the narrative demands of the Mutiny reports. To read the mystery itself as an effect of that colonial history, however, is to see in its indeterminacies the imprint of a racial memory. In the place of 'what happened in the caves?' I offer a different kind of question, one suggested by Adela's cry in the deleted assault scene. Managing to free herself from the grip of her attacker, Adela screams, 'Not this time.' What are the other times, the other assaults to which her triumphant cry alludes? I think I have already answered that question.

Bette London, section entitled 'On Mimicry: Towards a Performative Theory of Colonial Authority' from her chapter 'Of Mimicry and English Men: E. M. Forster and the Performance of Masculinity', in Tony Davies and Nigel Wood (eds), *A Passage to India*, Buckingham: Open University Press, 1994, pp. 93–101

Bette London's essay focuses on Aziz and his relation to English people, customs and authority. London begins with a consideration of Aziz's meeting with Mrs Moore at the mosque in terms of Edward Said's conception of Orientalism and the European assumption of cultural authority with military and economic power. She deepens this analysis, however, by then discussing Aziz in terms of Homi Bhabha's theories of ambivalence and mimicry: the subservient but also subversive and threatening status of the educated Indian, as Macaulay's Anglicized Indian who is never 'English', who is 'white but not quite'.

When a young Indian surgeon accosts an Englishwoman in a secluded Moslem holy place at the beginning of a widely acclaimed English novel, the scene should give us pause. Yet for most readers of E. M. Forster's *A Passage to India*,[1] Dr Aziz's chance encounter with Mrs Moore appears what it proclaims itself to be: a respite from the relentless performance of colonial authority, a moment of sanctuary from colonialism's prevailing inhumanity. Indeed, both parties to this encounter come to the mosque in retreat: Aziz, from the 'inevitable snub' (*PI*, 12) by Major Callendar (who, having sent for his subordinate, does not even await his arrival) and Mesdames Callendar and Lesley (who steal his tonga yet do not acknowledge his existence); Mrs Moore, from the Club's suffocating performance of *Cousin Kate*, sealed off from the gaze of Indian servants. Situated 'at the edge of the civil station' (*PI*, 13), the mosque thus defines the outer limits of colonial civility.

Within the mosque, by all accounts, Aziz behaves rudely, venting his anger on some unknown Englishwoman. But if the mosque would seem to be a place

1 References are to the Abinger edition of *A Passage to India* edited by Oliver Stallybrass.

beyond England's reach, colonial power asserts itself, as it always does, in the form of mimicry. For Aziz's 'rudeness' to Mrs Moore imitates, even as it inverts, the ambiguous enunciation of colonial authority, with its exclusionary codes of gender, custom, race, religion, nationality. As a woman, as English, and as Christian, Aziz implies, Mrs Moore occupies a space where she cannot be recognized:

> 'Madam, this is a mosque, you have no right here at all; you should have taken off your shoes; this is a holy place for Moslems' (*PI*, 14).

With the clarification of the muddle over the shoes – 'I have taken them off' – the scene assumes new configurations in which, ostensibly, the triumph of the personal over the political culminates in a moment of transcendent unity: Aziz's final address to Mrs Moore, 'Then you are an Oriental' (*PI*, 17). Yet a rereading of this scene in light of current theories of colonialist discourse might offer a more sobering view of its performance, a performance whose 'happy ending' identifies Aziz as both object and agent of what Edward Said has called 'Orientalism': the production, by and for the West, of 'the Orient' as a knowable entity. Indeed, the dialogue that produces this communion begins with the retraction of Aziz's authoritative position ('I am truly sorry for speaking'), the loss of his command of the rules of recognition (his power to confer or withhold the other's identity); and it requires that Aziz be recognized (that he recognize himself) through Mrs Moore's authority, in the terms of Mrs Moore's speech. For Mrs Moore's 'personal' disclosure of her own marital history elicits from Aziz these 'cryptic' words of identification: 'Then we are in the same box' (*PI*, 16), words that announce in their distortion of the idiom Aziz's distance from the 'common' language they speak.

Aziz's words, in fact, perform what Homi K. Bhabha has called 'colonial mimicry', proclaiming sameness even as they enact difference; in their close approximation to customary usage, they mark the speaker as 'almost the same, but not quite', the subject of a 'difference' – an ambivalence – upon which colonial power rests.[2] Aziz's elaboration (when he learns that, like himself, Mrs Moore has two sons and a daughter), 'Is not this the same box with a vengeance?' (*PI*, 16), underlines this dynamic: the 'box' is the same and not the same, the same *with an excess*. And Mrs Moore's gentle prodding, 'What are their names? Not also Ronny, Ralph, and Stella, surely?', reminds us of the power inscribed within their respective positions. For with the naming of his children – Ahmed, Karim, Jamila – Aziz declares what is unassimilable in the lingo of Anglo-India; inserting this un-English nomenclature into the language of sameness, Aziz reveals the political determinants of his mimetic dilemma where 'almost the same, but not quite' inevitably reduces to '*Almost the same but not quite*'.[3] Speaking 'inappropriately', he becomes what Bhabha calls a 'mimic man' (occupying a line of literary descent backward to Kipling and forward to Naipaul), 'the effect of a flawed colonial

2 Homi Bhabha, 'Of Mimicry and Man: The Ambivalence of Colonial Discouse', *October*, 28, spring, 1984, p. 126.
3 Ibid., p. 130.

mimesis, in which to be Anglicized, is *emphatically* not to be English'.[4] Indeed, the effort entailed in Aziz's acts of imitation and accommodation inevitably mark him as Other – one who must work to produce what the Englishman does naturally, what the Englishman inherits as his birthright and observes through an internalized code of behaviour.

'Is not this the same box *with a vengeance*?' (emphasis added). In these resonant words, it is as if Forster had underlined the un-English emphasis. But the phrase resonates, more generally, for a novel that turns upon a problem of identification: identification in the Caves, whose box-like sameness and resistance to differentiation produces Anglo-India's need for a vengeful agency (figured as 'India' or 'Indian'). It resonates, moreover, in the immediacy of the mosque scene, suggesting the mosque's problematic status as retreat, as a space *outside* colonial authority. And it resonates in what is edited out of the scene's normative humanist reading: the construction of Aziz's sexuality. For when Aziz surprises Mrs Moore – ''Oh! Oh!' the woman gasped' (*PI*, 14) – there is a definite hint of sexual menace in the scene; and when Mrs Moore is unveiled as inaccessible to Aziz's sexual fantasy ('She was older than Hamidullah Begum, with a red face and white hair'), Aziz's loss is construed as disproportionately devastating: 'A fabric bigger than the mosque fell to pieces' (*PI*, 15). Here, then, as elsewhere in the text, the representation of Aziz activates familiar fantasy formations of the Other's sexuality: the Other who, as the fear of miscegenation reflects, might share desires with his fellows in the West; who desiring *inappropriately* and *in excess* reveals himself to be sexed samely/differently.

Read in this light, the episode in the Caves (never fully represented) presents 'the same box' as the mosque – but with a vengeance – rendering explicit what the earlier scene masks with its spurious unity. Mrs Moore's retreat, for example, from a space of suffocating closeness (the Club, the Caves) sets the stage for Aziz's appearance as sexual predator; what appears in the aftermath of the Caves, then, as an 'unthinkable' development (Aziz's guilty sexuality) has already been thought in colonialism's collective fantasy (in the mind of Adela and the Anglo-Indian community; in the novel's logic of representation). Moreover, if Adela's 'tactless' question about polygamy prompts the Cave's catastrophe, its point of contention has been at least ambiguously conceded in the earlier scene; for if Mrs Moore acknowledges two (dead) husbands, for Aziz, what exactly does being 'in the same box' mean?

I cite this moment of indeterminacy to return to Homi Bhabha and the problem of text and theory. For in a series of essays of imposing density and complexity, Bhabha has made 'ambivalence' the trademark of his theory of colonial mimicry – a theory reworked, refined, and elaborated in the body of his writings. As he himself explains: 'These strategies of mimicry, hybridity, incommensurability or translation, which I've been trying to variously interpret, are, I think, the unspoken, unexplored moments of the history of modernity'.[5] Participating in the

4 Ibid., p. 128.
5 Homi Bhabha, 'Location, Intervention, Incommensurability: A Conversation with Homi Bhabha', *Emergences*, 1, pp. 63–88, 1989, p. 67.

breaking of the silence about colonialism's practices and history, Bhabha's work contributes to the ongoing study of colonial discourse that has been so important to the development of what has been variously called 'cultural studies', 'culture studies' and 'cultural critique'; this study, as Gayatri Spivak explains, constitutes 'an important (and beleaguered) part of the discipline now', with its own defined and contested place in the academy.[6] Cultural studies, in fact, as a recognizable academic practice and theory, has defined itself through contestation. Operating from explicitly articulated political positions, it has challenged both the traditional objects of literary study and the discipline's pose of disinterestedness; but it has also been contested from within, reflecting the inherent contradictions (and competing priorities) of an oppositional practice located *inside* the academy.

Among the workers in this new field of study, Bhabha has been the one perhaps most insistently attentive to the *discursive* construction of colonial authority, to the play of colonial power in a field of *textuality*. In this emphasis, he acknowledges two of the crucial components in his own 'hybrid position' as a critic: Derridean deconstruction and Lacanian psychoanalysis. Indeed, certain recent criticisms of Bhabha reproduce familiar critiques of Derrida's and Lacan's 'academic' theorizing: he is too distant from *real* political struggle; his work allows insufficient space for human agency (particularly the agency of those occupying marginal and oppositional positions); his project lacks historical specificity; his commitment to theory and the theory he articulates reproduces the 'silencing' of the Other it purportedly critiques, denying the Other an authentic identity.

Yet Bhabha's particular contribution to colonial and postcolonial studies lies precisely in his effort to appropriate these critical methodologies for the work of exposing and dismantling political oppression. If Bhabha's explication of mimicry, for example, as the articulation of sameness *as* difference (where what one utters is never identical to the thing 'repeated') requires, for its underpinnings, Derrida's concepts of *différance* and 'double inscription', Bhabha deploys these concepts differently. Turning away from Derrida's *literary* emphasis on 'the vicissitudes of interpretation' in the act of reading, Bhabha introduces the crucial question of 'the effects of power' in the particular scene of enunciation he investigates: the colonial theatre.[7] There, where power is distributed so unevenly, the production and circulation of 'identity' and 'difference' unleashed in the decisive meeting between colonizer and colonized cannot be read simply as the 'free play' of the signifier endemic to linguistic instability; rather one must ask whose interests are served and what desires fulfilled by the particular arrangement of these positions.

On the face of it, the answer would evidently be that colonial mimicry operates as the means by which colonial power shores up its authority through 'strategies of individuation and domination', through 'dividing practices' that differentiate

6 Gayatri Spivak, 'Poststructuralism, Marginality, Post-Coloniality and Value', in Peter Collier and Helga Geyer-Ryan (eds), *Literary Theory Today*, Oxford: Polity, 1990, p. 221.

7 Homi Bhabha, 'Signs Taken for Wonders', *'Race', Writing and Difference*, Chicago: Chicago University Press, 1985, p. 151.

'us' from 'them' while covering over internal contradictions.[8] Thus Bhabha defines colonial mimicry as

> the desire for a reformed, recognizable Other, as a *subject of a difference that is almost the same, but not quite*. Which is to say, that the discourse of mimicry is constructed around an *ambivalence*; in order to be effective, mimicry must continually produce its slippage, its excess, its difference.[9]

By this account, mimicry works as a complex strategy for reforming, regulating and disciplining an Other it partially 'invents' through these very strategies.

To take the Anglo-Indian situation Forster writes about, the Anglicized Indian, as the ultimate product of mimicry, must impersonate the English (thereby justifying the imposition of English authority) without ultimately threatening the integrity of English identity. Thus, as Aziz explains to Fielding (when he lends him his collar-stud), he wears Western dress 'to pass the police': 'If I'm biking in English dress – starch collar, hat with ditch – they take no notice. When I wear a fez, they cry, "Your lamp's out!"' (*PI*, 59). If the success of this mimetic performance allows Aziz to escape surveillance in the streets, the inevitable 'slippage' is produced when he comes under civil scrutiny, under the eye of Ronny Heaslop acting in his private capacity: 'Aziz was exquisitely dressed, from tie-pin to spats, but he had forgotten his back collar-stud, and there you have the Indian all over: inattention to detail; the fundamental slackness that reveals the race' (*PI*, 74). As Ronny's ill-informed judgement indicates, the native's 'slackness' serves colonialism's needs: the need to mark racial difference visibly, to uncover, as it were (to borrow Frantz Fanon's terms) the black skin beneath the white mask. For as Bhabha would read this scene, the Indian must slip up ('they all forget their back collar-studs sooner or later' (*PI*, 87), Ronny later explains) or slip out ('there you have the Indian all over') if mimicry is to remain an effective guarantee of English colonial superiority.

In this reading of mimicry, 'Colonial power produces the colonised as a fixed reality which is at once an "other" and yet entirely knowable and visible';[10] as Bhabha makes clear, such an understanding of the operation of desire and power depends upon psychoanalytic categories: disavowal, fetishism, fantasy. As an understanding of fetishism illustrates, the term 'disavowal' includes, simultaneously, both the recognition and non-recognition of difference; for the trauma of sexual difference (the discovery that the mother does not have a penis) provokes an elaborate denial – or disavowal – of that very thing. In the case of fetishism, this disavowal is achieved through the fixation on an object of substitution – the fetish (foot, shoe, etc.) – that masks that difference and thus restores the illusion of an original presence. If the mother *has* a penis, then the male subject

8 Ibid.

9 Homi Bhabha, 'Of Mimicry and Man: The Ambivalence of Colonial Discourse', *October*, 28, spring, 1984, p. 126; emphasis in original.

10 Francis Barker, et al. (eds) *The Politics of Theory*, Colchester: University of Essex, 1983, p. 199.

cannot be castrated; ultimately, then, fetishism fulfils a *masculine* fantasy of wholeness and integrity that requires both the *difference* of the mother (*she* is the one who is castrated) and her *sameness*.

For Bhabha, it is the *ambivalence* of fetishism that gives it its explanatory power for colonial mimicry; thus in his rewriting of the psychoanalytic scene, Bhabha grafts racial and cultural differences on to sexual difference to produce his own hybrid categories:

> For fetishism is always a 'play' or vacillation between the archaic affirmation of wholeness/similarity – in Freud's terms: 'All men have penises'; in ours 'All men have the same skin/race/culture'; and the anxiety associated with lack and difference – again, for Freud 'Some do not have penises'; for us 'Some *do not* have the same skin/race/culture.'[11]

The racial stereotypes produced through mimicry (the native's slackness, for example, or his sexual voracity) can thus be seen as fetishistic representations, compensatory fantasies. As such, in their reconstruction of difference as inappropriateness ('slippage', 'lack', 'excess'), they protect the colonizer's illusion of an *appropriate* (i.e. non-contradictory) identity: coherent, intact, bounded.

In this reading, mimicry figures the operation by which the colonial subject (colonizer) disavows the contradictions in his own position of authority: his *lack* of originality, authenticity, self-identity. Following Lacan, Bhabha locates the recognition of this lack (and the deployment of compensatory strategies) in the subject's entry into language – the entry into social relations that both reveal and compensate for the gap between self and world, language and reality. Language (and the 'Symbolic Order' it represents), in effect, splits the subject by articulating the 'Imaginary' wholeness from which the subject now knows itself to be forever dispossessed. As a speaking subject, the self can only perform the culturally scripted fictions of identity. Bhabha, however, extends this drama to the performance of national identity; as figured in the possession of a language (English) with the power to confer reality, national identity serves as a particularly seductive script, promising the restoration of an elusive wholeness.

But as Forster demonstrates (at least when read through Bhabha's critical machinery), for the colonizer as much as the colonized, the act of enunciation betrays the crucial splitting in the self required for the mimicry of English identity. For to 'make England in India' *(PI*, 66) entails more than 'doing what comes naturally'; even on the verbal terrain, as the production of *Cousin Kate* confirms, English middle-class identity must be *performed* – and reperformed – on a daily basis. Thus Fielding, in spite of the fact that 'all his best friends were English', finds that among his compatriots *in India* he cannot pull off a successful impersonation of an Englishman: 'he appeared to inspire confidence until he spoke' (*PI*, 55–6). And Ronny can achieve this apotheosis only at the cost of authenticity: 'When he said "Of course there are exceptions," he was quoting Mr Turton, while

11 Ibid., p. 202.

"increasing the izzat" was Major Callendar's own. The phrases worked and were in current use at the Club' (*PI*, 28). Moreover, as the response to 'the incident' in the Caves illustrates, a united Anglo-Indian front can be maintained only through careful vigilance and repressive discipline – the type of linguistic policing (the lookout for slippages) that contains native insurgency.

If Bhabha, then, remains deliberately vague around questions of agency, relying on such terms as 'the desire of colonial mimicry' (*whose* desire?) and 'the colonial subject' (*which* colonial subject – colonizer or colonized?), this ambivalence reflects his sense that mimicry operates both ways simultaneously. Indeed, this doubleness constitutes one of the most distinctive (and controversial) features of Bhabha's theory – a theory that locates in mimicry not only the inscription of the mechanisms of colonial authority but also the site of the dislocation, disruption or subversion of that authority. To follow the metaphor of fetishism, mimicry unmasks in the process of masking the desire in which it originates. Thus Bhabha explains: 'The effect of mimicry on the authority of colonial discourse is profound and disturbing.'[12] For mimicry, in effect, through the *fantasy* of difference it projects, continually produces and reproduces the threat against which its operation militates. Consequently, whatever *really* happened in the Caves, the emergence of Aziz as potential rapist can be understood as the logical extension of colonial mimicry, with its demand for the Other's lawlessness. In fact, at the moment of his arrest, Aziz slips up, attempting to escape rather than maintaining a stiff upper lip in the face of opposition. Acting the criminal, he stands as cause and effect of the 'normalizing' knowledge his transgression activates – in this case, the Superintendent of the Police's 'theory about climatic zones': 'The theory ran: "All unfortunate natives are criminals at heart, for the simple reason that they live south of latitude 30 . . ."' (*PI*, 158).

As this scenario demonstrates, the failure of mimicry (Aziz's inappropriate behaviour) is simultaneously the mark of mimicry's successful ability to discriminate the Anglicized from the English. If mimicry, then, lays bare the assumptions that govern colonial relations, what it exposes most emphatically are the contradictions that underwrite colonial authority. As Bhabha explains it, the mimetic performance alienates colonial authority from its own first principles, from the language of liberty and fairness, from the practice of civility. It works, then, to *split* the rhetoric of Anglo-India, by opening to view the space where the philanthropic colonial justification (the obligatory answer to uncomfortable political questions, 'England holds India for *her* good' (*PI*, 102)) meets its self-interested double: England holds India for her good – i.e. the good of the mother country. And it works to illuminate a 'civil administration' indifferent to the claims of common civility: 'We're not out here for the purpose of behaving pleasantly!' (*PI*, 43). If the 'unpleasantness' of the Caves, then, provokes extraordinary measures that unleash colonialism's sadistic fantasies ('He wanted to flog every native that he saw, but to do nothing that would lead to a riot or to the necessity

12 Homi Bhabha, 'Of Mimicry and Man: The Ambivalence of Colonial Discourse', *October*, 28, spring, 1984, p. 126.

for military intervention' (*PI*, 174)), these fantasies (circumscribed within the law) already inhabit colonial authority's *ordinary* operations.

Producing other knowledges of colonialism's norms, mimicry alienates colonial practice from its universalizing pretensions; exposing the contradictions that split the colonial subject, it disrupts the play of power in a single direction. For Bhabha, then, part of mimicry's subversive potential lies in its capacity to undermine colonial authority as a monolithic structure. In this operation, it opens a space for colonial resistance – a space that might tap the desire of the colonized to uncover and displace the grounds of their oppression, to turn 'the discursive conditions of dominance into the grounds of intervention'.[13] But for Bhabha, resistance need not be 'an oppositional act of political intention';[14] it exists as 'the effect of an ambivalence' within colonial authority. While Bhabha argues that this ambivalence enables 'a form of subversion, founded on that uncertainty'[15] he resists locating the subversive agency. Aziz's remark, then, with which I opened this discussion of Bhabha's concept of mimicry, 'Is not this the same box with a vengeance?' yields up a final echo in this 'vengeance' that enters without origin and trails off so indeterminately. Yet in such vengeance – the potential for subversion that adheres to all acts of mimicry – we might locate the grounds for a performative practice of reading.

David Dowling, 'Forster's Novels', *Bloomsbury Aesthetics and the Novels of Forster and Woolf*, London: Macmillan, 1985, pp. 71–84

This extract from Dowling's essay is concerned with questions of form, organisation and structure. He offers some glosses on previous readings and interpretations of the novel with regard to issues of harmony and unity. Particularly concerned with the friendship between Aziz and Fielding, he considers *A Passage to India* as a novel of ideas and as an exploration of personal relationships in the light of gender, sexuality and feminism. Above all, Dowling perceives the book to be at root not an exploration of colonialism, spirituality or liberal values but of one particular pair of men struggling to become friends.

> *It doesn't do to think. To follow the promptings of the eye and the imagination is quite complicated enough.*[1]

Forster's last and greatest novel has continually teased critics into endless debate about its completeness as a work of art. Virginia Woolf was clearly unimpressed

13 Homi Bhabha, 'Signs Taken for Wonders', *'Race', Writing and Difference*, Chicago: Chicago University Press, 1985, p. 154.
14 Ibid., p. 153.
15 Ibid., p. 154.

1 [Dowling's note.] E. M. Forster, *The Hill of Devi*, London: Edward Arnold, 1953, p. 73.

by the 'wholeness' of it when, after praising its observations and social satire, she rather archly commented, 'Mr Forster has almost achieved the great feat of animating this dense, compact body of observation with a spiritual light.'[2] 'Clear and triumphant beauty', she said, existed only in chapters. Wilfred Stone has been far more affirmative, calling it 'perhaps the greatest English novel of this century as an aesthetic accomplishment'.[3] His ensuing discussion toys with the principle of rhythm as the 'incarnation of the book's meaning'[4] but finally settles on the spatial metaphor of the mandala. The practice of applying Forster's critical principle of rhythm to *A Passage to India* was begun, of course, by E. K. Brown in his *Rhythm in the Novel*, where he praised the tripartite, symphonic structure of the novel in those terms which Forster used to describe *War and Peace*. So convinced is Elizabeth Heine that there is indeed an order in the novel, whether rhythmic or spatial, that she attributes an order to the metaphysical meaning of the novel as well:

> Thus this final development of Forster's consistent 'structure' in *A Passage to India*, where the characters' mental experiences are shaped in mysterious ways beyond the knowledge of psychology, indicates Forster's aesthetic faith in an order beyond 'humanism'. The paradoxical fact that he has created the ultimate order of the novel does not change the reader's conviction that the structure as created reflects a non-human absolute.[5]

This plethora of observations about the unity of the novel is a testimony to the deceptive confidence of Forster's habitual tone and of the three sections of the novel. But a genuine effort to explicate the unity and harmony inevitably lead one back to Woolf's reservation, though not, perhaps, with her overtone of censure.

When Forster revisited India in 1921 he recorded some revealing responses. Those responses were so strong that they inhibited his working on the novel while he was there; 'the gap between India remembered and India experienced was too wide'.[6] This gap between the organised memory and the chaotic experience was never resolved; indeed, it became itself the new centre of the completed novel. Forster recorded while he was in Dewas, 'I could never describe the muddle in this place. It is wheel within wheel.'[7] Of the festival of Gokul Ashtami he wrote, 'The noise the noise the noise which sucks one into a whirlpool . . . music has never existed.'[8] And in a letter to Dickinson he confessed that he found the Hindu character 'unaesthetic'.[9]

2 [Dowling's note.] Virginia Woolf, *Collected Essays*, London: Hogarth, 1966–7, 4 vols., volume 1, p. 351.
3 [Dowling's note.] Wilfred Stone, *The Cave and the Mountain*, Stanford: Stanford University Press, 1966, p. 345.
4 [Dowling's note.] Ibid., pp. 343, 346.
5 [Dowling's note.] Elizabeth Heine, 'The Significance of Structure in the Novels of E. M. Forster and Virginia Woolf' *English Literature in Transition*, 16 (1973) p. 296.
6 [Dowling's note.] Forster, *The Hill of Devi*, p. 155.
7 [Dowling's note.] Ibid., p. 77.
8 [Dowling's note.] Ibid., p. 108.
9 [Dowling's note.] Ibid., p. 87.

Such comments clearly explain why Forster could not write in India. He found the country inimical to the artistic endeavour itself, at least as it is conceived in the West as an effort towards balance, harmony, and a form which must have significance. This does not mean that Forster was antipathetic to Indian society, however. He found the life as congenial as ever, responding fully to the affection which he felt 'quivered through everything'.[10]

Analysing Forster's response to India over the years in his writings, G. K. Das concludes that, while Forster responded warmly to Islam, he was also drawn towards elements of Hinduism: not the obliterating pantheism of the 'Temple' section, but the paradoxical affirmation of the individual. In 1953 Forster recalled a Hindu temple:

> There often exists inside its complexity a tiny cavity, a central cell, where the individual may be alone with his god. . . . It is only a cell where the worshipper can for a moment face what he believes. He worships at the heart of the world-mountain, inside the exterior complexity. And he is alone. Hinduism, unlike Christianity and Buddhism and Islam, does not invite him to meet his god congregationally; and this commends it to me.[11]

Forster's attraction to Hinduism, this religion which, as he said in 1915, says 'I am different from everybody else' *and* 'I am the same as everybody else',[12] is at the heart of the meaning and technique of *A Passage to India*. The division of the novel into three sections – 'Mosque', 'Caves', 'Temple' – suggests such a religious patterning or debate. Where the novel differs from such other tripartite novels as *To the Lighthouse*, *The Longest Journey* and *Howards End* is in the disproportions of each section here. The quantitative relationship of 3:4:1 belies the emotional and symbolic importance given to the final section, 'Temple', which is only one-eighth of the novel's bulk.

The explanation of this feature goes a long way towards reconciling the various responses to the novel here summarised. The fact is that we cannot argue for the 'ultimate order of the novel' from the point of view of themes any more than we can from the point of view of three balanced sections. John Beer suggests we can read the novel 'in three quite differing ways'[13] according as we see the central character as Fielding, Mrs Moore or Adela. But what about Aziz, Godbole, or even Ronnie [*sic*]? Benita Parry also seizes on the number three, which Forster has so teasingly dangled before us, to argue that the novel presents 'three major Indian philosophical-religious systems'.[14] But can the Moslem religion be said to dominate the first section, and what about Christianity? Such attempts to impose

10 [Dowling's note.] Ibid., p. 116.
11 [Dowling's note.] *Listener*, 10 September 1953, p. 420.
12 [Dowling's note.] *Daily News and Leader*, 30 April 1915, p. 7.
13 [Dowling's note.] John Beer, foreword to G. K. Das, *E. M. Forster's India*, London: Macmillan, 1977, p. xi.
14 [Dowling's note.] Benita Parry, '*A Passage to India*: Epitaph or Manifesto?', in *Forster: A Human Exploration*, ed. G. K. Das and John Beer, New York: New York University Press, 1979, p. 137.

a neat thematic order on the novel are not only reductive but also ignore the constant ambiguities and bewildering multiplicity of perspectives which is the experience of reading *A Passage to India*.

Nevertheless, Parry is closest to the central issues of the novel by focusing on the issue of how to be, or how to see. She writes,

> The novel offers this triad as the form of paradoxical differences contained within the unbroken whole: incorporated in the enclosing frame is the gracious culture of Islam in India, a society where personal relations amongst Moslems do flourish; the unpeopled Jain caves, place of the ascetic renunciation of the world; and the buoyant religious community of the Hindus, internally divided and internally cohesive. The approach to the component meanings of these systems is, however, profoundly ambiguous, moving between responsiveness and rejection, making the myth and subverting it.[15]

This is a clear case of trying to have one's three-tiered cake and eating it, too. The insistence on an 'unbroken whole' and differences which are not differences is founded on the unnecessary assumption that novels, particularly this one with its three sections, should be watertight conceptual tanks. Again, it ignores the reading-experience, which focuses not on systems but on individuals, and which ends with two men on horseback alone in the wilderness.

It should be agreed, then, that *A Passage to India* looks like a novel of ideas. Indeed, as Edwin Thumboo puts it, 'The metaphysics . . . at key moments moves from background to middleground and foreground.'[16] Life does seem to be examined against the backdrop of the eternal verities – 'a continual recurrence, surge, or movement of man between the poles of being and nothing, between the primary and tertiary levels of experience and between birth and death.'[17] Even the habitual movement of the prose is from assertion to negation[18] or from language to silence.[19] But still, *A Passage to India* is not a religious meditation or a sociological tract, it is a novel. From first to last, from the meeting of Aziz with Mrs Moore to the ride of Aziz and Fielding, it is 'this man-to-man business' of human relations, and we must not lose sight of that fact in the seductive lure of the politics of Chandrapore or the metaphysics of Godbole.

The novel is essentially a love story – not that of Aziz and Mrs Moore, or Ronnie and Adela, or even Mrs Moore and India, but that of Aziz and Fielding. The question is whether friendship, that cardinal Moorean virtue, can flourish

15 [Dowling's note.] Ibid.

16 [Dowling's note.] Edwin Thumboo, 'E. M. Forster's *A Passage to India*: from Caves to Court', *Southern Review*, 9–10 (1976–7), p. 141.

17 [Dowling's note.] Avrom Fleischman, 'Being and Nothing in *A Passage to India*', *Criticism*, 15 (1973), p. 125.

18 [Dowling's note.] John Colmer, 'Promise and Withdrawal in *A Passage to India*', in *Forster: A Human Exploration*, ed. G. K. Das and John Beer, New York: New York University Press, 1979.

19 [Dowling's note.] Michael Orange, 'Language and Silence in *A Passage to India*', in *Forster: A Human Exploration*, ed. G. K. Das and John Beer, New York: New York University Press, 1979.

between individuals of different backgrounds and beliefs. For such a friendship to occur, the participants must stand apart from their communities, alone, confronting the nothingness of non-being itself, like the Hindu in the innermost cell of the temple or the tourist in the Marabar Caves. The only value that will sustain him in that extreme situation is the friendship itself. Luring him back from friendship is the comforting security of the group: the Anglo-Indian community, the circle of Moslem friends around the hookah, the swarming Hindu mass. If we restore individuals to their central place on Forster's canvas, we can see that the supposed philosophical dialectic between being and nothingness resolves itself into a debate between belonging to the group and belonging to the individual.

Forster's earlier novels had translated this issue into the conventions of the love story (*A Room with a View*) or the symbolic counters of an evolutionary parable (*The Longest Journey*, *Howards End*). In *A Passage to India* he was able to return more directly to the issue which concerned him in *Maurice*, but without feeling limited by the sexual debate within the mores of one restrictive society. The word 'homosexual' thus becomes ludicrously limiting, unless one can apply the word equally to the impulses underlying Forster's declarations in 'What I Believe': 'I believe in personal relationships. . . . If I had to choose between betraying my country and betraying my friend, I hope I should have the guts to betray my country.' Of course, the relationship of Aziz and Fielding is affected by their attitudes towards women and wives – indeed, this becomes the crisis at the end of the 'Caves' section and persists in 'Temple'. But marriage itself should be seen here as an aspect of a society's communal force – at least in the ways Aziz and Fielding regard their particular wives – and not as a demand on their spiritual resources equal to that of friendship.

A comparison with Lawrence's *Women in Love* will clarify this difference. Both novels end in a similar way, with the unfulfilled urge towards a homosexual friendship. Lawrence, however, gives us a drama hermetically sealed around four characters. Their response to the Austrian snow (so similar in many ways to Forster's placing his characters in the alien environment of the Marabar Caves) is in terms of pre-existing relationships being challenged. Forster's novel is far more tentative, theoretical almost. Fielding's friendship with Aziz is not welded and distorted in the heat of battle, as it were, but rather contemplated as a possibility, weighed up against the other possible strategies of returning to England, getting married, and so forth. This is why *A Passage to India* seems like a novel of ideas: the crucial point is that it is the ideas of Forster's characters, not of Forster, which are being formulated and challenged.

The proportional imbalance of the three sections, then, is a function of the rhythms involved in Fielding's inner debate and in our reading-experience. We shall appreciate the aesthetic shape of the novel only if we follow the fortunes of its characters through step by step.

The opening chapter takes us on a brilliant, bird's-eye view of Chandrapore, from the muddy Ganges to the Marabar Caves in the distance. Arranged like various strata are the quarters of the various races. The progression is not only hierarchical but also metaphysical, from the undifferentiated mass of the Hindu river-dwellers – 'like some low but indestructible form of life' – through the exclusive civil station to the individual's confrontation with self in the caves. Between these poles, social and philosophical, the story will play itself out. The movement of the novel from overview to intense personal drama is illustrated in the way this opening chapter contrasts with the beginning of 'Caves', which is an intimate description of the interior of the caves towards which the characters are hastening, and the beginning of 'Temple', which does not set the physical scene but concentrates on Godbole and the activities of the mass of celebrants.

The first scene of the Moslems gathered round their hookah defines the virtues and vices of that community. There is the congenial friendship, the beautiful poetry which reminds them of departed greatness, and 'for the time India seemed one and their own' (p. 17);[20] but there is also the antagonism towards the British, and what we should now call the male chauvinism in their attitude towards women. All these will be important elements in Aziz's friendship with Fielding.

Alone in the mosque, which 'alone signified' (p. 21) to Aziz, in the sense of making sense of the world of human affections through a work of art, Aziz stumbles upon Mrs Moore. It is important to note that Aziz approaches her initially only because he thinks she is a younger woman. The sexual possibilities however are soon replaced by warm friendship, partly because Mrs Moore is no longer sexually active and so Aziz sees no possible threat to his affections. That affection, the Forsterian narrator clearly states, is worth more than aesthetic satisfaction – 'the flame that not even beauty can nourish' (p. 25). This idea is supported later when Adela laments that, unlike Mrs Moore, she will see India only as a frieze (p. 50) and not as a living spirit.

The 'Indian problem' is beautifully and succinctly revealed in the bridge party, a term which itself betrays the ignorance of the British in supposing that the two societies are somehow on an equal level. Forster surrounds the episode with clues as to the real nature of reality as an indivisible whole, from the debate with the missionaries about where to draw the line concerning admission into Heaven (p. 41) to the narrator's own reminder that the physical setting is an infinite regression of spheres (p. 42). After the bridge party, however, we do see one momentary, casual example of a true communion, when Aziz plays polo with an unidentified subaltern on the Maidan. The two men, through physical exertion and concentration on the ball, achieve a warm fellowship. The scene prefigures the final scene in the novel, and also prefigures the limitations to Aziz's own abilities to bridge the gap between one individual and another.

The narrator's approval of Fielding is evident from his first introduction:

> The feeling grew that Mr Fielding was a disruptive force, and rightly, for ideas are fatal to caste, and he used ideas by that most potent method – interchange. Neither a missionary nor a student, he was happiest in the give-and-take of a private conversation. The world, he believed, was a globe of men who are trying to reach one another and can best do so by the help of good will plus culture and intelligence. . . . (p. 65)

20 References are to the Abinger edition of *A Passage to India* edited by Oliver Stallybrass.

But the eventual doom of Fielding's friendship with Aziz is also specified in this description, when Forster says, 'He had discovered that it is possible to keep in with Indians and Englishmen, but he who would also keep in with Englishwomen must drop the Indians' (p. 66). Indeed, despite the portentousness of Fielding's first words to Aziz – 'Make yourself at home' – we see Aziz, by tearing out his collar stud and offering it, almost repeating the same gesture of misplaced kindness which destroyed the bridge party. In keeping with the novel's general anti-art attitude, too, Aziz's mention of Post-Impressionism also leads to a confusion of meaning between the two men.

Once introduced, however, the relationship between Aziz and Fielding is left to simmer in the background, while we concentrate on Ronnie and Adela in their attempts to cope with the muddle which is India. Unable to face Godbole's haunting 'Come, come', which remains unanswered as a refrain throughout the novel (India itself is seen as singing the same words – p. 143), the couple reaffirm their engagement as if cowering from the unidentified beast which attacked their car. Adela, who becomes the focus for the central third of the novel, fails the first challenge of the spirit of India.

When we return to Aziz and Fielding, it is to learn about their relationships with their own communities. Aziz is ill and so is surrounded by his Moslem friends, while Fielding is seen more than once as the spectator of the play of his English colleagues (p. 81). This detachment from his own society makes him able to approach Aziz but at the same time unable to appreciate some of the values of community which Aziz holds. Aziz observes that his friend is 'truly warm-hearted and unconventional, but not what can be called wise' (p. 127), while the narrator warns us, 'Experience can do much, and all that he had learnt in England and Europe was an assistance to him, and helped him towards clarity, but clarity prevented him from experiencing something else' (p. 123).

Because the great stumbling-block to the friendship of the two men is the sexual impulse, Forster deliberately focuses on the two women, Mrs Moore and Adela, and takes them through the caves as a kind of harrowing of hell, a sort of unholy experiment to see what will happen to that impulse. He emulates Fielding's namesake Henry Fielding when he introduces one chapter with the observation that much of our lives is an emptiness of non-sensation, when 'a perfectly adjusted organism would be silent' (p. 139). This is why, Forster implies, I as author have been silent about the two women, who have nevertheless been continuing their spiritual pilgrimage since we last left them with Godbole's song. It is crucial in the lead-up to the caves that we see Adela and Mrs Moore engaged in a steady modification of their ideas by their confrontation with India.

Mrs Moore, being beyond the sexual impulse, is further on the road to 'enlightenment' than Adela, since she is in harmony with the nothingness of the caves and the landscape leading to it (the non-event of the sunrise, for example) by reflecting that relations between people are unimportant – 'in particular too much fuss has been made over marriage' (p. 141). Unlike the tradition of Forsterian mother figures (and even Mrs Ramsay), Mrs Moore here departs from the model of matchmaker, perceiving the sexual impulse to be something which actually militates against friendship. Discussing the Moslem heroes, Aziz and Adela cover the same ground theoretically. Aziz admires Babur because he never betrayed a friend (p. 150) and Adela searches for universal brotherhood.

Mrs Moore, then, is more ready for the experience of the caves and more ready to submit to the horror of it – 'the universe . . . offered no repose to her soul' (p. 157) – while Adela, theorising only, and a young girl, turns the conversation to sex and marriage even as she enters the fateful cave. All her biological instincts are pointing her towards Ronnie. Although she already has her doubts, when this basic impulse is questioned or rather exposed in the cave for the animal motivation which it is she panics, and in just those sexual terms. Even Forster's later comments on the incident are sexual; the caves were to 'engender an event like an egg'.

The result of this event, which comes at the exact centre of the novel, is to align the social groups along battle lines even as it has the opposite effect of breaking up the received ideas of the more enlightened principal characters. 'The Europeans', says Forster, 'were putting aside their normal personalities and sinking themselves in their community' (p. 173). Nowhere is his hatred of the mob more pronounced. Fielding is rejected by the Club – 'you can't run with the hare and hunt with the hounds' – and the experience is akin to that of the women in the caves: 'After forty years' experience, he had learnt to manage his life and make the best of it on advanced European lines . . . but as the moment passed, he felt he ought to have been working at something else the whole time' (p. 199). Fielding, unlike Aziz, has not cultivated a small circle of friends.

The considered reactions of the two women are now examined, and these too emerge as a reorientation of their attitudes towards personal relationships. Adela confesses, 'I'm not fit for personal relationships' (p. 105); Mrs Moore angrily rejects 'all this marriage, marriage' (p. 210). The same qualities which made Mrs Moore more accessible to the truth of the caves make her defenceless to its repercussions. She has no community and no friends, and she leaves the stage in a confusion of sentiments. One cannot even justifiably erect her death into a kind of noble suicide – it just happens. Adela, on the other hand, is young and resilient. Ironically, her turning-point towards the truth and towards a more genuine life comes in the courtroom when she sees the punkah wallah working the fan. This Indian, 'almost naked and splendidly formed' (p. 226), seems to her like a 'male fate, a winnower of souls'. The epiphany is, ironically, heavily sexual in origin, but its effect is to convince Adela that if life is to be lived at all it must be lived with dignity.

So she tells the truth and becomes an outcast, too, flung in the way of Fielding. This is the masterstroke of Forster's design, because the symbolic issue represented by Adela, which had pushed Aziz and Fielding towards each other, now becomes an actual, human issue which divides them again. Adela comes across Fielding's path at the moment when he is learning, by taking his stand for Aziz, the value of friendship, of involvement in personal relationships: 'He lost his usual sane view of human intercourse; and felt that we exist not in ourselves, but in terms of each other's minds' (p. 259). It is Fielding's answer to Ansell's problem of the cow in the quad, and it leads him to contemplate Mrs Moore's immortality as well as to try to reconcile Adela and Aziz. With Adela he finds he is able to approach the kinds of truth presented by the caves without breaking into violence or insanity, simply because he reaches them in the companionship of another human being, and Adela finds this too:

> A friendliness, as of dwarfs shaking hands, was in the air. Both man and woman were at the height of their powers – sensible, honest, even subtle. They spoke the same language, and held the same opinions, and the variety of age and sex did not divide them. (p. 274)

It is one of the rare moments of genuine friendship in the novel, notwithstanding Forster's rather brutal placing of them in perspective as 'dwarfs'. It is not insignificant that they can actually speak to each other, something which rarely happens in this novel.

But, while Fielding is moving towards Adela, he is moving away from Aziz. The prophecy of the beginning of the book is starting to come true, not because Fielding is inciting Aziz's jealousy, but because he is revealing the presumptions of his society in its attitude towards women. In no aspect is a society more distinctive than in its attitude towards women, a fact Aziz has always been acutely aware of. His own Islamic attitude was one which we would now call male chauvinism:

> It enraged him that he had been accused by a woman who had no personal beauty; sexually, he was a snob. This had puzzled and worried Fielding. Sensuality, as long as it is straightforward, did not repel him, but this derived sensuality – the sort that classes a mistress among motor-cars if she is beautiful, and among eye-flies if she isn't – was alien to his own emotions, and he felt a barrier between himself and Aziz whenever it arose. (p. 251)

Fielding is caught. Forster reminds us that it is 'essential in friendship' (p. 265) to respect the other's every opinion, but Fielding cannot go along with Aziz regarding Adela as a mindless creature. Aziz, in effect, wants Fielding to become 'a sort of Mohammed Latif': 'When they argued so about it something racial intruded – not bitterly, but inevitably, like the colour of their skins: coffee-colour versus pinko-grey' (p. 271).

Fielding recoils from this impasse to the familiar forms and here Forster neatly conflates the significant form of works of art and the social forms – of custom and sexual mores – of Italy:

> He had forgotton the beauty of form among idol temples and lumpy hills; indeed, without form, how can there be beauty? Form stammered here and there in a mosque, became rigid through nervousness even, but oh these Italian churches! . . . something more precious than mosaics and marbles was offered to him now: the harmony between the works of man and the earth that upholds them, the civilization that has escaped muddle, the spirit in a reasonable form, with flesh and blood subsisting. (p. 293)

When he returns to India, it is to the Hindu festival, which Forster describes as 'this approaching triumph of India . . . a muddle (as we call it), a frustration of reason and form' (p. 297). Once the muddle is cleared up over Fielding's wife, we might expect the two friends to come together again. Aziz has a kind of marriage, and Stella is 'after something' (p. 331) which she finds partly in the Hindu ceremony. The reader is left asking if the rocks and temples which deny their friendship are any more than Forster the narrator refusing the happy ending.

The ending does indeed seem perverse if one sees the novel as an abstract, allegorical structure. But I have suggested that it really tells the quite specific story of Aziz and Fielding, with the caves providing the metaphysical background and the experiences of the two women providing the plot complication which finally separates the two men into their two cultures. From Aziz's first contact with Mrs Moore, the question of the place of women has loomed as the central issue between the two men. The final section has little to say on the metaphysical level. It simply serves as the setting for the meeting of the two men again, and for the neatly symbolic collision of the boats when Stella is thrown into Aziz's lap. Fielding speaks of his wife as being ahead of him in the spiritual quest, something which the Moslem Aziz would never say of his woman. It reminds him of the very bitter row over Adela which began to kill their friendship two years earlier. As a result of that row, Aziz's poetry has become more and more nationalistic. Earlier, the Moslem poem had voiced 'our need for the Friend who never comes yet is not entirely disproved' (p. 111). Now, under the invitation of the Hindu Mr Bhattacharya, Aziz's poems look forward and salvation will come through the motherland of India (p. 279). In fact most recently he has become a 'feminist': 'His poems were all on one topic – Oriental womanhood. "The purdah must go," was their burden, "otherwise we shall never be free"' (p. 305). It is as if Aziz (in theory anyway) were looking to his own women as a counter to such Englishwomen as Adela and a substitute for the friendship offered by such as Fielding. But one suspects that it is only theory, and that for someone such as Aziz the fact would be very hard to stomach. Still, the whole complex of nationalism-feminism is what turns his horse away from Fielding's at the end. It is not a historically accurate symbolic conclusion, but was never intended to be. It is the natural conclusion of this particular muddle.

That we must read *A Passage to India* in this specific, contingent way is suggested also by the references to art in the novel. I have said that it is essentially an anti-art novel. This is not simply because it is set in India, a country inimical to the significant forms of art: 'Men yearn for poetry though they may not confess it; they desire that joy shall be graceful and sorrow august and infinity have a form, and India fails to accommodate them' (p. 219). But everywhere the confident assumptions of art are attacked. During Mrs Moore's disillusionment Forster observes, 'All heroic endeavour, and all that is known as art, assumes that there is such a background' (p. 216); at the moment of their communion Adela says to Fielding, 'I used to feel death selected people, it is a notion one gets from novels' (p. 274); and of the Hindu festival Forster writes, 'Did it succeed? Books written afterwards say "Yes." But how, if there is such an event, can it be remembered afterwards? How can it be expressed in anything but itself?' (p. 300). Forster even goes so far as to challenge the serious framework of his own novel, when he attempts to describe Mrs Moore's vision: 'Visions are supposed to entail profundity, but – Wait till you get one, dear reader!' (p. 217). Such an eruption into the fabric of the novel makes one wonder if Forster really means to say, 'Novels are supposed to entail profundity.'

This anti-art stance, then, underlines the idea that the meaning of the novel will not be got from standing back and toting up motifs and symbols, and balancing the three unbalanceable sections. The ending of the novel is far more like the ending of Forster's first novel, *Where Angels Fear to Tread* – equivocal and particular – than like the large symbolic tableaux at the end of his other novels. Thirteen years and one Great War after *Howards End*, Forster is no longer writing neat parables about the condition of India, England or the liberal soul. He is following through faithfully the tangled relationship between one Indian and one Englishman.

It is this specificity which gives *A Passage to India* its greatness. Readers looking for *The* Passage to India will be frustrated at the narrative tone of equivocality and non-involvement, and by the lack of significance in the juxtaposition of the stories of Mrs Moore, Adela, Fielding and Aziz. One may make much of the bee and Mrs Moore and Godbole, but in itself it counts for little until put up against the incident in 'Temple' when Ralph and Fielding are stung by a swarm of bees and the 'symbolic' moment is merged into part of the central ongoing narrative. The recurrences between being and nothingness, the stylistic affirmations and withdrawals, are in themselves dry, academic exercises until they are linked to the developing relationship of Aziz and Fielding, the delicate minuet of advance and withdrawal, closeness and alienation. For all his teasing attempts, Forster has no intention to 'bathe it all in a spiritual light', as Virginia Woolf wished.

While Woolf too reached a similar stage of scepticism about the efficacy of large statements near the end of her fictional career, she never abandoned the form of art to the extent that Forster did. Fielding may err like Forster's earlier heroes in overvaluing the form of Italian art, but in his earlier novels set in Europe Forster felt compelled to think of answers and to invent ideal heroes. In the muddled setting of India he felt liberated to offer no hero in Aziz, but to concentrate instead on the subtle pressures which are inevitably exerted on friendship, from without and from within. Forster wrote his novel in the spirit he recorded in 1921 in India – 'It doesn't do to think. To follow the promptings of the eye and the imagination is quite complicated enough' – and his imaginative grasp of the phenomenon of friendship itself helped create his greatest novel. But does the novel expand at the end, or leave us hearing great chords behind? I think not. The political and metaphysical possibilities of the novel have finally been abandoned in favour of the individual human being, with whom Forster's sympathies finally lie. The structure of the novel does not reverberate except as the memory of a series of conflicts between perspectives. The last section in particular seems to bear little relation to the point which Aziz and Fielding have reached in their friendship. Neither man seems to relate to the festival at all. The festival seems to signify a common, minimal humanity which friendship tries to rise above, and if the mystery of such friendship cannot be achieved then at least the two men can attain the clear sense of community which the Moslem or English society offers.

Extract from Charu Malik, 'To Express the Subject of Friendship: Masculine Desire and Colonialism in *A Passage to India*', in Robert K. Martin and George Piggford (eds), *Queer Forster*, Chicago: University of Chicago Press, 1997, pp. 221–6

This extract from Malik's essay focuses on the trial scene in the novel. In particular the analysis is concerned with the homoerotic image of the nearly naked punkah-wallah, lovingly described by Forster's narrator as a 'God'. Malik is interested to explore the way in which this figure subverts colonial authority and, by extension, masculinist stereotypes. The argument goes on to put forward the novel's interest in comradeship and feminised masculinity as further ways of undermining dominant discourses, concluding that the ultimate significance of the caves could be said to be in the fact of their primordial existence prior to social binaries such as masculine and feminine, heterosexual and homosexual, colonised and coloniser.

As Adela Quested enters the courtroom for the trial of the Indian she has charged with attempting to rape her, she is distracted by the 'person who had no bearing officially upon the trial,' the 'almost naked' punkah wallah (*PI*, 207).[1] Her attention immediately captured by the punkah wallah, Adela cannot resist thinking that 'he seemed to control the proceedings' (*PI*, 207). In his naked yet splendid, and humble yet beautiful form nourished by the city's garbage, in his 'strength,' 'physical perfection,' and 'aloofness,' the punkah wallah's figure 'prove[s] to society how little its categories' (*PI*, 207) matter. With every pull at the rope he swirls air for everyone in the room but remains excluded from any of it himself; nevertheless, he seems to refocus and relocate, for Adela, the central action to his humble, marginal position. From his excluded, aloof, yet beautifully compelling form, the punkah wallah rebukes 'the narrowness of [the] sufferings' (*PI*, 207) of this girl from middle-class England and challenges the civilizing presence of her compatriots:

> In virtue of what had she collected this roomful of people together? Her particular brand of opinions, and the suburban Jehovah who sanctified them – by what right did they claim so much importance in the world, and assume the title of civilization? (*PI*, 207)

Jolted in her perspective by a glimpse of subservient yet unknown, un-conquered human beauty, Adela begins to question her own charge of rape. Later in the legal proceedings, as she envisions the scene at the caves, finding that she could see herself both inside and outside the cave but failing to locate Aziz following her into it, 'the airs from the punkah behind her wafted her on . . .' (*PI*, 217). Soon after this recollection, Adela withdraws her charge.

1 E. M. Forster, *A Passage to India* [PI]. 1924. Abinger Ed. 6 Ed. Oliver Stallybrass. London: Edward Arnold, 1978.

This figure of the punkah wallah, mechanically blowing cooling air into the courtroom, provides the impetus that makes Adela change her mind. The punkah wallah disrupts the entire legal proceedings, which had been largely initiated so that the English could damn and convict as criminal an Indian, a conviction that would legitimize and prove their moral superiority to rule over the natives of India, the 'darker races' (*PI*, 208). But the punkah wallah not only makes the disruption of the trial possible. In his aloof servility and humbleness muted by striking physical beauty, he presents a contradictory figure who simultaneously reinforces colonial authority and disturbs it. In his study of colonial discourse, Homi Bhabha theorizes about such a contradictory figure in terms of 'mimicry.' He describes mimicry as a trope of partial presence that masks a threatening racial difference only to reveal the gaps in colonial power and knowledge, a 'double vision which in disclosing the ambivalence of colonial discourse also disrupts its authority'.[2]

But although the punkah wallah precipitates a resistance to colonial authority by disrupting and making ambivalent its representative, the system of justice – concurrently demonstrating that in this case law was being regarded as a matter of control, not justice – he does so in a manner somewhat different from Bhabha's mimic man, who is an imperfect double of the English gentleman, inhabiting the space of 'not quite/not white'.[3] In his menial, servile position, the punkah wallah does embody colonial authority. But through his physical perfection, his aloofness, his non-Anglicized person, he denies this authority in his refusal to mimic and in his lack of aggression. Strategically positioned across from the Indian assistant magistrate, who is seated on a platform as a sign of colonial authority, the punkah wallah offers an opposition to the 'good' colonial subject. The punkah wallah, an untouchable, negates everything that characterizes the magistrate – a Western-educated native, who is a 'cultivated, self-conscious, and conscientious' Indian civil servant (*PI*, 207). The punkah wallah initiates disruption of the legal place that legitimizes colonial authority through his contrast to the educated colonials: the magistrate; the urbane barrister from Calcutta; the Nawab Bahadur; Hamidullah; and even Aziz himself, a trained medical doctor – all of whom are the apparently privileged subjects of the colonizing mission. The punkah wallah is 'exorbitant' in Derrida's sense – an exteriority that is irreducible, cutting across the binary opposition of civilized and barbaric that allows the birth of the arrangement of colonizer and colonized.[4] He embodies that complete difference between the white and the dark races that makes possible the rule of the former over the latter but that also remains suppressed, its narrative untold. The courtroom dissolves into chaos after Adela's withdrawal of her charge. However, 'the beautiful naked god,' the punkah wallah, although the only one with nothing to say during this 'scene of . . . fantasy,' continues 'to pull at the cord of his punkah, to gaze at the empty dais . . .' (*PI*, 219) and creates a moment 'of

2 Homi K. Bhabha, *The Location of Culture*. London: Routledge, 1994 [p. 86].
3 Ibid., p. 92.
4 Jacques Derrida, *Of Grammatology*. Trans. G. Spivak. Baltimore: Johns Hopkins UP, 1978 [p. 162].

subversion that turn[s] the gaze of the discriminated back upon the eye of power'.[5]

Forster's *A Passage to India* enunciates this disruption of colonial authority by making visible 'the colonized other who is the essential other component or opposite number' of the 'imperial world system,' to use Fredric Jameson's version of modern imperialism.[6] If colonialism constitutes a loss of meaning because 'a significant structural segment of the economic system as a whole is now located elsewhere, beyond the metropolis, outside of the daily life and existential experience of the home country, in colonies over the water whose own life experiences and life world – very different from that of the imperial power – remain unknown and unimaginable,' it is the situation of just such a loss of meaning that, paradoxically, *A Passage to India* tries to reveal, to make visible in its narrative.[7] However, in order to imagine fictionally this colonial space – different from, yet essential to, the formation and identity of empire – without turning his own novel into an imperialist narrative, Forster desists from speaking for the punkah wallah, even at the price of leaving his story untold. In *A Passage to India*, we witness moments that the text refuses to master, disrupting the plenitude of representation and allowing difference to seep up to the surface.

In deliberate omissions, as figured in the incomplete narrative, the unknowable, opaque foreignness of the punkah wallah, *Passage* attempts not to create 'the other' as exotic – since it does not try to speak for the punkah wallah – but to leave gaps in representation for 'otherness' to show through. *Passage* thus presents an analysis and critique of the discourse of colonial authority in terms of the Indian situation. The text of the novel reinforces this critique in its ambiguities, gaps, secrets, and uncertainties, which disrupt and make ambivalent both colonial authority and an imperialist narrative. But Forster's awareness that positing a monolithic experience may constitute an act of imperialism, whether in the colonies or in the text, may be traced finally to the marginal vantage point dictated by the author's homosexuality, this enforced 'otherness' making urgent to him the dangerous possibility of excluding other experiences in privileging one kind of certainty. This frame of reference adds another resonance to the punkah wallah's marginal figure, on whose 'splendid form' and 'untouchable' beauty the text lingers lovingly, seeing the 'almost naked' 'Indian of low birth' as a 'beautiful [all] naked god' (*PI*, 219) by the end of the chapter. The narrative makes this moment of resistance to colonial dominance, provoked by the dignified and sensual presence of the punkah wallah, also a site for homoerotic desire. In using sexual ambivalence here to show the ambivalence of colonial authority, Forster not only questions the dominant discourse that appropriated his own sexuality but also shows its complicity with colonial power and unitary narratives that are based on imperialist, exclusionary models. And may we not also view as the novel's counter to these models both the queering of desire, as witnessed in the comradeship of

5 Bhabha, Homi, K. *The Location of Culture*. London: Routledge, 1994 [p. 112].
6 Jameson, Fredric. 'Modernism and Imperialism.' *Nationalism, Colonialism and Literature*. Ed. Seamus Deane. Minneapolis: U of Minnesota P, 1990 [p. 50].
7 Ibid., p. 51.

Aziz and Fielding, and the feminizing of masculinity made possible in the narrative's undulating, sinuous movement of affection and gentleness between Aziz and Ralph Moore? This moment, often overlooked, provides the framing context for the final horse-riding scene of expansive inconclusiveness and deferment.

The disruption that finally becomes embodied in the figure of the punkah wallah reverberates through the town of Chandrapore, echoing in its people and in particular in the courtroom before and during the trial: 'A new spirit seemed abroad, a rearrangement, which no one in the stern little band of whites could explain' (*PI*, 204). This rearrangement of the familiar structure of power is manoeuvered by the 'spontaneous forms of [rebellious] activity' that spurt up in Chandrapore, among its most disempowered and disenfranchised groups, disturbing the daily life of the city. As the Collector makes his way to the court, a pebble thrown by a child strikes his car in greeting. But it is the young students of Government College, the Collector's 'pawns' for whom 'he retained a contemptuous affection' (*PI*, 204), who take special delight in their 'sly civility' – another one of Bhabha's terms for insurrection[8] – and taunt the authority of the officer. In their sly resistance, they prevent the Collector's assertion of power by disallowing his entry into the front of the Courthouse and countermand the mark of his official privilege.

In the courtroom, the proceedings of the trial are interrupted from the very start with disruptive comments that sometimes seem to '[fall] from nowhere, from the ceiling perhaps' (*PI*, 208). The Englishman's tendency to regard the situation of the attempted rape and this 'formal' trial as an appropriate staging of 'Oriental Pathology' (*PI*, 208) invites resistance that results in painful and naked revelation of the pathology of empire itself. Thus, when the Superintendent, in his testimony, declares as a 'general truth' that the 'darker races are physically attracted by the fairer, but not vice versa,' the Indian side of the Courtroom erupts with this rejoinder: 'Even when the lady is so uglier than the gentleman?' (*PI*, 208). Although present in the courtroom to punish the perpetrator of an assault on her body, Adela's body nevertheless trembles in resentment as it registers this (re)mark of undesirability. And in this trembling, Adela's body signals itself as a site for the play of colonial authority, emphasizing colonialism's mixed economy not only of power and domination but also of pleasure and desire that prevents its authority from being total or complete.

The charge of alleged assault made by an English woman against an Indian man makes concrete the polarized relationship between the Indians and the English. For the English, the situation reinforces their sense of mission and superiority reflected in their communal sense of outraged virtue: 'All over Chandrapore that day the Europeans were putting aside their normal personalities and sinking themselves in their community. Pity, wrath, heroism, filled them' (*PI*, 156). For the Indians, it serves to unite Hindus and Muslims, the privileged and the ordinary, into a 'confederacy' (*PI*, 182) for a common cause against a common enemy. Thus the trial, seen by the English as a vindication of the moral impulse

8 Homi K. Bhabha, *The Location of Culture*. London: Routledge, 1994 [p. 97].

underpinning the imperial power's civilizing mission, also becomes an occasion for the English to exhort each other to keep fueled the colonial enterprise, with its now evident heterosexual, masculinist rhetoric and ideology:

> And remember it afterwards, you men. You're weak, weak, weak. Why, [the Indians] ought to crawl from here to the caves on their hands and knees whenever an Englishwoman's in sight, they oughtn't to be spoken to, they ought to be spat at, they ought to be ground into the dust, we've been far too kind with our Bridge Parties and the rest. (*PI*, 206)

In these vicious sentiments of Mrs Turton, the novel enacts a twisted parody of the colonial situation: the civilizing mission of the imperial power – experienced by the subjected people as ravishment and pillaging – when threatened is defended by the outraged British as an assault on *their* virtue. What should have been rightly an appropriate appeal for the Indians to make is appropriated here by the English to promote their own cause. As Salman Rushdie comments: 'It is useless, I'm sure, to suggest that if a rape must be used as the metaphor of the Indo-British connection, then surely, in the interests of accuracy, it should be the rape of an Indian woman by one or more Englishmen of whatever class . . .'.[9]

The answer, or nonanswer (to use a term which *Passage* nudges us toward), to why the trial and the courtroom become such contested sites for colonial, heterosexist authority lurks within the Marabar caves and is suggested by Adela's panic in one of them. In the novel, which finds both the Indian landscape and its people finally beyond its utterance, the circular Marabar caves and what does (or does not) happen in them offer a hermeneutical frame for the elusiveness and sexual ambivalence troped in the figure of the punkah wallah and for the comradeship between Aziz and Fielding, as for the questions of masculinity and relation between races determining the fate of this comradeship.

The text concedes that it cannot ultimately master these caves, suggesting that by age alone – since in their outlines the sun may recognize 'forms that were his before our globe was torn from his bosom' (*PI*, 116) – the caves lie before the discernment that is necessary to bring into play binary oppositions (self/other, inside/outside) upon which hinges Western knowledge. These caves, which have (only) nothing attached to them, are 'empty as an Easter egg' (*PI*, 118). In their 'terrifying echo . . . entirely devoid of distinction' (*PI*, 138) and their kissing/expiring flames that testify to the alienation at the heart of identification, these caves become a means by which *Passage* recognizes and confronts the racial and sexual other as 'other,' while it attempts not to participate in the fundamental imperialist structure of (literary) colonial appropriation. In this novel, then, India, as the 'other imperial nation-state,' 'as the colonized other who is [the imperial system's] essential other component or opposite number,' occupies the space of

9 Salman Rushdie, 'Outside the Whale.' *American Film*. 10:4 (1985): 70.

the 'prototypical paradigm of the Other';[10] but, India becomes visible in the structure of the caves as an autonomous entity that has its secrets and that cannot be known in its entirety.

10 Fredric Jameson, 'Modernism and Imperialism.' *Nationalism, Colonialism and Literature*. Ed. Seamus Deane. Minneapolis: U of Minnesota P, 1990 [pp. 49, 50].

The Work in Performance[1]

There have been two adaptations of *A Passage to India*. The first was a play, later filmed by the BBC, by Santha Rama Rau, the daughter of an Indian diplomat. Forster commended, and wrote a Programme Note for, the first production when it was premiered in 1960. The second was David Lean's well-known 1984 film.

Rau embarked on an adaptation for the stage of Forster's novel in 1955, and was greatly surprised when Forster approved her script. The adaptation took five years to reach production, however. It was eventually first staged in Forster's presence by the Oxford Playhouse (for information about the gestation of the play see 'Remembering E. M. Forster' by Santha Rama Rau and 'A Late Debut' by Frank Hauser, both in J. H. Stape (ed.), *E. M. Forster: Interviews and Recollections*, London: Macmillan, 1993). A success, the production moved to London and then to New York. Though it was filmed by the BBC, Forster himself was against a film adaptation because he distrusted 'Hollywood'. He wrote to Rau in 1967 'I didn't and I don't want *A Passage* filmed'; and he was unconvinced even by the proposal from the Bengali director Satyajit Ray. Earlier, in 1947, he had refused £25,000 from Fox for the film rights to *A Room with a View* (see *Selected Letters*, vol. 2, p. 227). The play by Rau is a truncated version of the novel and ends after the trial scene. Forster's Programme Note endorses this decision for the dramatization by saying 'I tried to indicate the human predicament in a universe which is not, so far, comprehensible to our minds. This aspect in the novel is described in its final chapters. It is obviously unsuitable for the stage . . .'.

The play was nonetheless filmed for BBC television in Forster's lifetime. The TV adaptation was made by John Maynard, directed by Waris Hussein, and starred Sybil Thorndike (Mrs Moore), Zia Mohyeddin (Aziz), Cyril Cusack (Fielding) and Virginia McKenna (Adela). Like the David Lean film version that followed, the role of Godbole was taken by an Englishman, Michael Bates, who also played the main Indian character in the 1970s television series *It Ain't Half Hot, Mum*. The TV play condenses the novel into six scenes, which have the rhythm of three long sections preceded by three shorter ones: Aziz and Mrs

1 See p. 161 for a list of further reading relating to this topic.

Moore at the mosque, Fielding's party, the train journey to the hills, at the Marabar Caves, at the Club and the trial scene. The play accentuates Aziz's sexual significance for Adela by his reciting, at Fielding's party, a sensual speech about a beautiful Moghul Princess. The intimacy between them immediately before Adela enters the second cave is also pronounced. When Adela capitulates at the end of the play she says she has been 'unwell', possibly from before the visit to the caves. She says she has been 'In a state of sadness' and that the caves suggested to her that 'everything I had ever believed in amounted to nothing'. She describes her experience as a kind of 'hallucination', and concludes that 'India is too big for me'. She and Fielding speculate that the experience of India forces one to 'destroy what one cannot cope with', whether it be 'India', 'life in India', or 'love'. The parting between Aziz and Fielding is staged at the courthouse and when Aziz asserts that Fielding cannot be both with Adela and with him, they acknowledge that they cannot be friends now but might be in the future. Significantly, the play ends with a long shot of the young, almost naked, punkah-wallah, who is left alone in the court after the others have left.

An adaptation of the novel that is also indebted to the play, David Lean's 1984 film, by contrast, attempts to add to Forster's novel by introducing extra material. It is particularly notable for its decision to frame Forster's text with two scenes, both set back in a rainy England. The film opens outside the P&O offices in London as Adela (Judy Davis) goes to buy tickets to India for herself and Mrs Moore (Peggy Ashcroft). There, while admitting that she has never left England before, Adela stares at photographs of India and in particular at one that, she is told, shows 'The Marabar Caves – about 20 miles from you at Chandrapore.' Her look suggests both curiosity and anxiety, and it is from this moment onwards that Lean's take on Forster's novel becomes apparent. This is to be a film primarily about Adela's desire, repeatedly suggested by her gaze, which is characterised by a mixture of unexpressed passion and a fascinated fear of the unfamiliar. While the film will follow many characters in the novel, Adela's perceptions are frequently foregrounded.

Adela is told that the Viceroy will be on board her boat and when the film then cuts to Bombay there are all the signs of imperial pomp and the red-carpet splendour of the raj, in contrast to the banal informality of rainy London. This is replicated when the train conveying Mr and Mrs Turton, as well as Adela and Mrs Moore, arrives in Chandrapore to be greeted by a reception committee for the Collector. From here, met by Ronny (Nigel Havers), the characters proceed by road, and the literal passage to India absent from Forster's novel is underlined by the journeys by first ship, next train, and then car for the Turtons but horse and carriage for Adela and Mrs Moore. All this time, as the English pass by, the Indian characters are seen at the periphery, lying on platforms, cycling, walking, cheering and staring. To complete her own journey from the P&O office, when Adela arrives at Ronny's house, Fairholme, her very first words confirm Lean's sense of her as fated: 'Are those the Marabar Hills?' she asks from the veranda.

The first interior shot we see of Aziz (Victor Bannerjee) has him questioned about marriage, just as Adela will question him as they proceed up to the second group of caves. The scenes with the Anglo-Indians that follow underline Adela's

***Figure 1* Film still from David Lean's *A Passage to India*, 1984, Columbia EMI Warner Dist. Ltd.**

Source: Photo courtesy of the Ronald Grant Archive

dissatisfaction, as solitary shots intimate her desire for passion while scenes with Ronny emphasise his restraint: a kiss on the cheek on her arrival, a goodnight called from the hall to Adela in her bedroom. The result of this, after Fielding's (James Fox) party, is Adela's decision not to marry Ronny. However, Lean now introduces the major invention of his adaptation, a scene set at a temple ruin. Here, having cycled alone to this spot 12 miles outside of Chandrapore, Adela scrutinises several erotic carvings with the same expression she had when she stared at the photographs in the P&O office at the film's start (Forster did write an article on 'Erotic Indian Sculpture' for *The Listener*, 12 March 1959). The camera then closes in on her face to suggest her intense curiosity. The music soundtrack at this point, for the only time in the film, includes a human voice, humming wistfully and singing wordlessly, which fades away when Adela becomes aware of a menacing feral call and chatter. This causes her to notice for the first time the monkeys perched on top of the temple. They are portrayed as violent by the sudden shift to kettle drums and dramatic brass on the soundtrack. The monkeys then descend to chase Adela as the music builds to a crescendo (the scene is unintentionally reminiscent of the 'king of the swingers' episode in Disney's *Jungle Book*). Adela is seen escaping the monkeys on her bicycle, which echoes Aziz trying to escape Turton's car as it careered through the market-place after Turton's reception at Chandrapore station. (The animals feature again just before Aziz's trial as protesting Indians dressed in monkey costumes try to taunt or intimidate Adela; also, when Aziz is declared innocent, it is those Indians dressed as monkeys who lead the charge into the courtroom to celebrate.)

Immediately on her return from the temple Adela overturns her decision not to marry. After dancing with Ronny, she is shown alone in bed that night thinking back on the erotic images she has seen at the temple. The camera then cuts to Aziz in bed looking at revealing pictures of women in a magazine. To underline the connection between Adela's desire and Aziz, it is revealed that Aziz is in bed with a fever while 'the hot weather is coming'. Any homoerotic suggestion, between Aziz and Fielding, or in the scene of the beautiful young punkah-wallah at the courtroom, is excised from Lean's version of the story. (In a letter to Rau, Forster had said of the first stage production that the absence of 'the nude beautiful punkah wallah', who was to end the play, was of all his concerns the 'MOST IMPORTANT OF ALL'.)

Lean explains Adela's experience in the caves in terms of her relationship with Ronny. On the witness stand at the trial, she says at first that she thinks she was partly to blame because, seeing Chandrapore in the distance from the Marabar Hills, she had realised she didn't love Ronny and this had led to her questioning Aziz on his marriage, introducing a note of intimacy into their relationship. Lean then follows Forster's dialogue, but his decision to introduce Adela's thoughts on her relationship with Ronny as speech positions her capitulation as the realisation of a delusion prompted by her preoccupation with sex, love and marriage.

Excising Godbole's celebration of Krishna's birth in 'Temple', the film ends with Aziz and Fielding's reconciliation at Srinagar (Stella appears, but does not speak; Ralph Moore does not appear at all), interspersed with shots of Adela back in England, once more in the cold, rainy climate that Lean contrasts so pointedly with the heat of India in the middle part of the film. The 'Temple' section is significantly truncated and Lean chooses reconciliation over ambivalence for his ending. Fielding and Aziz part firm friends, with no suggestion of difficulty in the friendship, if also with no immediate prospect of their meeting again. Meanwhile, in a prolepsis, Adela receives a letter from Aziz offering her his forgiveness, and also his thanks. The narrative moves back to her from Srinagar three times and closes with her staring out of a window at the rain just as she was introduced at the very start of the film from the other side of the rain-covered windows of the P&O office. The changes that India has wrought on Adela are suggested by the change in the style of her hair, which she wears down for the first time. Where Forster ended with a point about the intersection of the personal and the political, Lean ignores the political element of the novel in his ending and foregrounds the personal, reconciling the characters to each other in a way that Forster thought impossible in 1924 for political reasons. Lean's decision to use an English actor, Alec Guinness, to play the role of Godbole, was in many ways the most controversial of the many decisions in a film that served to foreground English elements and downplay Indian ones.

3

Key Passages

Introduction

This section of the Sourcebook is concerned with some of the novel's key passages that are individually important but that also, collectively, go to the heart of the most discussed aspects of the book. To place the key passages that follow into the context of the whole novel, I will here summarise the main incidents of the narrative. This precis does not include everything that occurs, but is intended as a reminder of the chief characters and the sequence of principal events.

A Passage to India's setting is Chandrapore, a seemingly unremarkable small Indian city. After an unfavourable tourist-book overview of the ordinary city, twenty miles from which are the extraordinary Marabar Caves, the opening section of the novel, 'Mosque', concerns itself with journeys, meetings and friendships. The first passage/journey the reader learns about is that of Adela Quested and Mrs Moore to visit Ronny Heaslop, who is the Chandrapore city magistrate, Mrs Moore's son and Adela's fiancé. Mrs Moore is a spiritual figure with a similar significance to Mrs Wilcox in Forster's previous novel, *Howards End*, and Adela is a serious-minded, callow young woman keen to see the 'real India'. The first key meeting of the novel is Mrs Moore's encounter with the Muslim Dr Aziz, the book's Indian protagonist, at a mosque by the Ganges. The next attempt at connection, at Indo-British friendship, is the failed 'Bridge Party', which the city's standoffish officials organise so that the two women can meet the local Indian community. By contrast, the third meeting of the novel's opening section is an unofficial get-together organised at his home by Cyril Fielding, a liberal college principal, at which Adela, Mrs Moore, Aziz and the Hindu Brahman Professor Godbole congregate. The next section of the novel is set up by Aziz inviting the group to be his guests on a trip to the Marabar Caves. However, this party at Fielding's house is soured when Ronny arrives and ruins the atmosphere with his high-handed sahib demeanour. His coldness and snobbery push Adela to the decision not to marry him but a mysterious car accident changes her mind. 'Mosque' moves to its conclusion with Aziz and Fielding becoming closer and culminates in Aziz showing a photograph of his dead wife to the Englishman as a token of their friendship. Set during India's cold season, the section overall has been characterised by attempts at, mostly, good-natured hospitality and invitation undermined by Anglo-Indian prejudice as well as cultural difference and misunderstanding, which Forster characterises as 'muddle'.

Part II, 'Caves', is set in the hot weather. Its principal subject is the journey to the caves, which Aziz is obliged to undertake despite everyone's lethargy over the prospect. The trip is dogged by false starts and unpleasantness as Fielding misses the train and Mrs Moore feels physically and spiritually unwell in the first cave they visit. Adela and Aziz continue alone with only a guide to the second group of caves and become separated after a moment of embarrassment caused by Adela asking Aziz if he has more than one wife. They enter separate caves but shortly afterwards Adela rushes down the hills to stop a car and return to Chandrapore. Though the reader will never know what actually happened, Adela believes she has been assaulted in the caves by Dr Aziz. The car in which she travels back to the city is the one that brings Fielding to the expedition. Perplexed by the situation at the caves, Fielding returns with Aziz to find his friend is arrested at Chandrapore station. Basing their views on knowledge of his character rather than on prejudiced assumptions about 'Orientals', Fielding and Mrs Moore believe Aziz to be innocent. The rest of the Anglo-Indians rally behind Adela and Ronny, convinced that, 'naturally', an Indian must be guilty of the crime if he has been accused by one of their own people. Fielding is ostracised by the other members of the Anglo-Indian community and resigns from the English club. Mrs Moore decides to sail home and she dies aboard ship, news of the event reaching the others shortly after Aziz's trial. In the courtroom, Adela says that she has made a mistake and Aziz is acquitted. She is shunned by the English but Fielding decides to support her, his friendship with Aziz suffering as a result. Aziz thinks that a romance is developing between Adela and Fielding but the two sail home to England separately.

Two years later, the narrative shifts to Mau, where Godbole is Minister of Education and Aziz is doctor to the Rajah. It is now the rainy season and the final section, 'Temple', begins with a description of the Gokul Ashtami festival, celebrating the birth of Krishna, at which Godbole officiates. Fielding arrives back in India and is on tour with his wife and her brother. He has come to Mau to inspect the local school. Aziz has no desire to meet him as he believes Fielding to have married Adela but he has actually wedded Mrs Moore's daughter from her second marriage, Stella. Aziz however is only calmed when he meets Stella's diffident brother Ralph, who has the same spiritual qualities, as well as openness and goodwill, that Aziz had responded to in Mrs Moore. Aziz's reconciliation with Fielding is achieved when their boats collide on the Mau Tank at the height of the festival and each falls into the water. The famous ending of the novel has them riding together in the jungle, still wishing to be friends but aware that the political situation makes it impossible in the here and now.

Key Passages

The Opening Chapter

A cinematic beginning pans across Chandrapore from the sacred Ganges, through the human communities, and up to the sky. As well as the physical, this also sets the political scene for the rest of the novel in symbolical terms.

Except for the Marabar[1] Caves – and they are twenty miles off – the city of Chandrapore[2] presents nothing extraordinary. Edged rather than washed by the river Ganges,[3] it trails for a couple of miles along the bank, scarcely distinguishable from the rubbish it deposits so freely. There are no bathing-steps on the river front, as the Ganges happens not to be holy here; indeed there is no river front, and bazaars shut out the wide and shifting panorama of the stream. The streets are mean, the temples ineffective, and though a few fine houses exist they are hidden away in gardens or down alleys whose filth deters all but the invited guest. Chandrapore was never large or beautiful, but two hundred years ago[4] it lay on the road between Upper India, then imperial, and the sea, and the fine houses date from that period. The zest for decoration stopped in the eighteenth century, nor was it ever democratic. In the bazaars there is no painting and scarcely any carving. The very wood seems made of mud, the inhabitants of mud moving. So

1 The name appears to be a hybrid of Malabar and Barabar. The Barabar Hills are near Benares and Patna, north of Calcutta.

2 Forster said that, geographically, Chandrapore was suggested by the Indian city of Bankipore, where he stayed in 1913. It is placed on the Ganges below Benares. 'Pore' means 'town'.

3 The Ganges is the river of the goddess Ganga and represents baptism and redemption. Its waters supposedly have magical healing properties, though Forster says the river is not holy at Chandrapore.

4 The exact time setting of Forster's novel is hard to pinpoint, and critics have made different claims for situating it before or after the First World War.

abased, so monotonous is everything that meets the eye,[5] that when the Ganges comes down it might be expected to wash the excrescence back into the soil. Houses do fall, people are drowned and left rotting, but the general outline of the town persists, swelling here, shrinking there, like some low but indestructible form of life.

Inland, the prospect alters. There is an oval maidan,[6] and a long sallow hospital. Houses belonging to Eurasians[7] stand on the high ground by the railway station. Beyond the railway – which runs parallel to the river – the land sinks, then rises again rather steeply. On this second rise is laid out the little Civil Station,[8] and viewed hence Chandrapore appears to be a totally different place. It is a city of gardens. It is no city, but a forest sparsely scattered with huts. It is a tropical pleasance, washed by a noble river. The toddy palms and neem trees and mangoes and peepul that were hidden behind the bazaars now become visible and in their turn hide the bazaars. They rise from the gardens whose ancient tanks nourish them, they burst out of stifling purlieus and unconsidered temples. Seeking light and air, and endowed with more strength than man or his works, they soar above the lower deposit to greet one another with branches and beckoning leaves, and to build a city for the birds. Especially after the rains[9] do they screen what passes below, but at all times, even when scorched or leafless, they glorify the city to the English people who inhabit the rise, so that newcomers cannot believe it to be as meagre as it is described, and have to be driven down to acquire disillusionment. As for the Civil Station itself, it provokes no emotion. It charms not, neither does it repel. It is sensibly planned, with a red-brick Club[10] on its brow, and further back a grocer's and a cemetery, and the bungalows are disposed along roads that intersect at right angles. It has nothing hideous in it, and only the view is beautiful; it shares nothing with the city except the overarching sky.

The sky too has its changes, but they are less marked than those of the vegetation and the river. Clouds map it up at times, but it is normally a dome of blending tints, and the main tint blue. By day the blue will pale down into white where it touches the white of the land, after sunset it has a new circumference – orange, melting upwards into tenderest purple. But the core of blue persists, and so it is by

5 Forster is at pains to emphasise the ordinariness of daily life in comparison with the experience of the extraordinary caves. This perspective is most baldly stated by the opening sentence of Chapter 14: 'Most of life is so dull that there is nothing to be said about it, and the books and talk that would describe it as interesting are obliged to exaggerate, in the hope of justifying their own existence.'
6 A *maidan* is an open space of ground used for recreation in a town.
7 The words 'Anglo-Indian' and 'Eurasian' have swapped meanings and are used differently by different people. For Forster 'Anglo-Indian' means the British in India and 'Eurasian' means of mixed parentage.
8 The name given to the area of town occupied by the non-military European community.
9 The Indian year is divided into three seasons: the cold weather, which peaks around the new year, the hot weather, beginning around mid-April, and the monsoon, which arrives around November. Forster said that the novel's three sections represent the divisions of the Indian year into seasons: cold weather, hot weather, rains.
10 The Club was the hub of the social life of any Anglo-Indian civil and military station. One would be found in all stations, except for the very smallest. George Orwell wrote in his 1935 novel *Burmese Days* that 'In any town in India the European club is the spiritual citadel, the real seat of the British power.'

night. Then the stars hang like lamps from the immense vault. The distance between the earth and them is as nothing to the distance behind them; and that further distance, though beyond colour, last freed itself from blue.

The sky settles everything – not only climates and seasons, but when the earth shall be beautiful. By herself she can do little – only feeble outbursts of flowers. But when the sky chooses, glory can rain into the Chandrapore bazaars, or a benediction pass from horizon to horizon. The sky can do this because it is so strong and so enormous. Strength comes from the sun, infused in it daily, size from the prostrate earth. No mountains infringe on the curve. League after league the earth lies flat, heaves a little, is flat again. Only in the south, where a group of fists and fingers are thrust up through the soil, is the endless expanse interrupted. These fists and fingers are the Marabar Hills, containing the extraordinary caves.

The opening to *A Passage to India* immediately illustrates Forster's distinctive style: it appears to be in a realist mode, with a third-person omniscient narrator introducing the reader systematically to the story's setting, yet is heavily symbolic and uses the devices of unusual sentence construction and of description by absence or denial (e.g. 'there is no painting' and 'It is no city . . .'). In this strongly visual introductory chapter, the narrator establishes a number of contrasts. The immediate opposition is clearly between the city, which presents 'nothing' – as the litany of negatives in the first paragraph amply details – and the 'extraordinary' caves. These two words will occur repeatedly in the book to express Forster's conviction that existence is astonishing and yet ultimately meaningless. At the centre of the book's metaphysical concerns is an echoing hollowness, which reverberates throughout the narrative – and the caves are the chief symbol of this nullity or vacancy. The second sentence decides that Chandrapore is 'Edged rather than washed', and then Forster proceeds to accumulate negative images around the city: 'there are no bathing-steps'; 'the Ganges happens not to be holy here'; 'there is no river front'; 'bazaars shut out'; 'streets are mean'; 'temples ineffective'; 'houses . . . hidden away'. This opening paragraph ends by reducing the city to the dirt that results from mixing water and soil, as though the Ganges, which is not holy here, were turning the riverbanks and also the city to sludge: 'The very wood seems made of mud, the inhabitants of mud moving.' The Indian people are figured as 'some low but indestructible form of life', in which phrase Forster reveals his Western conditioning and prejudices but also wishes to convey the fact that Indians inhabited 'their' country for centuries before the arrival of the British, or the Moghuls, and will probably do so for centuries after they have left. Forster's other association here is between land and people: he portrays India as a vast country of almost limitless time and space, which dwarfs the British islanders.

It is with the second paragraph that Forster's images of circling and demarcation, inclusion and exclusion come to dominate. On the high ground above Chandrapore are the Eurasians, who are symbolically positioned between the Indian city and the English Civil Station on the higher second rise. From this vantage point it is possible to see another encampment: 'a city for the birds' in the tall trees. All these many communities – Indian, Eurasian, English and animal – share only 'the overarching sky'. This 'dome of blending tints' is an 'immense vault' beyond which there are distances to which 'the distance between the earth and [the stars] is as nothing'. With these various descriptions, up to the final paragraph, Forster has arranged a series of separations and ever-increasing distances that creates a pattern of arcs moving away from the starting-point of the Ganges. In an artful progression, the omniscient third-person narration has moved from the (un)holy river through three artificial levels of humanity to the natural animal kingdom and up to the immense vault of the sky, beyond which are still greater distances. The pattern is of circles or arches radiating out from the Ganges as though a pebble had been dropped in the water and the ripples had spread out to encompass each of these places in turn.

In this second paragraph, after the part-British, part-Indian insertion of the Eurasians, Forster accentuates the difference between the city and the Civil Station. From the second rise Chandrapore appears to be 'no city' but 'a totally different place', a forest of huts, gardens and trees; to the extent that it is now 'washed' and no longer only edged by the Ganges. Above all this 'soar' the trees that screen the Indians and English from each other because they are 'endowed with more strength than man or his works' just as later in the chapter the sky 'is so strong and so enormous'.

After the detail in the second paragraph about the communities that live above the Indian city, the third paragraph moves to the sky. The dominant subject of the paragraph is colour, and it should strike the reader that up to this point there has been no mention of any colour, except for the 'red-brick Club'. In this paragraph there are several colours: white, orange, purple and *above all* blue (the colour of not just the sky but also the Hindu god Krishna whom Godbole invites to come to him). The sky too has its changes, which are less than those of Chandrapore but are infinitely greater than those of the distances beyond colour that exist behind the stars. It is with reference to this ultimate scheme of things – the dark, colourless cosmic order – that Forster will describe the petty wranglings of human beings as minuscule and insignificant (which is the conclusion Mrs Moore comes to before the trial, and why, for example, Adela and Fielding are later described as like 'dwarfs shaking hands' in Chapter 29). But, at the level of the earth, the important arbiter is the sky, with its many colours, tints, and shades of difference. It is the sky that forms the weather, so its influence in the novel can be easily noted from the fact that *A Passage to India* proceeds from the initial cold weather of 'Mosque', when everyone is cordial and courteous, if cool, to the middle part's hot weather (as metaphor for the passions and tempers aroused by the Marabar Caves incident) and finally the release that comes with the rains of the monsoon in 'Temple'. So, the last paragraph of Chapter I begins by stating that, on earth, the sky settles everything. This idea runs throughout the novel to the very final line's prohibition on a friendship between Aziz and Fielding: 'and the sky said, "No, not there."' On a political level it is arguable therefore that the sky is itself an overarching metaphor for imperial rule – it hangs over the country (the world even) and 'colours' everything that happens beneath, settling whether Indians and Europeans can be friends and when the earth shall be beautiful, as the 'native' city and the Civil Station of Chandrapore are not.

Chapter 4

In this chapter, following Adela's desire to see the 'real India', the Collector sends out invitations to a Bridge Party on the lawns of the English Club and his gesture is debated by several of the Indian characters. The chapter is a key exposition of Anglo-Indian differences.

The Collector[1] kept his word. Next day he issued invitation cards to numerous Indian gentlemen in the neighbourhood, stating that he would be at home in the garden of the Club between the hours or five and seven on the following Tuesday, also that Mrs Turton would be glad to receive any ladies of their families who were out of purdah.[2] His action caused much excitement and was discussed in several worlds.

'It is owing to orders from the L.G.,'[3] was Mahmoud Ali's explanation. 'Turton would never do this unless compelled. Those high officials are different – they sympathize, the Viceroy[4] sympathizes, they would have us treated properly. But they come too seldom and live too far away. Meanwhile –'

'It is easy to sympathize at a distance,' said an old gentleman with a beard. 'I value more the kind word that is spoken close to my ear. Mr Turton has spoken it, from whatever cause. He speaks, we hear. I do not see why we need discuss it further.' Quotations followed from the Koran.[5]

'We have not all your sweet nature, Nawab Bahadur, nor your learning.'

'The Lieutenant-Governor may be my very good friend, but I give him no trouble – "How do you do, Nawab[6] Bahadur?" "Quite well, thank you, Sir Gilbert; how are you?" – and all is over. But I can be a thorn in Mr Turton's flesh,

1 The head of administration for a district (Mr Turton).
2 Purdah is the custom of keeping women in seclusion and clothing them completely in public. It is practised in many Hindu and Muslim countries. A purdah screen in a Hindu home is used to conceal women from visitors.
3 The Lieutenant-Governor, or Governor for short, of the province (his name is Mellanby; see extract from Chapter 23 and commentary on pp. 144–7).
4 The governor of a colony who acts in the name of the government or the monarch. Lord Hardinge became the Indian Viceroy in 1910 and was succeeded by Lord Chelmsford (1916–21).
5 The sacred Islamic book. It is believed by Muslims to be the holy word of God as told to Mohammed.
6 A title of nobility; a Muslim official acting as deputy governor of a province.

and if he asks me I accept the invitation. I shall come in from Dilkusha specially, though I have to postpone other business.'

'You will make yourself chip,' suddenly said a little black man.

There was a stir of disapproval. Who was this ill-bred upstart, that he should criticize the leading Mohammedan landowner of the district? Mahmoud Ali, though sharing his opinion, felt bound to oppose it. 'Mr Ram Chand!' he said, swaying forward stiffly with his hands on his hips.

'Mr Mahmoud Ali!'

'Mr Ram Chand, the Nawab Bahadur can decide what is cheap without our valuation, I think.'

'I do not expect I shall make myself cheap,' said the Nawab Bahadur to Mr Ram Chand, speaking very pleasantly, for he was aware that the man had been impolite and he desired to shield him from the consequences. It had passed through his mind to reply, 'I expect I shall make myself cheap,' but he rejected this as the less courteous alternative. 'I do not see why we should make ourselves cheap. I do not see why we should. The invitation is worded very graciously.' Feeling that he could not further decrease the social gulf between himself and his auditors, he sent his elegant grandson, who was in attendance on him, to fetch his car. When it came, he repeated all that he had said before, though at greater length, ending up with 'Till Tuesday, then, gentlemen all, when I hope we may meet in the flower-gardens of the Club.'

This opinion carried great weight. The Nawab Bahadur was a big proprietor and a philanthropist, a man of benevolence and decision. His character among all the communities in the Province stood high. He was a straightforward enemy and a staunch friend, and his hospitality was proverbial. 'Give, do not leave; after death who will thank you?' was his favourite remark; He held it a disgrace to die rich. When such a man was prepared to motor twenty-five miles to shake the Collector's hand, the entertainment took another aspect. For he was not like some eminent men, who give out that they will come, and then fail at the last moment, leaving the small fry floundering. If he said he would come, he would come, he would never deceive his supporters. The gentlemen whom he had lectured now urged one another to attend the party, although convinced at heart that his advice was unsound.

He had spoken in the little room near the courts where the pleaders waited for clients; clients, waiting for pleaders, sat in the dust outside. These had not received a card from Mr Turton. And there were circles even beyond these – people who wore nothing but a loincloth, people who wore not even that, and spent their lives in knocking two sticks together before a scarlet doll – humanity grading and drifting beyond the educated vision, until no earthly invitation can embrace it.

All invitations must proceed from heaven perhaps; perhaps it is futile for men to initiate their own unity, they do but widen the gulfs between them by the attempt. So at all events thought old Mr Graysford and young Mr Sorley, the devoted missionaries who lived out beyond the slaughter-houses, always travelled third on the railways,[7] and never came up to the Club. In our Father's house are

7 Third class on the railways was the cheapest. Most English would be expected to travel first, and most Indians third class. The missionaries are showing their humility and their willingness to mix with their 'flock' in India.

many mansions,[8] they taught, and there alone will the incompatible multitudes of mankind be welcomed and soothed. Not one shall be turned away by the servants on that veranda,[9] be he black or white, not one shall be kept standing who approaches with a loving heart. And why should the divine hospitality cease here? Consider, with all reverence, the monkeys. May there not be a mansion for the monkeys also? Old Mr Graysford said No, but young Mr Sorley, who was advanced, said Yes; he saw no reason why monkeys should not have their collateral share of bliss, and he had sympathetic discussions about them with his Hindu friends. And the jackals? Jackals were indeed less to Mr Sorley's mind, but he admitted that the mercy of God, being infinite, may well embrace all mammals. And the wasps? He became uneasy during the descent to wasps, and was apt to change the conversation. And oranges, cactuses, crystals and mud?[10] And the bacteria inside Mr Sorley? No, no, this is going too far. We must exclude someone from our gathering, or we shall be left with nothing.

In the novel's opening (see passage and commentary on pp. 115–17), the 'monotonous' ordinariness of Chrandrapore, which was 'never large or beautiful', is pejoratively presented to the point where its filth keeps away all but the 'invited guest'. In Chapter 4, one of the key social, political and religious themes of the novel is reintroduced: that of invitation. *A Passage to India* is structured around attempts to bring people together: the Bridge Party (at which Mrs Bhattacharya encourages Mrs Moore to call on her); Fielding's gathering with Adela, Aziz and Mrs Moore; the invitation to the caves; Godbole's milkmaid's song of invitation to Krishna at Fielding's and his similar invocation on behalf of Mrs Moore at the Gokul Ashtami Festival that starts the third part of the novel. It is integral to Forster's anti-colonial agenda that none of these invitations ends well (even the party at Fielding's house is ruined by Ronny): the English are not invited guests in India, and their desire for formality and for forms of exclusion will prevent, as we see at the end of the novel, even Aziz and Fielding from being friends though they both want to be. The political realities of colonialism overpower the force of goodwill, which Forster, who famously said he would sooner betray his country than his friend, places at the centre of his liberal humanist philosophy. The Bridge Party should be a force for connection, to bring people together; however, it is not motivated by goodwill. The invitations are not sincere

8 There are many biblical references and allusions in Forster's novel. This comes from John 14:2, when Jesus says 'In my Father's house are many mansions: if it were not so, I would have told you. I go to prepare a place for you.'

9 An open porch-like gallery surrounding a house. Though its etymological origin is open to debate, 'veranda' is one of the many words that have entered the English language from India. Such words are themselves called 'Anglo-Indian'.

10 It is worth noting that Forster describes Chandrapore as 'mud' on the first page of the novel. 'Mud', to be followed by 'bacteria', not only represents the smallest things, but also the building blocks of life, in terms of the primordial slime from which humanity evolved and the living organisms that we consider parasites but without which we could not survive.

inasmuch as the Anglo-Indian community has no intention of getting to know the invited Indians.

Forster's novel was received in 1924 as an imaginative and fictional but political treatise on 'the India question' (whether the country should be given independence), which he denied. Certainly, the book's symbolic and suggestive descriptions seem repeatedly to divide the national characters and religions from each other. The English are physically separate but also emotionally predisposed to segregate and differentiate, a point alluded to by repeated references to 'roads that intersect at right angles'. For example, to underline the idea of a gridwork of power and hierarchies, in Chapter 2 we are told that 'The roads, named after victorious generals and intersecting at right angles, were symbolic of the net Great Britain had thrown over India' (p. 39). Indians and India however are associated with invitations and a friendliness that the English take for lack of discrimination, as illustrated by Aziz's insistence on giving his own collar-stud to Fielding at their first meeting in Chapter 7, or when we are told that 'no Indian animal has any sense of an interior' at the end of Chapter 3.

Turning to this short chapter, it is evident that Forster is focusing on issues of invitation and goodwill: on the connections between the circles outlined in the novel's opening chapter and further illustrated here.

> [The Nawab Bahadur] had spoken in the little room near the courts where the pleaders waited for clients; clients, waiting for pleaders, sat in the dust outside. These had not received a card from Mr Turton. And there were circles even beyond these – people who wore nothing but a loincloth, people who wore not even that, and spent their lives in knocking two sticks together before a scarlet doll – humanity grading and drifting beyond the educated vision, until no earthly invitation can embrace it.

Once more the tropes of exclusion on earth, circles beyond circles, and humanity's inconsequence surface in a chapter that ends with two missionaries debating whether there are sufficient rooms in God's mansion for all people, and for monkeys, and for wasps, or even bacteria (reminding the reader of 'a low but indestructible form of life'): 'No, no, this is going too far. We must exclude someone from our gathering, or we shall be left with nothing.' Humans, or at least the English and their religion, must separate, exclude, and compartmentalise, while Forster's narrator says in the first chapter that the sky (the abode of the weather and the gods) can rain 'glory' or pass a benediction 'from horizon to horizon'. This benign influence of the sky could be seen as also within the power of the raj over India, but for Forster the political, religious and social divisions of the Empire amount only to a constricting net of right angles thrown over the subcontinent. It is important also to note that the chapter ends with the keyword 'nothing' that appeared in the novel's opening sentence. Where the Indians see earthly inclusiveness echoing the divine embrace symbolised by the sky, the British consider it a sign of disorder, a muddle. Mr Sorley is unsure, for example, about whether wasps will have a place in heaven, but both Mrs Moore (p. 55) and Godbole (p. 283) show love for the creature. Suggesting the wider significance of this creature, Forster said that the wasp was 'the Indian social wasp'.

The extract highlights the book's interest with Indian inclusion as opposed to British exclusion: a theme that resonates with Forster's perennial concern with connection and operates on many levels in the novel from the overarching sky down to the Bridge Party. Probably the most common statement about the novel is that it is a book about omissions, gaps, fissures and absences. The pivotal event of the narrative, in the Marabar Caves, is of course missing from the text. Similarly, Godbole's song to Krishna asking him to 'Come' will always be unanswered and this is echoed in Mrs Moore's refusal to appear at the trial, though of course she, or her spirit, is invoked as 'Esmiss Esmoor'.

The book is full of negatives and is a catalogue of exclusions. As the missionaries say of events such as the Bridge Party: 'We must exclude someone from our gathering or we shall be left with nothing.' This attitude is meant to be representative of the raj and its hierarchies, and is opposed to an inclusiveness and lack of discrimination Forster ascribes to Hinduism – particularly evident in the last section, 'Temple'.

The End of Chapter 5

Following the Bridge Party, Mrs Moore and her son Ronny, the magistrate, argue over the reason for Britain's presence in India. They begin by considering the Anglo-Indians' attitude towards Ronny's proposed marriage to Adela.

When the guests had gone, and Adela gone to bed, there was another interview between mother and son. He wanted her advice and support – while resenting interference. 'Does Adela talk to you much?' he began. 'I'm so driven with work, I don't see her as much as I hoped, but I hope she finds things comfortable.'

'Adela and I talk mostly about India. Dear, since you mention it, you're quite right – you ought to be more alone with her than you are.'

'Yes, perhaps, but then people'd gossip.'

'Well, they must gossip sometime! Let them gossip.'

'People are so odd out here, and it's not like home – one's always facing the footlights, as the Burra Sahib[1] said. Take a silly little example: when Adela went out to the boundary of the Club compound,and Fielding followed her. I saw Mrs

1 Literally, 'Burra Sahib' means the 'great man' and usually refers to a senior official but might be used as a term of deference to anyone in charge.

Callendar notice it. They notice everything, until they're perfectly sure you're their sort.'[2]

'I don't think Adela'll ever be quite their sort – she's much too individual.'

'I know, that's so remarkable about her,' he said thoughtfully. Mrs Moore thought him rather absurd. Accustomed to the privacy of London, she could not realize that India, seemingly so mysterious, contains none, and that consequently the conventions have greater force. 'I suppose nothing's on her mind,' he continued.

'Ask her, ask her yourself, my dear boy.'

'Probably she's heard tales of the heat, but of course I should pack her off to the hills every April – I'm not one to keep a wife grilling in the plains.'[3]

'Oh, it wouldn't be the weather.'

'There's nothing in India but the weather, my dear mother; it's the alpha and omega of the whole affair.'[4]

'Yes, as Mr McBryde was saying, but it's much more the Anglo-Indians themselves who are likely to get on Adela's nerves. She doesn't think they behave pleasantly to Indians, you see.'

'What did I tell you?' he exclaimed, losing his gentle manner. 'I knew it last week. Oh, how like a woman to worry over a side-issue!'

She forgot about Adela in her surprise. 'A side-issue, a side-issue?' she repeated. 'How can it be that?'

'We're not out here for the purpose of behaving pleasantly!'

'What do you mean?'

'What I say. We're out here to do justice and keep the peace. Them's my sentiments. India isn't a drawing-room.'

'Your sentiments are those of a god,' she said quietly, but it was his manner rather than his sentiments that annoyed her.

Trying to recover his temper, he said, 'India likes gods.'[5]

'And Englishmen like posing as gods.'

'There's no point in all this. Here we are, and we're going to stop, and the country's got to put up with us, gods or no gods. Oh, look here,' he broke out, rather pathetically, 'what do you and Adela want me to do? Go against my class, against all the people I respect and admire out here? Lose such power as I have for doing good in this country, because my behaviour isn't pleasant? You neither of you understand what work is, or you'd never talk such eyewash. I hate talking

2 Ronny is not overstating the case or describing a situation peculiar to Chandrapore. The raj was well known for being obsessed with not just class and status but conformity.

3 This sentence brings to mind Kipling's first India book, *Plain Tales from the Hills* (1889), which any British person going to India might be expected to have read. The book made Kipling a household name and by the turn of the century he was one of the world's most famous and popular authors. In the hot months women and children usually relocated to the hill stations while the men continued working in the plains.

4 Ronny here is in agreement with Forster's narrator but has different reasons. To Ronny, the rhythms of official and social life are dictated by the transition of the seasons. For the narrator, as we saw in Chapter 1, the importance of the sky is still greater. Alpha and omega are the first and last letters of the Greek alphabet.

5 Ronny is alluding to the fact that Hinduism is a polytheistic religion. An added significance is the fact that the top administrators of the Indian Civil Service were known as the 'twice-born', which is the name of the Brahmans, the highest, priestly class in the Hindu caste system.

like this, but one must occasionally. It's morbidly sensitive to go on as Adela and you do. I noticed you both at the Club today – after the Collector had been at all that trouble to amuse you. I am out here to work, mind, to hold this wretched country by force. I'm not a missionary or a Labour Member[6] or a vague sentimental sympathetic literary man. I'm just a servant of the Government; it's the profession you wanted me to choose myself, and that's that. We're not pleasant in India, and we don't intend to be pleasant. We've something more important to do.'

He spoke sincerely. Every day he worked hard in the court trying to decide which of two untrue accounts was the less untrue, trying to dispense justice fearlessly, to protect the weak against the less weak, the incoherent against the plausible, surrounded by lies and flattery. That morning he had convicted a railway clerk of overcharging pilgrims for their tickets, and a Pathan[7] of attempted rape. He expected no gratitude, no recognition for this, and both clerk and Pathan might appeal, bribe their witnesses more effectually in the interval, and get their sentences reversed. It was his duty. But he did expect sympathy from his own people, and except from newcomers he obtained it. He did think he ought not to be worried about Bridge Parties when the day's work was over and he wanted to play tennis with his equals or rest his legs upon a long chair.

He spoke sincerely, but she could have wished with less gusto. How Ronny revelled in the drawbacks of his situation! How he did rub it in that he was not in India to behave pleasantly, and derived positive satisfaction therefrom! He reminded her of his public-school days. The traces of young-man humanitarianism had sloughed off, and he talked like an intelligent and embittered boy. His words without his voice might have impressed her, but when she heard the self-satisfied lilt of them, when she saw the mouth moving so complacently and competently beneath the little red nose, she felt, quite illogically, that this was not the last word on India. One touch of regret – not the canny substitute but the true regret from the heart – would have made him a different man, and the British Empire[8] a different institution.

'I'm going to argue, and indeed dictate,' she said, clinking her rings. 'The English *are* out here to be pleasant.'

'How do you make that out, mother?' he asked, speaking gently again, for he was ashamed of his irritability.

'Because India is part of the earth. And God has put us on the earth in order to be pleasant to each other. God . . . is . . . love.' She hesitated, seeing how much he disliked the argument, but something made her go on. 'God has put us on earth to love our neighbours and to show it, and He is omnipresent, even in India, to see how we are succeeding.'

He looked gloomy, and a little anxious. He knew this religious strain in her, and that it was a symptom of bad health; there had been much of it when his

6 Formed at the turn of the century, the Labour Party gained an increasing number of seats in elections up to 1922 when it replaced the Liberals as the main party of opposition. Labour first took government office in January 1924, the year Forster's novel was published.

7 The Pathans are Indian tribes from around the north-west frontier.

8 The British government only took over official rule in India in 1858 following the Indian 'Mutiny' of the previous year. Queen Victoria was declared Empress of India in 1876.

stepfather died. He thought, 'She is certainly ageing, and I ought not to be vexed with anything she says.'

'The desire to behave pleasantly satisfies God . . . The sincere if impotent desire wins His blessing. I think everyone fails, but there are so many kinds of failure. Goodwill and more goodwill and more goodwill. Though I speak with the tongues of . . .'

He waited until she had done, and then said gently: 'I quite see that. I suppose I ought to get off to my files now, and you'll be going to bed.'

'I suppose so, I suppose so.' They did not part for a few minutes, but the conversation had become unreal since Christianity had entered it. Ronny approved of religion as long as it endorsed the National Anthem, but he objected when it attempted to influence his life. Then he would say in respectful yet decided tones, 'I don't think it does to talk about these things, every fellow has to work out his own religion,' and any fellow who heard him muttered, 'Hear!'

Mrs Moore felt that she had made a mistake in mentioning God, but she found Him increasingly difficult to avoid as she grew older, and He had been constantly in her thoughts since she entered India, though oddly enough He satisfied her less. She must needs pronounce His name frequently, as the greatest she knew, yet she had never found it less efficacious.[9] Outside the arch there seemed always an arch, beyond the remotest echo a silence.[10] And she regretted afterwards that she had not kept to the real serious subject that had caused her to visit India – namely the relationship between Ronny and Adela. Would they, or would they not, succeed in becoming engaged to be married?

It is worth noting to begin with that Adela (1062–1137) was the name of the youngest daughter of William the Conqueror and mother of King Stephen of England. *Chambers Biographical Dictionary* describes her as 'cultured and pious': terms that could apply to Adela Quested, who presumably first appears very briefly as the 'Miss Quested' who is a lunch-guest of the free-thinking Schlegel sisters in *Howards End* (E. M. Forster, *Howards End*, Harmondsworth: Penguin, 1975, p. 88). It is Adela's spirit of piety that makes Mrs Moore think she will never be accepted by the Anglo-Indians as 'their sort'. By contrast, Ronny's rejection of his 'young-man humanitarianism' has occasioned his acceptance of his role as a sahib.

It has been said that 'only connect', the motto of Forster's previous novel, *Howards End* (1910), could also be the epigraph to *A Passage to India*. This is partly because the English, though they were proud of an intercontinental *pax Britannica*, were unable after centuries of rule to bring the people of India's two major religions, Hinduism and Islam, into harmony. Emblematic of this, the

9 This alludes to the spiritual crisis Mrs Moore is undergoing, which will culminate in her discovery that the Marabar Caves echo back 'Ou-boum' to any name or word she might pronounce.

10 This is an allusion to the symbolism initiated by the first chapter of the novel and it places Mrs Moore in sympathy both with Godbole and with the pronouncements of Forster's narrator.

Collector attempts and fails to make a bridge between the British colonisers and the Indian colonised with his party in Chapter 5. But the novel argues that politics and cultural misunderstandings (Forster calls them 'muddles') will always intrude, and it is only the overarching sky that can connect the 'native' city and the 'sensibly planned' Civil Station – on a physical level, because the sky dictates the heat and dust that India is reduced to in the Orientalist imagination and on a metaphysical level, because it represents the universal values that Forster believed in, and which are, in the absence of religious unity, summed up in his repeated term 'goodwill', which is a touchstone in this argument between Mrs Moore and Ronny. The book's tripartite structure reflects this: the parts are called 'Mosque', 'Caves', 'Temple' to represent Islam and Hinduism as book-ends between which intervene the ancient pre-deistic caves that seem to have been substituted in this triad for the European Church. The English and their religion have not brought Muslims and Hindus together in India but have instead suffered a crisis of their own religious and moral values (cf. J. G. Farrell's novel *The Siege of Krishnapur*).

Mrs Moore here voices the conviction that personal relationships are more important than political ones, and that the purpose of every human being is to be pleasant and to act out of goodwill. She sees this as an extension of God's overarching role, connecting all humanity, a theme later mused on by Aziz to Fielding: 'I was a child when you knew me first. Everyone was my friend then. The Friend: a Persian expression for God' (p. 273). Mrs Moore's belief that 'God is love' is transformed to 'God si love' in the final section of the novel (p. 283), when Godbole concludes about Mrs Moore herself: 'It was his duty, as it was his desire, to place himself in the position of the God and to love her, and to place himself in her position and to say to the God, "Come, come, come, come"' (p. 287). By contrast, Ronny sees his role in relation to God to be one of emulation: to pose as a divine authority because 'India likes gods'. Against him, Mrs Moore quotes the opening of I Corinthians 13: 'Though I speak with the tongues of men and of angels, and have not charity, I am become as sounding brass, or a tinkling cymbal . . . and though I have all faith, so that I could remove mountains, and have not charity, I am nothing'. Also presaged here is Mrs Moore's spiritual crisis prompted by the Marabar Caves at the end of Chapter 14.

Chapter 7 (pp. 81–7)

After the Bridge Party, this extract from near the start of chapter 7 features the alternative informal party where Aziz and Fielding first meet, and the novel's four main characters discuss goodwill, cultural differences between India and England, and 'muddles'.

Lifting up his voice, he shouted from the bedroom, 'Please make yourself at home.' The remark was unpremeditated, like most of his actions; it was what he felt inclined to say.

To Aziz it had a very definite meaning. 'May I really, Mr Fielding? It's very good of you,' he called back; 'I like unconventional behaviour so extremely.' His spirits flared up, he glanced round the living-room. Some luxury in it, but no order – nothing to intimidate poor Indians. It was also a very beautiful room, opening into the garden through three high arches of wood. 'The fact is I have long wanted to meet you,' he continued. 'I have heard so much about your warm heart from the Nawab Bahadur. But where is one to meet in a wretched hole like Chandrapore?' He came close up to the door. 'When I was greener here, I'll tell you what: I used to wish you to fall ill so that we could meet that way.' They laughed, and encouraged by his success he began to improvise. 'I said to myself, "How does Mr Fielding look this morning? Perhaps pale. And the Civil Surgeon is pale too, he will not be able to attend upon him when the shivering commences." I should have been sent for instead. Then we would have had jolly talks, for you are a celebrated student of Persian poetry.'[1]

'You know me by sight, then.'

'Of course, of course. You know me?'

'I know you very well by name.'

'I have been here such a short time, and always in the bazaar. No wonder you have never seen me, and I wonder you know my name. I say, Mr Fielding?'

'Yes?'

'Guess what I look like before you come out. That will be a kind of game.'

'You're five feet nine inches high,' said Fielding, surmising this much through the ground glass of the bedroom door.

'Jolly good. What next? Have I not a venerable white beard?'

'Blast!'

'Anything wrong?'

'I've stamped on my last collar-stud.'

'Take mine, take mine.'

'Have you a spare one?'

'Yes, yes, one minute.'

'Not if you're wearing it yourself.'

'No, no, one in my pocket.' Stepping aside, so that his outline might vanish, he wrenched off his collar, and pulled out of his shirt the back stud, a gold stud, which was part of a set that his brother-in-law had brought him from Europe. 'Here it is,' he cried.

'Come in with it if you don't mind the unconventionality.'

'One minute again.' Replacing his collar, he prayed that it would not spring up at the back during tea. Fielding's bearer, who was helping him to dress, opened the door for him.

1 Poetry in the modern Persian language of the Islamic era, written in Arabic script. Persian poetry was not confined to Persia (Iran) but was also fertile in Turkey and northern India. A highly ornate and stylised genre, it remained remarkably stable for a millennium, right up to the time *A Passage to India* is set.

'Many thanks.' They shook hands, smiling. He began to look round, as he would have with any old friend. Fielding was not surprised at the rapidity of their intimacy. With so emotional a people it was apt to come at once or never, and he and Aziz, having heard only good of each other, could afford to dispense with preliminaries.

'But I always thought that Englishmen kept their rooms so tidy. It seems that this is not so. I need not be so ashamed.' He sat down gaily on the bed; then, forgetting himself entirely, drew up his legs and folded them under him. 'Everything ranged coldly on shelves was what *I* thought. – I say, Mr Fielding, is the study going to go in?'

'I hae ma doots.'

'What's that last sentence, please? Will you teach me some new words and so improve my English?'

Fielding doubted whether 'everything ranged coldly on shelves' could be improved. He was often struck by the liveliness with which the younger generation handled a foreign tongue. They altered the idiom, but they could say whatever they wanted to say quickly; there were none of the babuisms[2] ascribed to them up at the Club. But then the Club moved slowly; it still declared that few Mohammedans[3] and no Hindus would eat at an Englishman's table, and that all Indian ladies were in impenetrable purdah. Individually it knew better; as a club it declined to change.

'Let me put in your stud. I see . . . the shirt back's hole is rather small and to rip it wider a pity.'

'Why in hell does one wear collars at all?' grumbled Fielding as he bent his neck.

'We wear them to pass the police.'

'What's that?'

'If I'm biking in English dress – starch collar, hat with ditch – they take no notice. When I wear a fez, they cry, "Your lamp's out!" Lord Curzon[4] did not consider this when he urged natives of India to retain their picturesque costumes. – Hooray! Stud's gone in. – Sometimes I shut my eyes and dream I have splendid clothes again and am riding into battle behind Alamgir.[5] Mr Fielding, must not India have been beautiful then, with the Mogul Empire at its height and Alamgir reigning at Delhi upon the Peacock Throne?'[6]

'Two ladies are coming to tea to meet you – I think you know them.'

'Meet me? I know no ladies.'

'Not Mrs Moore and Miss Quested?'

'Oh yes – I remember.' The romance at the mosque had sunk out of his

2 'Babu', which means 'father' in Hindi, is a title of respect and can be placed before a man's full name or after his first name. To Anglo-Indians such as Ronny or Mr Turton, the term 'Babu' would imply the opposite of respect. 'Babuisms' is a denigratory term implying the periphrases of Indians with a little English education.

3 Followers of the Prophet Mohammed: another term for Muslims.

4 Viceroy of India from 1899 to 1905.

5 Alamgir was the imperial title of Aurangzeb, the last of the great Moghul emperors (1618–1707).

6 The Moghuls were a Muslim dynasty overthrown by the British in India. Their empire ran from the mid-sixteenth century to the beginning of the nineteenth. The peacock throne, until its theft, was kept inside the palace at Delhi where the dynasty was founded.

consciousness as soon as it was over. 'An excessively aged lady; but will you please repeat the name of her companion?'

'Miss Quested.'

'Just as you wish.' He was disappointed that other guests were coming, for he preferred to be alone with his new friend.

'You can talk to Miss Quested about the Peacock Throne if you like – she's artistic, they say.'

'Is she a Post-Impressionist?'[7]

'Post-Impressionism, indeed! Come along to tea. This world is getting too much for me altogether.'

Aziz was offended. The remark suggested that he, an obscure Indian, had no right to have heard of Post-Impressionism – a privilege reserved for the Ruling Race, that. He said stiffly, 'I do not consider Mrs Moore my friend, I only met her accidentally in my mosque,' and was adding, 'A single meeting is too short to make a friend,' but before he could finish the sentence the stiffness vanished from it, because he felt Fielding's fundamental goodwill. His own went out to it, and grappled beneath the shifting tides of emotion which can alone bear the voyager to an anchorage but may also carry him across it onto the rocks.[8] He was safe really – as safe as the shore-dweller who can only under-stand stability and supposes that every ship must be wrecked, and he had sensations the shore-dweller cannot know. Indeed, he was sensitive rather than responsive. In every remark he found a meaning, but not always the true meaning, and his life, though vivid, was largely a dream. Fielding, for instance, had not meant that Indians are obscure, but that Post-Impressionism is; a gulf divided his remark from Mrs Turton's 'Why, they speak English,' but to Aziz the two sounded alike. Fielding saw that something had gone wrong, and equally that it had come right, but he didn't fidget, being an optimist where personal relations were concerned, and their talk rattled on as before.

'Besides the ladies I am expecting one of my assistants – Narayan Godbole.'

'Oho, the Deccani Brahman!'[9]

'He wants the past back too, but not precisely Alamgir.'

'I should think not. Do you know what Deccani Brahmans say? That England conquered India from them - from them, mind, and not from the Moguls. Is not that like their cheek? They have even bribed it to appear in textbooks, for they are so subtle and immensely rich. Professor Godbole must be quite unlike all other Deccani Brahmans from all I can hear say. A most sincere chap.'

'Why don't you fellows run a club in Chandrapore, Aziz?'

'Perhaps – some day . . . Just now I see Mrs Moore and – what's her name – coming.'

7 Post-Impressionism was a largely French art movement brought to Britain by Roger Fry's London exhibition in 1910. Artists included in the movement are Gaugin, Cézanne, Seurat and van Gogh.

8 This not only emphasises the importance of connection in the need for Aziz to take Fielding's comments in a spirit of mutual goodwill, it is also an example of the novel's use of metaphorical imagery to add meaning to its title.

9 As a Brahman, Godbole is a member of the highest Hindu caste. More specifically he is a member of the Chitpavans, a powerful and proud sect of the Brahmans of the Deccan.

How fortunate that it was an 'unconventional' party, where formalities are ruled out. On this basis Aziz found the English ladies easy to talk to, he treated them like men. Beauty would have troubled him, for it entails rules of its own, but Mrs Moore was so old and Miss Quested so plain that he was spared this anxiety. Adela's angular body and the freckles on her face were terrible defects in his eyes, and he wondered how God could have been so unkind to any female form. His attitude towards her remained entirely straightforward in consequence.

'I want to ask you something, Dr Aziz,' she began. 'I heard from Mrs Moore how helpful you were to her in the mosque, and how interesting. She learned more about India in those few minutes' talk with you than in the three weeks since we landed.'

'Oh, please do not mention a little thing like that. Is there anything else I may tell you about my country?'

'I want you to explain a disappointment we had this morning; it must be some point of Indian etiquette.'

'There honestly is none,' he replied. 'We are by nature a most informal people.'

'I am afraid we must have made some blunder and given offence,' said Mrs Moore.

'That is even more impossible. But may I know the facts?'

'An Indian lady and gentleman were to send their carriage for us this morning at nine. It has never come. We waited and waited and waited; we can't think what happened.'

'Some misunderstanding,' said Fielding, seeing at once that it was the type of incident that had better not be cleared up.

'Oh no, it wasn't that,' Miss Quested persisted. 'They even gave up going to Calcutta to entertain us. We must have made some stupid blunder, we both feel sure.'

'I wouldn't worry about that.'

'Exactly what Mr Heaslop tells me,' she retorted, reddening a little. 'If one doesn't worry, how's one to understand?'

The host was inclined to change the subject, but Aziz took it up warmly, and on learning fragments of the delinquents' name pronounced that they were Hindus.

'Slack Hindus – they have no idea of society; I know them very well because of a doctor at the hospital. Such a slack unpunctual fellow! It is as well you did not go to their house, for it would give you a wrong idea of India. Nothing sanitary. I think for my own part they grew ashamed of their house and that is why they did not send.'

'That's a notion,' said the other man.

'I do so hate mysteries,' Adela announced.

'We English do.'

'I dislike them not because I'm English, but from my own personal point of view,' she corrected.

'I like mysteries but I rather dislike muddles,' said Mrs Moore.

'A mystery is a muddle.'

'Oh, do you think so, Mr Fielding?'

'A mystery is only a high-sounding term for a muddle. No advantage in stirring it up, in either case. Aziz and I know well that India's a muddle.'

'India's – oh, what an alarming idea!'

'There'll be no muddle when you come to see me,' said Aziz, rather out of his depth. 'Mrs Moore and everyone – I invite you all – oh, please.'

The old lady accepted: she still thought the young doctor excessively nice; moreover, a new feeling, half languor, half excitement, bade her turn down any fresh path. Miss Quested accepted out of adventure. She also liked Aziz, and believed that when she knew him better he would unlock his country for her. His invitation gratified her, and she asked him for his address.

Aziz thought of his bungalow with horror. It was a detestable shanty near a low bazaar. There was practically only one room in it, and that infested with small black flies. 'Oh, but we will talk of something else now,' he exclaimed. 'I wish I lived here. See this beautiful room! Let us admire it together for a little. See those curves at the bottom of the arches. What delicacy! It is the architecture of Question and Answer.[10] Mrs Moore, you are in India; I am not joking.'

Here we have the opening of the major scene of interaction between the four principal characters in the novel, who are joined later by the fifth, Professor Godbole. The passage emphasises that Forster aims to construct a narrative about progressive, liberal-minded people trying to be friends against the backdrop of imperial administration: Fielding, we are told, has come neither to preach nor to learn: as an individual he is there 'because he needed a job': 'Neither a missionary nor a student, he was happiest in the give-and-take of private conversation. The world, he believed, is a globe of men who are trying to reach one another and can best do so by the help of goodwill plus culture and intelligence' (p. 80). Goodwill is one of the words most frequently mentioned in the novel. Personal factors are seen as ways of uniting people, and political factors as sources of division. The easy familiarity of Aziz and Fielding's first meeting is contrasted with the formal and impersonal attempts of the Collector's Bridge Party.

The extract ends with one of the prime examples of Forster's view of India, of Indo-British relations, and of human relationships themselves, characterised by muddle, as I discussed in the introduction to this section. An excellent minor example of 'muddle' occurs in the passage when Fielding expresses astonishment at Aziz's mention of Post-Impressionism. Aziz thinks this is a comment on

10 This appears to represent the 'Mosque' section: an architecture of call and response compared with the unchanging feedback of 'Ou-boum' to any utterance in 'Caves' and the lack of reply to the invitation to 'Come' that is associated with Godbole, whose name means 'sweet-mouthed', and the Hindu festival in 'Temple'.

him, as an Indian, whereas Fielding means it to convey something about his own attitude to art. It is an example for Forster of a personal remark about the self misinterpreted as a political remark about the other. The passage contains other misunderstandings and small deceptions, but no unkindnesses, from the gift of Aziz's collar-stud to the mix-up over Adela and Mrs Moore's visit to the Bhattacharayas. Such incidents become of greater importance when they are not marked by goodwill, as when Ronny later remarks that Aziz's lack of a collar-stud is typical of Indians. The ultimate example of such prejudiced accusations is the Club's response to Adela's allegation of rape against Aziz.

The Start of Chapter 11

To cement their friendship, Aziz shows his wife's photograph to Fielding.

Although the Indians had driven off, and Fielding could see his horse standing in a small shed in the corner of the compound, no one troubled to bring it to him. He started to get it himself, but was stopped by a call from the house. Aziz was sitting up in bed, looking dishevelled and sad. 'Here's your home,' he said sardonically. 'Here's the celebrated hospitality of the East. Look at the flies. Look at the chunam[1] coming off the walls. Isn't it jolly? Now I suppose you want to be off, having seen an oriental interior.'

'Anyhow, you want to rest.'

'I can rest the whole day, thanks to worthy Dr Lal. Major Callendar's spy,[2] I suppose you know, but this time it didn't work. I am allowed to have a slight temperature.'

'Callendar doesn't trust anyone, English or Indian; that's his character, and I wish you weren't under him; but you are, and that's that.'

'Before you go, for you are evidently in a great hurry, will you please unlock that drawer? Do you see a piece of brown paper at the top?'

'Yes.'

'Open it.'

'Who is this?'

'She was my wife. You are the first Englishman she has ever come before. Now put her photograph away.'

1 Lime.

2 Aziz elaborates on this on p. 132: 'whatever you say or do in this damned country there is always some envious fellow on the lookout. You may be surprised to know that there were at least three spies sitting here when you came to inquire.'

He was astonished, as a traveller who suddenly sees, between the stones of the desert, flowers. The flowers have been there all the time, but suddenly he sees them. He tried to look at the photograph, but in itself it was just a woman in a sari, facing the world. He muttered, 'Really, I don't know why you pay me this great compliment, Aziz, but I do appreciate it.'

'Oh, it's nothing, she was not a highly educated woman or even beautiful, but put it away. You would have seen her, so why should you not see her photograph?'

'You would have allowed me to see her?'

'Why not? I believe in the purdah,[3] but I should have told her you were my brother, and she would have seen you. Hamidullah saw her, and several others.'

'Did she think they were your brothers?'

'Of course not, but the word exists and is convenient. All men are my brothers, and as soon as one behaves as such he may see my wife.'

'And when the whole world behaves as such, there will be no more purdah?'

'It is because you can say and feel such a remark as that, that I show you the photograph,' said Aziz gravely. 'It is beyond the power of most men. It is because you behave well while I behave badly that I show it you. I never expected you to come back just now when I called you. I thought, "He has certainly done with me; I have insulted him." Mr Fielding, no one can ever realize how much kindness we Indians need, we do not even realize it ourselves. But we know when it has been given. We do not forget, though we may seem to. Kindness, more kindness, and even after that more kindness. I assure you it is the only hope.' His voice seemed to arise from a dream. Altering it, yet still deep below his normal surface, he said: 'We can't build up India except on what we feel. What is the use of all these reforms,[4] and Conciliation Committees for Mohurram, and shall we cut the tazia[5] short or shall we carry it another route, and Councils of Notables and official parties where the English sneer at our skins?'

'It's beginning at the wrong end, isn't it? I know, but institutions and the Government don't.' He looked again at the photograph. The lady faced the world at her husband's wish and her own, but how bewildering she found it, the echoing contradictory world!

3 Aziz's opinions on matters of gender are not as traditional or inflexible as this comment might suggest: his later view expressed in his poetry is 'Free our women and India will be free' (p. 314).

4 Aziz is talking about steps taken towards Indian self-government. Depending on when the story is placed, Aziz could be considered to be referring to the Morley–Minto reforms of 1909 or the Montagu–Chelmsford reforms of 1919.

5 Mohurram is a period of commemoration for the death in the seventh-century of the Prophet's descendants Hasan and Husain. Carried in the Mohurram procession, the tazia is a representation of their tomb. Mohurram takes place shortly before the trial (p. 198 ff.) and leads to 'riots' that make the British all the keener to make an example of Aziz (as was the case for Indians mistreated at Amritsar and after the Mutiny).

'Put her away, she is of no importance, she is dead,' said Aziz gently. 'I showed her to you because I have nothing else to show. You may look round the whole of my bungalow now, and empty everything. I have no other secrets, my three children live away with their grandmamma, and that is all.'

Chapter 11 includes a very brief account of Aziz's wife, who is now dead (p. 128). She, which is to say her photograph, is hidden away in Aziz's drawer, and this in itself suggests parallels. Most importantly, she is kept in darkness and only shown to special visitors – like the Marabar Caves. Aziz says the picture is nothing when he shows it to Fielding, but it is all he has to show – which is also how he feels about the Marabar Caves: they are all that Chandrapore has to show the Europeans. But primarily, Aziz's wife is an object of exchange and a 'sign' of friendship between men – her picture is effectively revealed or uncovered in order to bring Aziz and Fielding closer together. This is similarly the purpose of Mrs Moore and Adela – to bring Aziz and Fielding together – and it is also Adela's 'crime' to part the men, to break the friendship between Aziz and Fielding, which is also the subject of the book, from another perspective. Women are used to bring together or to separate men: they are means not ends. Concealed in his drawer, Aziz's wife is also in purdah – hidden away, like Aziz's second wife in Mau – about whom we hear nothing except a short remark in relation to purdah (see Aziz's poetry on 'oriental womanhood' (p. 290)).

The relevance of this to colonialism, especially in India, is quite important because of the way in which deteriorating relations between Indians and Anglo-Indians were often attributed to the memsahibs. Women only started coming to India in large numbers when rule was taken from the East India Company by the British government in 1858, the year after the 'Indian Mutiny'. The whole novel is arguably shot through with this attitude towards women from the Bridge Party to the trial. (Adela's hysteria/hallucination has also been read in terms of a 'masculinist' cliche.)

Chapter 12

The opening to the second section of the novel, 'Caves', provides further indications of Forster's construction of India and the significance of the Marabar Caves.

The Ganges, though flowing from the foot of Vishnu and through Siva's hair, is not an ancient stream.[1] Geology, looking further than religion, knows of a time when neither the river nor the Himalayas that nourish it existed, and an ocean flowed over the holy places of Hindustan.[2] The mountains rose, their debris silted up the ocean, the gods took their seats on them and contrived the river, and the India we call immemorial came into being. But India is really far older. In the days of the prehistoric ocean the southern part of the peninsula already existed, and the high places of Dravidia[3] have been land since land began, and have seen on the one side the sinking of a continent that joined them to Africa, and on the other the upheaval of the Himalayas from a sea. They are older than anything in the world. No water has ever covered them, and the sun who has watched them for countless aeons may still discern in their outlines forms that were his before our globe was torn from his bosom. If flesh of the sun's flesh is to be touched anywhere, it is here, among the incredible antiquity of these hills.

Yet even they are altering. As Himalayan India rose, this India, the primal, has been depressed, and is slowly re-entering the curve of the earth. It may be that in aeons to come an ocean will flow here too, and cover the sun-born rocks with slime. Meanwhile the plain of the Ganges encroaches on them with something of the sea's action. They are sinking beneath the newer lands. Their main mass is untouched, but at the edge their outposts have been cut off and stand knee-deep, throat-deep, in the advancing soil. There is something unspeakable in these outposts. They are like nothing else in the world, and a glimpse of them makes the breath catch. They rise abruptly, insanely, without the proportion that is kept by the wildest hills elsewhere, they bear no relation to anything dreamt or seen. To call them 'uncanny' suggests ghosts, and they are older than all spirit. Hinduism has scratched and plastered a few rocks, but the shrines are unfrequented, as if pilgrims, who generally seek the extraordinary, had here found too much of it.

1 The three most important gods in Hindu religion are Brahma the creator, Vishnu the preserver, and Shiva the destroyer and re-creator. According to Hindu mythology, entreaties to heaven caused the river Ganges to descend to earth, emerging from Vishnu's foot and flowing through Shiva's hair.

2 The mountains of the Himalayas (which means 'abode of snow' in Sanskrit) are the highest mountain range in the world and extend across northern India. 'Hindustan' (which means 'land of the Hindus') is not a precise term: it is generally taken to include either the Ganges Plain in northern India or all of northern India where Hindustani (Hindi) is spoken. 'Hindustan' is sometimes used to mean the country of India or even the entire Indian subcontinent.

3 'Dravidian' is a term applied to linguistically related Indian peoples from the south of the country, such as the Tamil and the Ghats. Spoken over most of southern India, the Dravidian language was probably the main language over the whole of the subcontinent before Indo-Europeans invaded. It remains the fourth most spoken language in the world.

Some saddhus[4] did once settle in a cave, but they were smoked out, and even Buddha, who must have passed this way down to the Bo Tree of Gaya,[5] shunned a renunciation more complete than his own, and has left no legend of struggle or victory in the Marabar.

The caves are readily described. A tunnel eight feet long, five feet high, three feet wide, leads to a circular chamber about twenty feet in diameter. This arrangement occurs again and again throughout the group of hills, and this is all, this is a Marabar cave. Having seen one such cave, having seen two, having seen three, four, fourteen, twenty-four, the visitor returns to Chandrapore uncertain whether he has had an interesting experience or a dull one or any experience at all. He finds it difficult to discuss the caves, or to keep them apart in his mind, for the pattern never varies, and no carving, not even a bees' nest or a bat, distinguishes one from another. Nothing, nothing attaches to them, and their reputation – for they have one – does not depend upon human speech. It is as if the surrounding plain or the passing birds have taken upon themselves to exclaim 'Extraordinary!' and the word has taken root in the air, and been inhaled by mankind.

They are dark caves. Even when they open towards the sun, very little light penetrates down the entrance tunnel into the circular chamber. There is little to see, and no eye to see it, until the visitor arrives for his five minutes, and strikes a match. Immediately another flame rises in the depths of the rock and moves towards the surface like an imprisoned spirit; the walls of the circular chamber have been most marvellously polished. The two flames approach and strive to unite, but cannot, because one of them breathes air, the other stone. A mirror inlaid with lovely colours divides the lovers, delicate stars of pink and gray interpose, exquisite nebulae, shadings fainter than the tail of a comet or the midday moon, all the evanescent life of the granite, only here visible. Fists and fingers thrust above the advancing soil – here at last is their skin, finer than any covering acquired by the animals, smoother than windless water, more voluptuous than love. The radiance increases, the flames touch one another, kiss, expire. The cave is dark again, like all the caves.

Only the wall of the circular chamber has been polished thus. The sides of the tunnel are left rough, they impinge as an afterthought upon the internal perfection. An entrance was necessary, so mankind made one. But elsewhere, deeper in the granite, are there certain chambers that have no entrances? Chambers never unsealed since the arrival of the gods? Local report declares that these exceed in number those that can be visited, as the dead exceed the living – four hundred of them, four thousand or million. Nothing is inside them, they were sealed up before the creation of pestilence or treasure; if mankind grew curious and excavated, nothing, nothing would be added to the sum of good or evil. One of them is rumoured within the boulder that swings on the summit of the highest of the hills; a bubble-shaped cave that has neither ceiling nor floor, and mirrors its own darkness in every direction infinitely. If the boulder falls and smashes, the cave will

4 Wandering Hindu holy men.

5 Guatama Buddha (563–483 BC) was the founder of Buddhism. The Bo Tree, known as the tree of perfect knowledge or intelligence, was a peepul tree under which Buddha meditated.

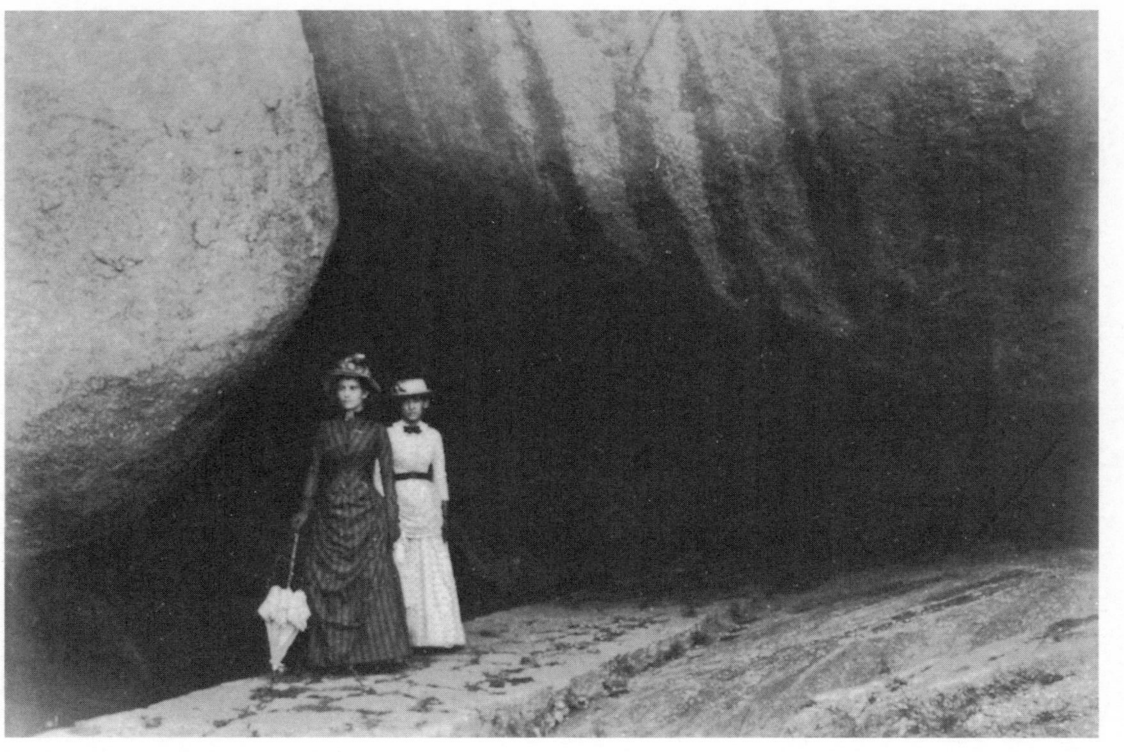

Figure 2 **Two Victorian women (c. 1886) visit the Bangalore caves.**

Source: By permission of The British Library (image 447/3: A visit to caves near Bangalore)

smash too – empty as an Easter egg. The boulder because of its hollowness sways in the wind, and even moves when a crow perches upon it; hence its name and the name of its stupendous pedestal: the Kawa Dol.[6]

I noted when looking at the novel's introductory pages that underneath the sky there is only one thing extraordinary to be mentioned in Forster's narrative. There are 'no mountains' to break the narrator's camera-eye scanning the landscape, and the earth lies flat *except* where the 'endless expanse [is] interrupted' by the 'fists and fingers' of the Marabar Hills. The first chapter's narrative works full circle back to the 'extraordinary caves' carved in hills that stretch up to the sky. Forster intimates that the caves were once a part of the sun, and are therefore linked with the sky's position above everything that occurs on earth, from religion to politics. The major image of the novel that this anticipates is the strange and disturbing echo, 'Ou-boum', that oppresses Mrs Moore and haunts Adela after their experience of the caves. One of the explicit links between these tropes is given in one of the passages considered above (pp. 123–7), at the end of Chapter 5, when Mrs Moore decides that 'Outside the arch there seemed always an arch, beyond the remotest echo a silence.' These images on the one hand are of inclusion and encircling and on the other hand they suggest the impact on the English of both the huge physical geography of the subcontinent and India's spiritual and cultural antiquity.

In one respect, the narrative concerns Adela's quest (hence her name) to find 'the real India'. What she actually finds is the Marabar Hills and an accompanying atmosphere of spiritual nullity, sexual confusion and human inconsequence in the universe. As I suggested in the introduction to this section, there are arguments that say that India is reduced to the Marabar Caves in the novel. Everything reported about the caves also applies to orientalist notions of the country: dark, oppressive and mysterious. The common way of imagining India as a land occupied by monsoons, heat and dust rather than people is repeated in the fetishising of the caves in the novel. The caves are considered inexplicable and unknowable: remote and timeless, like India.

It is significiant that the opening to each of the novel's three sections refers to the Marabar, and this provides another way of thinking about differences between representations of East and West. The first section begins with a dislocation in space – 'Except for the Marabar Caves, and they are twenty miles off' – and with the narrator describing the caves as 'extraordinary'. The first paragraph of 'Caves' signals a disjunction in time, as the narrator explains that the 'high places of Dravidia', such as the Marabar Hills, are 'older than anything in the world'. On this occasion, it 'is as if the surrounding plain or the passing birds have taken upon themselves to exclaim "Extraordinary!"'. Later in 'Caves',

6 Forster visited the (Buddhist) Barabar Caves near Gaya in 1913, where there is a hill called the Kauwa Doll.

in Chapter 23 (see extract and commentary on pp. 144–7), the narrator says that what Mrs Moore found in the caves was not only very old but 'Before time, it was before space also' (p. 212). The third section starts with the observation that the narrative has shifted 'Some hundreds of miles westward of the Marabar Hills, and two years later in time' (p. 281). Repeatedly, Forster accentuates breaks in time and space when describing India. Against this is pitted Europe, from which the 'Passage to India' is made. For example, we are told: 'though Venice was not Europe it was part of the Mediterranean harmony. The Mediterranean is the human norm' (p. 253). Thus a Western scene is apparently universalised into a human standard. India, by contrast, is 'extraordinary' but contains 'nothing': like the Marabar Caves.

The End of Chapter 20

After Aziz's arrest and imprisonment for his alleged attack on Adela, Fielding resigns from the Club. This extract illustrates the character of Fielding, Forster's chief representative in the novel, who is standing up for his friend against his country. It also reveals the 'hysteria' with which the Anglo-Indians greet the primal scene of an attack on an Englishwoman by 'natives'.

'Heard about Miss Quested's servant?' reinforced the Major.[1]

'No, what about him?'

'Heaslop warned Miss Quested's servant last night never to lose sight of her. Prisoner got hold of this and managed to leave him behind. Bribed him. Heaslop has just found out the whole story, with names and sums – a well-known pimp to those people gave the money, Mohammed Latif by name. So much for the servant. What about the Englishman – our friend here? How did they get rid of him? Money again.'

Fielding rose to his feet, supported by murmurs and exclamations, for no one yet suspected his integrity.

'Oh, I'm being misunderstood, apologies,' said the Major offensively. 'I didn't mean they bribed Mr Fielding.'

'Then what do you mean?'

'They paid the other Indian to make you late – Godbole. He was saying his prayers. I know those prayers!'

'That's ridiculous . . .' He sat down again, trembling with rage; person after person was being dragged into the mud.

1 Major Callendar, with his network of spies, has been established by this point as the primary stirrer amongst the Anglo-Indians (see extract from Chapter 11 and commentary, pp. 133–5).

Having shot this bolt, the Major prepared the next. 'Heaslop also found out something from his mother. Aziz paid a herd of natives to suffocate her in a cave. That was the end of her, or would have been, only she got out. Nicely planned, wasn't it? Neat. Then he could go on with the girl. He and she and a guide, provided by the same Mohammed Latif. Guide now can't be found. Pretty.' His voice broke into a roar. 'It's not the time for sitting down. It's the time for action. Call in the troops and clear the bazaars.'[2]

The Major's outbursts were always discounted, but he made everyone uneasy on this occasion. The crime was even worse than they had supposed - the unspeakable limit of cynicism, untouched since 1857.[3] Fielding forgot his anger on poor old Godbole's behalf, and became thoughtful; the evil was propagating in every direction, it seemed to have an existence of its own, apart from anything that was done or said by individuals, and he understood better why both Aziz and Hamidullah had been inclined to lie down and die. His adversary saw that he was in trouble, and now ventured to say, 'I suppose nothing that's said inside the Club will go outside the Club?' winking the while at Lesley.

'Why should it?' responded Lesley.

'Oh, nothing. I only heard a rumour that a certain member here present has been seeing the prisoner this afternoon. You can't run with the hare and hunt with the hounds, at least not in this country.'

'Does anyone here present want to?'

Fielding was determined not to be drawn again. He had something to say, but it should be at his own moment. The attack failed to mature, because the Collector did not support it. Attention shifted from him for a time. Then the buzz of women broke out again. The door had been opened by Ronny.

The young man looked exhausted and tragic, also gentler than usual. He always showed deference to his superiors, but now it came straight from his heart. He seemed to appeal for their protection in the insult that had befallen him, and they, in instinctive homage, rose to their feet. But every human act in the East is tainted with officialism, and while honouring him they condemned Aziz and India. Fielding realized this, and he remained seated. It was an ungracious, a caddish thing to do, perhaps an unsound thing to do, but he felt he had been passive long enough, and that he might be drawn into the wrong current if he did not make a stand. Ronny, who had not seen him, said in husky tones, 'Oh, please – please all sit down, I only want to listen to what has been decided.'

'Heaslop, I'm telling them I'm against any show of force,' said the Collector apologetically. 'I don't know whether you will feel as I do, but that is how I am situated. When the verdict is obtained, it will be another matter.'

'You are sure to know best; I have no experience, I can't tell.'

'How is your mother, old boy?'

'Better, thank you. I wish everyone would sit down.'

2 A reference to General Dyer's actions at Amritsar in April 1919, when about 1,600 Indians were killed or wounded under British orders in the public meeting ground called the Jallianwallah Bagh.

3 The year of the 'Indian Mutiny', when Indian sepoys (soldiers) turned against the British in several towns and cities across India.

'Some have never got up,' the young soldier said. 'And the Major brings us an excellent report of Miss Quested,' Turton went on.

'I do, I do, I'm satisfied.'

'You thought badly of her earlier, did you not, Major? That's why I refused bail.'

Callendar laughed with friendly inwardness, and said:

'Heaslop, Heaslop, next time bail's wanted, ring up the old doctor before giving it; his shoulders are broad, and, speaking in the strictest confidence, don't take the old doctor's opinion too seriously. He's a blithering idiot, we can always leave it at that, but he'll do the little he can towards keeping in quod[4] the –' He broke off with affected politeness. 'Oh, but he has one of his friends here.'

The subaltern called, 'Stand up, you swine.'

'Mr Fielding, what has prevented you from standing up?' said the Collector, entering the fray at last. It was the attack for which Fielding had waited, and to which he must reply.

'May I make a statement, sir?'

'Certainly.'

Seasoned and self-contained, devoid of the fervours of nationality or youth, the schoolmaster did what was for him a comparatively easy thing. He stood up and said, 'I believe Dr Aziz to be innocent.'

'You have a right to hold that opinion if you choose, but pray is that any reason why you should insult Mr Heaslop?'

'May I conclude my statement?'

'Certainly.'

'I am waiting for the verdict of the courts. If he is guilty I resign from my service, and leave India. I resign from the Club now.'

'Hear, hear!' said voices, not entirely hostile, for they liked the fellow for speaking out.

'You have not answered my question. Why did you not stand when Mr Heaslop entered?'

'With all deference, sir, I am not here to answer questions, but to make a personal statement, and I have concluded it.'

'May I ask whether you have taken over charge of this District?'

Fielding moved towards the door.

'One moment, Mr Fielding. You are not to go yet, please. Before you leave the Club, from which you do very well to resign, you will express some detestation of the crime, and you will apologize to Mr Heaslop.'

'Are you speaking to me officially, sir?'

The Collector, who never spoke otherwise, was so infuriated that he lost his head. He cried: 'Leave this room at once, and I deeply regret that I demeaned myself by meeting you at the station. You have sunk to the level of your associates; you are weak, weak, that is what is wrong with you –'

'I want to leave the room, but cannot while this gentleman prevents me,' said Fielding lightly; the subaltern had got across his path.

4 British slang for jail.

'Let him go,' said Ronny, almost in tears.

It was the only appeal that could have saved the situation. Whatever Heaslop wished must be done. There was a slight scuffle at the door, from which Fielding was propelled, a little more quickly than is natural, into the room where the ladies were playing cards. 'Fancy if I'd fallen or got angry,' he thought. Of course he was a little angry. His peers had never offered him violence or called him weak before, besides, Heaslop had heaped coals of fire on his head. He wished he had not picked the quarrel over poor suffering Heaslop, when there were cleaner issues at hand.

However, there it was, done, muddled through, and to cool himself and regain mental balance he went onto the upper veranda for a moment, where the first object he saw was the Marabar Hills. At this distance and hour they leapt into beauty; they were Monsalvat, Valhalla, the towers of a cathedral peopled with saints and heroes, and covered with flowers.[5] What miscreant lurked in them, presently to be detected by the activities of the law? Who was the guide, and had he been found yet? What was the 'echo' of which the girl complained? He did not know, but presently he would know. Great is information, and she shall prevail. It was the last moment of the light, and as he gazed at the Marabar Hills they seemed to move graciously towards him like a queen, and their charm became the sky's. At the moment they vanished they were everywhere, the cool benediction of the night descended, the stars sparkled, and the whole universe was a hill. Lovely, exquisite moment – but passing the Englishman with averted face and on swift wings. He experienced nothing himself; it was as if someone had told him there was such a moment, and he was obliged to believe. And he felt dubious and discontented suddenly, and wondered whether he was really and truly successful as a human being. After forty years' experience, he had learned to manage his life and make the best of it on advanced European lines, had developed his personality, explored his limitations, controlled his passions – and he had done it all without becoming either pedantic or worldly. A creditable achievement, but as the moment passed he felt he ought to have been working at something else the whole time – he didn't know at what, never would know, never could know, and that was why he felt sad.[6]

Major Callendar's comment that they should 'Call in the troops and clear the bazaars' appears to be an allusion to the the Amritsar Incident of 1919, while the year of the 'Indian Mutiny', 1857, is invoked directly (as it had already been on p. 178 and will be again by Aziz towards the end of 'Caves' on p. 273). A key

5 Monsalvat is an alternative name for Mont Salvage, the mountain on which is situated the castle of the Holy Grail in Arthurian legend (sometimes taken to be Monserrat in Spain). Valhalla is Odin's hall at Asgard in Old Norse mythology.

6 While emphasis is invariably placed on Mrs Moore's and Adela's experience of the caves, this paragraph is the closest Fielding gets to crisis and to understanding something of the effect of the Marabar Hills: a Forsterian muddle of discontented thoughts and self-doubt.

aspect to the aftermath of the Mutiny was the brutal recriminations sought by British officers for alleged assaults and rapes of English women. The air of the Mutiny is explicitly suggested by the likening of the Club to the Residency at Lucknow at the start of the chapter, on p. 188, because this was the scene of a famous siege in 1857. The Club, after the attack on Adela, generates similar fear and recriminations to those evident at the time of the Amritsar Massacre, which was ordered by a British officer, General Dyer, after an attack on an English missionary woman. Perhaps most directly, it is suggested on p. 220 that Indians ought to be made to crawl to the caves on their hands and knees whenever they see an Englishwoman, and this is in reference to an order imposed by the English at Amritsar, forcing Indians to crawl along the street where the missionary was assaulted.

This context is important to the passage that focuses on male hysteria at the threat to 'their' women, 'the unspeakable limit of cynicism': rape. It is important to the dynamics of the scene that Adela is not present: her role of 'victim' is assumed in her absence by the man to whom she is betrothed. Fielding's putative insult of Heaslop at the Club, when he refuses to stand, thus offers another way of seeing gender relations. In the passage it is said that Aziz, by supposedly assaulting Adela, has also given an 'insult' to Ronny. That Fielding can also insult Heaslop in this way suggests two things: that Adela's ordeal is shared by Heaslop and that rape is an issue between men – that Heaslop, more than the absent and hidden-away Adela, is the public victim, the official injured party. This reading is accentuated in the colonial context, where Heaslop's manhood seems more challenged by the attack on his fiancée by a subordinate and a native – raising the issue of the sexual threat that is commonly associated with both India and Africa in the Western colonial imagination. In this same vein, Aziz's wife is assumed by McBryde, when he sees her photograph, to be a prostitute – which is the reading that would follow from the idea of Aziz as sexual threat and Indian women as commodities. Their identities are reduced by the Anglo-Indian Club to a projection of British fears about violated property and sexual threats. The incident at the Club is considered in an article by Brenda Silver[1] in terms of 'periphrasis': using many words where one would do (the prime example is the fact that 'rape' is never mentioned but constantly talked about). Members of the Anglo-Indian community generate numerous views, theories and accusations themselves, but they silence Adela, keep her in hiding, as though she were in purdah or locked away like Aziz's photograph of his wife in the drawer. While the hollow Marabar Caves symbolise the absent event at the centre of the narrative, the hysterical reactions at the Club stand in for Adela's, or Aziz's, testimony.

1 Brenda R. Silver, 'Periphrasis, Power and Rape in *A Passage to India*', *Novel* 22, Fall 1988, pp. 86–105.

Chapter 23

Focusing on Mrs Moore, who has escaped Aziz's trial to return to England, this chapter discusses the 'twilight of the double vision'. It also contains Mrs Moore's exit from the novel as well as her departure from India.

Lady Mellanby, wife to the Lieutenant-Governor of the Province, had been gratified by the appeal addressed to her by the ladies of Chandrapore. She could not do anything – besides, she was sailing for England; but she desired to be informed if she could show sympathy in any other way. Mrs Turton replied that Mr Heaslop's mother was trying to get a passage, but had delayed too long, and all the boats were full; could Lady Mellanby use her influence? Not even Lady Mellanby could expand the dimensions of a P. and O.,[1] but she was a very, very nice woman, and she actually wired offering the unknown and obscure old lady accommodation in her own reserved cabin. It was like a gift from heaven; humble and grateful, Ronny could not but reflect that there are compensations for every woe. His name was familiar at Government House owing to poor Adela, and now Mrs Moore would stamp it on Lady Mellanby's imagination, as they journeyed across the Indian Ocean and up the Red Sea. He had a return of tenderness for his mother – as we do for our relatives when they receive conspicuous and unexpected honour. She was not negligible, she could still arrest the attention of a high official's wife.

So Mrs Moore had all she wished; she escaped the trial, the marriage, and the Hot Weather; she would return to England in comfort and distinction, and see her other children. At her son's suggestion, and by her own desire, she departed. But she accepted her good luck without enthusiasm. She had come to that state where the horror of the universe and its smallness are both visible at the same time – the twilight of the double vision in which so many elderly people are involved. If this world is not to our taste, 'well, at all events there is Heaven, Hell, Annihilation – one or other of those large things, that huge scenic background of stars, fires, blue or black air. All heroic endeavour, and all that is known as art, assumes that there is such a background, just as all practical endeavour, when the world is to our taste, assumes that the world is all. But in the twilight of the double vision a spiritual muddledom is set up for which no high-sounding words can be found; we can neither act nor refrain from action, we can neither ignore nor respect Infinity. Mrs Moore had always inclined to resignation. As soon as she landed in India it seemed to her good, and when she saw the water flowing through the mosque-tank, or the Ganges, or the moon, caught in the shawl of night with all the other stars, it seemed a beautiful goal and an easy one. To be

1 The Peninsular and Oriental Steam and Navigation Company was the largest shipping company for travellers to the East. David Lean opens his film of Forster's novel in their offices in London.

one with the universe! So dignified and simple. But there was always some little duty to be performed first, some new card to be turned up from the diminishing pack and placed, and, while she was pottering about, the Marabar struck its gong.

What had spoken to her in that scoured-out cavity of the granite? What dwelt in the first of the caves? Something very old and very small. Before time, it was before space also. Something snub-nosed, incapable of generosity – the undying worm itself. Since hearing its voice, she had not entertained one large thought, she was actually envious of Adela. All this fuss over a frightened girl! Nothing had happened, 'and if it had,' she found herself thinking with the cynicism of a withered priestess, 'if it had, there are worse evils than love.' The unspeakable attempt presented itself to her as love: in a cave, in a church – boum, it amounts to the same. Visions are supposed to entail profundity, but – wait till you get one, dear reader![2] The abyss also may be petty, the serpent of eternity made of maggots; her constant thought was: 'Less attention should be paid to my future daughter-in-law and more to me, there is no sorrow like my sorrow,' although when the attention was paid she rejected it irritably.

Her son couldn't escort her to Bombay, for the local situation continued acute, and all officials had to remain at their posts. Antony couldn't come either, in case he never returned to give his evidence. So she travelled with no one who could remind her of the past. This was a relief. The heat had drawn back a little before its next advance, and the journey was not unpleasant. As she left Chandrapore the moon, full again, shone over the Ganges and touched the shrinking channels into threads of silver, then veered and looked into her window. The swift and comfortable mail-train slid with her through the night, and all the next day she was rushing through Central India, through landscapes that were baked and bleached but had not the hopeless melancholy of the plain. She watched the indestructible life of man and his changing faces, and the houses he has built for himself and God, and they appeared to her not in terms of her own trouble but as things to see. There was, for instance, a place called Asirgarh[3] which she passed at sunset and identified on a map – an enormous fortress among wooded hills. No one had ever mentioned Asirgarh to her, but it had huge and noble bastions and to the right of them was a mosque. She forgot it. Ten minutes later, Asirgarh reappeared. The mosque was to the left of the bastions now. The train in its descent through the Vindhyas[4] had described a semicircle round Asirgarh. What could she connect it with except its own name? Nothing; she knew no one who lived there. But it had looked at her twice and seemed to say: 'I do not vanish.' She woke in the middle of the night with a start, for the train was falling over the western cliff. Moonlit pinnacles rushed up at her like the fringes of a sea; then a brief episode of pain, the real sea, and

2 An unusual and rare address. Probably the most famous such breaking of the narrative frame is in *Jane Eyre* when Jane declares 'Reader, I married him' at the opening of Chapter 38.
3 Asirgarh is a hill-fortress in Madhya Pradash. Mention of it occurs again in 'Temple' (e.g. p. 292).
4 A low mountain range running east to west in central India.

the soupy dawn of Bombay. 'I have not seen the right places,' she thought, as she saw embayed in the platforms of the Victoria terminus the end of the rails that had carried her over a continent and could never carry her back. She would never visit Asirgarh or the other untouched places; neither Delhi nor Agra nor the Rajputana cities nor Kashmir, nor the obscurer marvels that had sometimes shone through men's speech: the bilingual rock of Girnar, the statue of Shri Belgola, the ruins of Mandu and Hampi, temples of Khajuraho, gardens of Shalimar.[5] As she drove through the huge city which the West has built and abandoned with a gesture of despair, she longed to stop, though it was only Bombay, and disentangle the hundred Indias that passed each other in its streets. The feet of the horses moved her on, and presently the boat sailed and thous-ands of cocoanut palms appeared all round the anchorage and climbed the hills to wave her farewell. 'So you thought an echo was India; you took the Marabar Caves as final?' they laughed. 'What have we in common with them, or they with Asirgarh? Goodbye!' Then the steamer rounded Colaba,[6] the continent swung about, the cliff of the Ghats melted into the haze of a tropic sea. Lady Mellanby turned up and advised her not to stand in the heat; 'We are safely out of the frying-pan,' said Lady Mellanby, 'it will never do to fall into the fire.'

The idea of travelling is important to an appreciation of the book, which from the first sentence emphasises the distance and the difference between places. The title of the novel, from a poem by Walt Whitman, refers to several journeys to India: the English colonial enterprise, Mrs Moore's and Adela's voyage (and Adela's subsequent desire to find the 'real' India), and the train ride to the caves, as well as, metaphorically, the reader's introduction to India by Forster.

Mrs Moore has had a vision, but it has not helped her to make contact with others or with God. Approaching death, she becomes increasingly conscious of a lack of spiritual response in the universe. Her vision has revealed to her simply the 'undying worm': an intimation of death, whose approach she cannot come to spiritual terms with. She again considers it a 'muddle' for which can be found no 'high-sounding words', as Fielding called a 'mystery' in Chapter 7 (see pp. 127–32), and here we should remember the religious sense of the word, as in 'Mystery Plays'.

The last extract I discussed also has a resonance in this passage. The sympathy expressed for Ronny by the members of the Club, in the light of his 'insults' from Aziz and from Fielding, is put in context by his reflection that the

5 Forster is here suggesting the wide variety of Indian history and culture. The Girnar Hills in Gujarat have inscriptions in two languages, the statue of Shri Belgola is an enormous nude of a Jain sage in Karnataka, Mandu and Hampi were ancient royal cities, the temples of Khajuraho have erotic carvings such as those Adela sees in Lean's film of the novel, and the Shalimar gardens in Kashmir and Lahore were built by the Moghul emperors.

6 A promontory off Bombay Island.

incident has had its 'compensations': making his name known to influential people.

Mrs Moore's crisis seemingly occurs because neither the 'practical' nor the 'heroic' endeavour, as the narrator calls them, seem worthwhile any longer. With Mrs Moore's vision, as Benita Parry says, 'the novel passes back to the world-rejecting atheist tradition of the Jains, a post-Vedic heterodoxy of the C5th BC ... rooted in the ancient, aboriginal metaphysics of primal, Dravidian India'[1] (see p. 225 for mention of the Jains). Fielding says later, with respect to Mrs Moore, that 'it is difficult, as we get on in life, to resist the supernatural' (p. 241). Mrs Moore has indeed been drawn to 'those large things' beyond the material world but has been unable to think about them since the Marabar incident. Neither the material nor the spiritual world offers her any comfort.

Chapter 24

Extract from chapter 24: the trial scene at which Adela 'renounced her own people'. The centrepiece of the novel and the public confrontation between Indians and representatives of the Raj.

The court was crowded and of course very hot, and the first person Adela noticed in it was the humblest of all who were present, a person who had no bearing officially upon the trial: the man who pulled the punkah. Almost naked, and splendidly formed, he sat on a raised platform near the back, in the middle of the central gangway, and he caught her attention as she came in, and he seemed to control the proceedings. He had the strength and beauty that sometimes come to flower in Indians of low birth. When that strange race nears the dust and is condemned as untouchable,[1] then nature remembers the physical perfection that she accomplished elsewhere, and throws out a god – not many, but one here and

1 Benita Parry, *Delusions and Discoveries*, London: Verso, 1998.

1 Untouchables are the underclass of the Hindu caste system. According to India's ancient literature, Aryan priests divided society into a basic caste system sometime around the time of Christ, creating the four great hereditary social divisions that survive to this day. The priests placed themselves at the summit of this caste system with the title of earthly gods, or Brahmans. Godbole is one of these. Next were the warriors, the Kshatriyas, then the farmers and merchants, the Vaisyas, and fourth the labourers, the Sudras. Those outside the social order were the people of no caste, the Harijans or Untouchables. These were the Dravidians, the aboriginal inhabitants of India, but the category swelled to include outcasts of various kinds.

there, to prove to society how little its categories impress her. This man would have been notable anywhere; among the thin-hammed, flat-chested mediocrities of Chandrapore he stood out as divine, yet he was of the city, its garbage had nourished him, he would end on its rubbish-heaps. Pulling the rope towards him, relaxing it rhythmically, sending swirls of air over others, receiving none himself, he seemed apart from human destinies, a male Fate, a winnower of souls. Opposite him, also on a platform, sat the little Assistant Magistrate, cultivated, self-conscious and conscientious. The punkah-wallah was none of these things; he scarcely knew that he existed and did not understand why the court was fuller than usual, indeed he did not know that it was fuller than usual, didn't even know he worked a fan, though he thought he pulled a rope. Something in his aloofness impressed the girl from middle-class England, and rebuked the narrowness of her sufferings. In virtue of what had she collected this roomful of people together? Her particular brand of opinions, and the suburban Jehovah who sanctified them – by what right did they claim so much importance in the world, and assume the title of civilization? Mrs Moore – she looked round, but Mrs Moore was far away on the sea; it was the kind of question they might have discussed on the voyage out, before the old lady had turned disagreeable and queer.

While thinking of Mrs Moore she heard sounds, which gradually grew more distinct. The epoch-making trial had started, and the Superintendent of Police was opening the case for the prosecution.

Mr McBryde was not at pains to be an interesting speaker; he left eloquence to the defence, who would require it. His attitude was, 'Everyone knows the man's guilty, and I am obliged to say so in public before he goes to the Andamans.'[2] He made no moral or emotional appeal, and it was only by degrees that the studied negligence of his manner made itself felt, and lashed part of the audience to fury. Laboriously did he describe the genesis of the picnic. The prisoner had met Miss Quested at an entertainment given by the Principal of Government College, and had there conceived his intentions concerning her: prisoner was a man of loose life, as documents found upon him at his arrest would testify, also his fellow assistant, Dr Panna Lal, was in a position to throw light on his character, and Major Callendar himself would speak. Here Mr McBryde paused. He wanted to keep the proceedings as clean as possible, but Oriental Pathology, his favourite theme, lay all around him, and he could not resist it. Taking off his spectacles, as was his habit before enunciating a general truth, he looked into them sadly, and remarked that the darker races are physically attracted by the fairer, but not vice versa – not a matter for bitterness this, not a matter for abuse, but just a fact which any scientific observer will confirm.

'Even when the lady is so uglier than the gentleman?'

The comment fell from nowhere, from the ceiling perhaps. It was the first interruption, and the Magistrate felt bound to censure it. 'Turn that man out,' he said. One of the native policemen took hold of a man who had said nothing, and

2 Islands in the Bay of Bengal to which convicts were shipped. People from the islands are described in stereotypically colonialist terms in Arthur Conan Doyle's Sherlock Holmes story 'The Sign of Four'.

turned him out roughly. Mr McBryde resumed his spectacles and proceeded. But the comment had upset Miss Quested. Her body resented being called ugly, and trembled.

'Do you feel faint, Adela?' asked Miss Derek, who tended her with loving indignation.

'I never feel anything else, Nancy. I shall get through, but it's awful, awful.'

This led to the first of a series of scenes. Her friends began to fuss around her, and the Major called out: 'I must have better arrangements than this made for my patient; why isn't she given a seat on the platform? She gets no air.'

Mr Das looked annoyed and said: 'I shall be happy to accommodate Miss Quested with a chair up here in view of the particular circumstances of her health.' The chuprassies[3] passed up not one chair but several, and the entire party followed Adela onto the platform, Mr Fielding being the only European who remained in the body of the hall.

'That's better,' remarked Mrs Turton, as she settled herself.

'Thoroughly desirable change for several reasons,' replied the Major.

The Magistrate knew that he ought to censure this remark, but did not dare to. Callendar saw that he was afraid, and called out authoritatively, 'Right, McBryde, go ahead now; sorry to have interrupted you.'

'Are you all right yourselves?' asked the Superintendent.

'We shall do, we shall do.'

'Go on, Mr Das, we are not here to disturb you,' said the Collector patronizingly. Indeed, they had not so much disturbed the trial as taken charge of it.

While the prosecution continued, Miss Quested examined the hall – timidly at first, as though it would scorch her eyes. She observed to left and right of the punkah-man many a half-known face. Beneath her were gathered all the wreckage of her silly attempt to see India – the people she had met at the Bridge Party, the man and his wife who hadn't sent their carriage, the old man who would lend his car, various servants, villagers, officials, and the prisoner himself. There he sat – strong, neat little Indian with very black hair, and pliant hands. She viewed him without special emotion. Since they last met, she had elevated him into a principle of evil, but now he seemed to be what he had always been – a slight acquaintance. He was negligible, devoid of significance, dry like a bone, and though he was 'guilty' no atmosphere of sin surrounded him. 'I suppose he *is* guilty. Can I possibly have made a mistake?' she thought. For this question still occurred to her intellect, though since Mrs Moore's departure it had ceased to trouble her conscience.

Pleader Mahmoud Ali now arose, and asked with ponderous and unjudged irony whether his client could be accommodated on the platform too: even Indians felt unwell sometimes, though naturally Major Callendar did not think so, being in charge of a Government hospital. 'Another example of their exquisite sense of humour,' sang Miss Derek. Ronny looked at Mr Das to see how he would handle the difficulty, and Mr Das became agitated, and snubbed Pleader Mahmoud Ali severely.

3 Messengers, but also general dogsbodies.

'Excuse me –' It was the turn of the eminent barrister from Calcutta. He was a fine-looking man, large and bony, with gray closely cropped hair. 'We object to the presence of so many European ladies and gentlemen up on the platform,' he said in an Oxford voice. 'They will have the effect of intimidating our witnesses. Their place is with the rest of the public in the body of the hall. We have no objection to Miss Quested remaining on the platform, since she has been unwell; we shall extend every courtesy to her throughout, despite the scientific truths revealed to us by the District Superintendent of Police; but we do object to the others.'

'Oh, cut the cackle and let's have the verdict,' the Major growled.

The distinguished visitor gazed at the Magistrate respectfully.

'I agree to that,' said Mr Das, hiding his face desperately in some papers. 'It was only to Miss Quested that I gave permission to sit up here. Her friends should be so excessively kind as to climb down.'

'Well done, Das, quite sound,' said Ronny with devastating honesty.

'Climb down, indeed, what incredible impertinence!' Mrs Turton cried.

'Do come quietly, Mary,' murmured her husband.

'Hi! My patient can't be left unattended.'

'Do you object to the Civil Surgeon remaining, Mr Amritrao?'[4]

'I should object. A platform confers authority.'

'Even when it's one foot high; so come along all,' said the Collector, trying not to laugh.

'Thank you very much, sir,' said Mr Das, greatly relieved. 'Thank you, Mr Heaslop; thank you, ladies all.'

And the party, including Miss Quested, descended from its rash eminence. The news of their humiliation spread quickly, and people jeered outside. Their special chairs followed them. Mahmoud Ali (who was quite silly and useless with hatred) objected even to these; by whose authority had special chairs been introduced, why had the Nawab Bahadur not been given one? etc. People began to talk all over the room, about chairs ordinary and special, strips of carpet, platforms one foot high.

But the little excursion had a good effect on Miss Quested's nerves. She felt easier now that she had seen all the people who were in the room. It was like knowing the worst. She was sure now that she should come through 'all right' – that is to say, without spiritual disgrace, and she passed the good news on to Ronny and Mrs Turton. They were too much agitated with the defeat to British prestige to be interested. From where she sat, she could see the renegade Mr Fielding. She had had a better view of him from the platform, and knew that an Indian child perched on his knee. He was watching the proceedings, watching her. When their eyes met, he turned his away, as if direct intercourse was of no interest to him.

4 The Calcutta barrister's name seems to be another allusion to the Amritsar incident.

Tangentially, this extract is concerned with the right of the British to rule India, not just in political terms, but in the most fundamental sense of anyone's right to impose themselves on others: 'by what right did they claim so much importance in the world, and assume the title of civilization?'. The extract opens with a figure Forster thought crucial to the novel. The punka-wallah is representative of the majority of the Indian people, who Forster saw as largely unconcerned with the raj, but is also a figure who exemplifies his main theme of the universe's indifference to human concerns: this aloof 'god' who declines the invitation to enter into the drama around him is one of nature's examples of physical perfection, born into what Forster sees as the chaos of Hindu life (like Krishna in the 'Temple' section). The beauty of the lowliest member of the courtroom illustrates the artificiality of human forms of exclusion, from the Indian caste system to the English class system. The punkah-wallah thus represents the continuity, stoicism and resilience of what Adela has called 'the real India'. For this reason, Forster agreed with Santha Rama Rau that the play adaptation should end on the impassive figure of the punkah-wallah operating the fan in the now deserted courtroom after the commotion of the trial (see pp. 107–8).

From another perspective, Forster's depiction of the beautiful and serene punkah-wallah can be read as conforming to the stereotype of the sensuous and mystical East. Yet this is an easy and dangerous caricature of which Forster is acutely aware. In the middle of the extract, he explores this Orientalist construction of the East. Because India has been figured so often in Western writing as a place of sexual excess, much proclivity and little inhibition, McBryde feels entirely justified in assuming Aziz must have attacked Adela (after the trial, Aziz alludes to this stereotype of the 'licentious oriental imagination' (p. 270)). The exchange at the trial between McBryde and an unknown indian spectator (p. 222) restates the idea of Indians as a sexual threat and can be read in terms of colonial psychology. McBryde's belief that the darker races are attracted to the fairer arguably asserts a fear of theft and violation while the response from the audience that Aziz is more attractive than Adela exposes another fear of sexual threat: the seductive allure of the East. The implication is that Adela as representative Englishwoman may be drawn to Aziz, as representative Indian man. This is of course, once more, all argument between men. In terms of colonial discourse it is also important that McBryde states his opinion as 'a fact which any scientific observer will confirm'. This is a familiar Orientalist standpoint, which claims science as the preserve of the West: an antidote to Eastern mysticism that can be claimed by any European in any argument.

Lastly, the need for the Anglo-Indians of Chandrapore to assert their authority, thereby implying that they feel it is either 'hollow' or under threat, occurs when they take the stage. The spurious superiority conferred by 'chairs ordinary and special, strips of carpet, platforms one foot high' is used by the Anglo-Indians to increase their chance of winning the trial (it can be put in this way because they see Aziz's trial as a test case for their right to rule). Consequently, Mr Das has to ask them literally to 'climb down'.

The Start of Chapter 33

The opening of the final section, 'Temple', this chapter contains Forster's transcription into fiction of his own experience of the Gokul Ashtami festival (described in *The Hill of Devi*), from which he drew many of his beliefs about Hinduism and India.

Some hundreds of miles westward of the Marabar Hills, and two years later in time, Professor Narayan Godbole stands in the presence of God. God is not born yet – that will occur at midnight ' – but He has also been born centuries ago, nor can He ever be born, because He is the Lord of the Universe, who transcends human processes. He is, was not, is not, was. He and Professor Godbole stood at opposite ends of the same strip of carpet.

> 'Tukaram, Tukaram,[1]
> Thou art my father and mother and everybody.
> Tukaram, Tukaram,
> Thou art my father and mother and everybody.
> Tukaram, Tukaram,
> Thou art my father and mother and everybody.
> Tukaram, Tukaram,
> Thou art my father and mother and everybody.
> Tukaram . . .'

This corridor in the palace at Mau[2] opened through other corridors into a courtyard. It was of beautiful hard white stucco, but its pillars and vaulting could scarcely be seen behind coloured rags, iridescent balls, chandeliers of opaque pink glass, and murky photographs framed crookedly. At the end was the small but famous shrine of the dynastic cult, and the God to be born was largely a silver image the size of a teaspoon. Hindus sat on either side of the carpet where they could find room, or overflowed into the adjoining corridors and the courtyard – Hindus, Hindus only, mild-featured men, mostly villagers, for whom anything outside their villages passed in a dream. They were the toiling ryot, whom some call the real India. Mixed with them sat a few tradesmen out of the little town, officials, courtiers, scions of the ruling house. Schoolboys kept inefficient order. The assembly was in a tender, happy state unknown to an English crowd; it seethed like a beneficent potion. When the villagers broke cordon for a glimpse of

1 A Maratha saint (the Maratha people live chiefly in Maharashtra). This scene should be compared to Forster's account of the Gokul Ashtami festival he attended. Gokul was the birthplace of Krishna.

2 There are several Maus in India, but the one Forster said had a slight connection with his fictional Mau is probably that in Central India, as this is where Fielding is said to be touring.

the silver image, a most beautiful and radiant expression came into their faces, a beauty in which there was nothing personal, for it caused them all to resemble one another during thee moment of its indwelling, and only when it was withdrawn did they revert to individual clods. And so with the music. Music there was, but from so many sources that the sum total was untrammelled. The braying banging crooning melted into a single mass which trailed round the palace before joining the thunder. Rain fell at intervals throughout the night.

It was the turn of Professor Godbole's choir. As Minister of Education, he gained this special honour. When the previous group of singers dispersed into the crowd, he pressed forward from the back, already in full voice, that the chain of sacred sounds might be uninterrupted. He was barefoot and in white, he wore a pale blue turban; his gold pince-nez had caught in a jasmine garland, and lay sideways down his nose. He and six colleagues who supported him clashed their cymbals, hit small drums, droned upon a portable harmonium, and sang:

> 'Tukaram, Tukaram,
> Thou art my father and mother and everybody.
> Tukaram, Tukaram,
> Thou art my father and mother and everybody.
> Tukaram, Tukaram . . .'

They sang not even to the God who confronted them, but to a saint; they did not one thing which the non-Hindu would feel dramatically correct; this approaching triumph of India was a muddle (as we call it), a frustration of reason and form. Where was the God Himself,[3] in whose honour the congregation had gathered? Indistinguishable in the jumble of His own altar, huddled out of sight amid images of inferior descent, smothered under rose-leaves, overhung by oleographs, outblazed by golden tablets representing the Rajah's[4] ancestors, and entirely obscured, when the wind blew, by the tattered foliage of a banana. Hundreds of electric lights had been lit in His honour (worked by an engine whose thumps destroyed the rhythm of the hymn). Yet His face could not be seen. Hundreds of His silver dishes were piled around Him with the minimum of effect. The inscriptions which the poets of the state had composed were hung where they could not be read, or had twitched their drawing-pins out of the stucco, and one of them (composed in English to indicate His universality) consisted, by an unfortunate slip of the draughtsman, of the words, 'God si Love.'

God si Love. Is this the final message of India?

This description of the Gokul Ashtami festival is based on Forster's own experience at Dewas Senior (see the extract from *The Hill of Devi* on pp. 30–2).

3 Krishna.
4 A ruler or landlord. The shortened term 'raj' thus means 'rule'.

It opens the third section of the novel by again referring to the Marabar Hills, as though they are a kind of Greenwich for Forster: the place from which time and space are measured.

Many of the book's themes, of inclusion, muddle, and travel, are developed in the 'Temple' section. Later, we are told that the God, and other offerings thrown into the river, were: 'emblems of passage; a passage not easy, not now, not here, not to be apprehended except when it is unattainable' (p. 309). This mystery and misunderstanding spills over into the metaphysical in all aspects of the book – particularly in this extract which culminates in the universal but misspelled message 'God si Love'. The chief Indian exponent of muddle is Godbole, who is privileged with praeternatural powers and with a 'telepathic appeal' that links him with Mrs Moore. He, typically, says 'everything is anything and nothing something' (p. 186). Yet Forster also tries here to suggest that this philosophy is fundamental to Hinduism, particularly in the description of Krishna: 'He is, was not, is not, was'. This is a logic beyond 'human processes' and can no more be understood than the Marabar Caves can. Its spirit of universality and inclusion is suggested by Forster's depiction of 'muddle' but also by the description of the effect of the ceremony on the people: 'When the villagers broke cordon for a glimpse of the silver image, a most beautiful and radiant expression came into their faces, a beauty in which there was nothing personal, for it caused them all to resemble one another.'

The Closing Pages of the Novel

At the end of chapter 37, reunited for the first time after they parted at Chandrapore, Aziz and Fielding, who have both since married, consider whether they can be friends. This is a much-debated scene and can be read in many different ways depending upon one's overall approach to the novel.

All the way back to Mau they wrangled about politics. Each had hardened since Chandrapore, and a good knock-about proved enjoyable. They trusted each other, although they were going to part, perhaps because they were going to part. Fielding had 'no further use for politeness,' he said, meaning that the British Empire really can't be abolished because it's rude. Aziz retorted, 'Very well, and we have no use for you,' and glared at him with abstract hate. Fielding said: 'Away from us, Indians go to seed at once. Look at the King-Emperor High School! Look at you, forgetting your medicine and going back to charms. Look at your poems.' – 'Jolly good poems, I'm getting published Bombay side.' – 'Yes, and what do they say? Free our women and India will be free. Try it, my lad. Free your own lady in the first place, and see who'll wash Ahmed, Karim and Jamila's faces. A nice situation!'

Aziz grew more excited. He rose in his stirrups and pulled at his horse's head in the hope it would rear. Then he should feel in a battle. He cried: 'Clear out, all you Turtons and Burtons. We wanted to know you ten years back – now it's too late. If we see you and sit on your committees, it's for political reasons, don't you make any mistake.' His horse did rear. 'Clear out, clear out, I say. Why are we put to so much suffering? We used to blame you, now we blame ourselves, we grow wiser. Until England is in difficulties we keep silent, but in the next European war – aha, aha! Then is our time.' He paused, and the scenery, though it smiled, fell like a gravestone on any human hope. They cantered past a temple to Hanuman[1] – God so loved the world that he took monkey's flesh upon him – and past a Saivite temple,[2] which invited to lust, but under the semblance of eternity, its obscenities bearing no relation to those of our flesh and blood. They splashed through butterflies and frogs; great trees with leaves like plates rose among the brushwood. The divisions of daily life were returning, the shrine had almost shut.

'Who do you want instead of the English? The Japanese?' jeered Fielding, drawing rein.

'No, the Afghans. My own ancestors.'

'Oh, your Hindu friends will like that, won't they?'

'It will be arranged – a conference of oriental statesmen.'

'It will indeed be arranged.'

'Old story of "We will rob every man and rape every woman from Peshawar to Calcutta",[3] I suppose, which you get some nobody to repeat and then quote every week in the *Pioneer*[4] in order to frighten us into retaining you! We know!' Still he couldn't quite fit in Afghans at Mau, and, finding he was in a corner, made his horse rear again until he remembered that he had, or ought to have, a motherland. Then he shouted: 'India shall be a nation! No foreigners of any sort! Hindu and Moslem and Sikh and all shall be one! Hurrah! Hurrah for India! Hurrah! Hurrah!'

India a nation! What an apotheosis! Last comer to the drab nineteenth-century sisterhood! Waddling in at this hour of the world to take her seat! She, whose only peer was the Holy Roman Empire, she shall rank with Guatemala and Belgium perhaps! Fielding mocked again. And Aziz in an awful rage danced this way and that not knowing what to do, and cried: 'Down with the English anyhow. That's certain. Clear out, you fellows, double quick, I say. We may hate one another, but we hate you most. If I don't make you go, Ahmed will, Karim will, if it's fifty or five hundred years we shall get rid of you, yes, we shall drive every blasted Englishman into the sea, and then' – he rode against him furiously – 'and then,' he concluded, half kissing him, 'you and I shall be friends.'

1 The monkey general who helps Rama in the Sanskrit ancient epic *The Ramayana* ('story of Rama').
2 Temples to Shiva.
3 These cities were at the ends of the Grand Trunk Road. Aziz's reference to rape is not solely in relation to the accusations made against himself: they also allude to stories of Indians abusing English women at the time of the Mutiny in 1857 and Amritsar in 1919.
4 Aziz means the *Allahabad Pioneer*, a widely respected newspaper for which Kipling wrote.

'Why can't we be friends now?' said the other, holding him affectionately. 'It's what I want. It's what you want.'

But the horses didn't want it – they swerved apart; the earth didn't want it, sending up rocks through which riders must pass single-file; the temples, the tank, the jail, the palace, the birds, the carrion, the Guest House, that came into view as they issued from the gap and saw Mau beneath: they didn't want it, they said in their hundred voices, 'No, not yet,' and the sky said, 'No, not there.'

> Oh East is East, and West is West, and never the twain shall meet,
> Till Earth and Sky stand presently at God's great Judgment seat;
> But there is neither East nor West, Border, nor Breed, nor Birth,
> When two strong men stand face to face, though they come from the
> ends of the earth!
>
> (Kipling, 'The Ballad of East and West')

The whole of this first stanza of Kipling's famous ballad seems to stand in dialogue with the end of Forster's novel. Friendship is what both men want, yet the earth and the sky do not. Forster is again emphasising his symbolic geography: here, it is not British rule but the Indian soil that keeps Aziz and Fielding apart; in the second section, it is the Marabar Caves that are to blame for Mrs Moore's and Adela's crises; and back at the start of the first section, it is the sky, we were told on p. 32, that 'settles everything'. The ambiguity in this symbolism has allowed a wide variety of interpretations, and most of them have been touched upon earlier. So, I want here only to emphasise one way of thinking about this ending. The fact that Aziz and Fielding are parted is commonly thought to be a statement of the inability for an Indian and an Englander to be friends under the raj, but it is also a statement about the social unacceptability of two men being lovers in the early twentieth century. The book Forster wrote before *A Passage to India* was *Maurice*, a novel about a homosexual relationship across not races but classes. Though it remained unpublished until after Forster's death in 1970, if we place it in its proper place in Forster's writing it suggests that the contemporary reader might consider sexuality in Forster's last novel in a very different way from most readers prior to 1970. At the least, Fielding and Aziz are presented by Forster in homosocial environments: Aziz with Hamidullah and his other male friends, Fielding with Godbole and his boys' school. At the most, there are several pointers to a sexual tension between Aziz and Fielding (Aziz almost pays court to Fielding and behaves at times like a jealous lover, and in this finale they half-kiss and then embrace).

Ultimately, in a book in which almost no human contact results in happiness, *A Passage to India* suggests that politics is opposed to friendship: particularly that between Fielding and Aziz, who are on different sides of the colonial divide. Looking back, it is now clear that the book's tripartite structure even works on this level. At the end of 'Mosque', we are told: 'But they were friends, brothers. That part was settled, their compact had been subscribed by the photograph, they trusted one another, affection had triumphed for once in a way' (p. 133). At the end of 'Caves', Aziz and Fielding are separated and Fielding returns to England. This last section, 'Temple', concludes with a statement on the difficulty of their friendship: an ambivalent ending that is pessimistic about the present and only by implication optimistic about the future.

4

Further Reading

Recommended Editions and Further Reading

The best available version of the text is the Abinger Edition of 1978, edited by Oliver Stallybrass. The edition of the novel used in this study is that published in 2000 by Penguin: a reprint of the Abinger Edition without the Textual Notes on errors in and differences between previous editions.

The texts I would recommend students to read after finishing this book are as follows:

John Beer (ed.), A Passage to India*: Essays in Interpretation*, London: Macmillan, 1985.

A fine assembly of essays, which tend to see Forster's novel as either a socio-political text or a richly symbolical one. With an equal number of male and female contributors, the book constitutes a major re-examination of the text from a variety of perspectives, both thematic and structural.

Malcolm Bradbury (ed.), *E. M. Forster: A Passage to India*, London: Macmillan, 1970.

Bradbury's 'Casebook' is an excellent collection of critical essays up to 1970. Its emphasis is thus on questions of form, Forster's modernism, liberalism and spiritual crisis, rather than issues of gender or colonialism. It also contains reviews from 1924 and early criticism.

G. K. Das, *E. M. Forster's India*, London: Macmillan, 1977.

In addition to the extract included on pp. 64–75, the other sections of Das's study of Forster are useful background reading in terms of the contexts in which *A Passage to India* can be read: nationalist, cultural and social as well as literary.

Tony Davies and Nigel Wood (eds), *A Passage to India*, Buckingham: Open University Press, 1994.

An excellent introduction to the critical history of the novel is followed by four wide-ranging but substantial readings, which respectively centre on nationalism and sexuality, colonial law and order, hybridity and masculinity, and representation and gender.

Judith Scherer Herz, *A Passage to India: Nation and Narration*, Boston: Twayne, 1993.
A detailed and extensive discussion of *A Passage*, which seeks to balance emphases on the colonial and formal aspects to criticism of the novel.

Betty Jay, *E. M. Forster's* A Passage to India, Harmondsworth: Icon books, 1998.
A review of criticism of the novel with greater emphasis on recent readings. The introductory chapter provides a helpful overview of traditional interpretations of Forster's novel, while later chapters concentrate on two or three specific essays from such angles as gender criticism and post-colonial studies.

Andrew Rutherford (ed.), *Twentieth Century Interpretations of* A Passage to India, Englewood Cliffs: Prentice-Hall, 1970.
A useful and only slightly overlapping volume to place alongside Bradbury's 'Casebook' (see above). Contains a chronology in addition to a wide variety of essays from the 1950s and 1960s.

Edward Said, *Culture and Imperialism*, London: Chatto and Windus, 1993.
Contains Said's own reading of the novel, following on from his pioneering work *Orientalism*. The book covers a wide range of figures, from Austen to Verdi, and submits specific works to extended readings. The consideration of *A Passage* emphasises Forster's attempt to fit into the book subjects not usually attempted in fiction: 'vastness, incomprehensible creeds, secret motions, histories, and social forms.'

J. H. Stape, *E. M. Forster: Critical Assessments*, Sussex: Croom, 1998.
Four volumes of criticism divided into: Memories and Impressions, Reviews (volume 1); The Critical Response 1907–44, Criticism of the Short Fiction, Forster's Criticism, Miscellaneous Writings (volume 2); Relations and Aspects, General Critcism on Forster 1945–90 (volume 3); The Modern Critical Response to the six novels (volume 4). The fourth volume contains six valuable essays on *A Passage to India*, but there is useful material in all the books.

Jeremy Tambling (ed.), *E. M. Forster*, London: Macmillan, 1995.
The collection of contemporary critical essays in Tambling's 'New Casebook' adds to those in Bradbury's earlier volume devoted to *A Passage*. This new volume has four essays on the novel, plus one on film and an insightful discussion by Rustom Bharucha on 'Forster's Friends', which is especially illuminating on Syed Ross Masood, the dedicatee of *A Passage*.

Texts relating to the work in performance:

Laura. E. Donaldson, 'A Passage to India: Colonialism and Filmic Representation', *Decolonizing Feminisms*, London: Routledge, 1992.

Peter J. Hutchings, 'A Disconneted View: Forster, Modernity and Film', in Jeremy Tambling (ed.), *E. M. Forster: Contemporary Critical Essays*, London: Macmillan, 1995.

June Perry Levine, 'Passage to the Odeon: Too Lean', in J. H. Stape (ed.), *E. M. Forster: Critical Assessments*, vol. 4, Sussex: Helm, 1998.

Index